On Main Street

On Main Street

A Memoir

Prudence Hatch McMann

Writer's Showcase
presented by *Writer's Digest*
San Jose New York Lincoln Shanghai

On Main Street
A Memoir

Writer's Showcase
presented by *Writer's Digest*
an imprint of iUniverse.com, Inc.

For information address:
iUniverse.com, Inc.
5220 S 16th, Ste. 200
Lincoln, NE 68512
www.iuniverse.com

ISBN: 0-595-13735-0

Printed in the United States of America

For those who lived and those who remember.

Epigraph

Any one who had a childhood, has enough material to write for a lifetime.

Flannery O'Connor

Contents

GENEALOGY

Walter and Jenny Hill

Estelle Hill (Aunt Teddy) Elsie Hill Sharpe (Auntie) Winnifred H. Hatch
Tim Hill

Children	**Children**
Jimmy	Barbara
Bunny	Harvey
Margaret	Mac

Children	**Children**
Ricky Sharpe	Nancy Rust
Marilyn Sharpe	Donnie Rust
	David Rust
Miles Mulcahy	
	Prudy Hatch
John G. Dyer	Randy Hatch
Barry Dyer	Sally Hatch
	Susie Hatch
	Patty DeForest

FOREWORD

Dear Reader,

This memoir is written with some chronology, but not in the chrono-logical way you might expect. The stories, which are written primarily about family members who are now dead, include only a few of my teen age years. I mention my friends, my sisters, and mother who is alive and well. My mother has been, and continues to be, an important person in my life, but I have not written a great deal about her influence.

This book is about the Hatch, Hill, and Sharpe relatives and how their lives affected mine. I am indebted to Peg Shore, my final editor, who has helped me see what I must cut—pages and pages of details—so I would not distance you, the reader. I am to blame for the abundance of details that remain. I couldn't part with them. Some of details and stories cut from this book will appear in my second book which is already partially written. A list of people, who also helped me as I wrote and revised this book, can be found in the acknowledgments.

PHM

PROLOGUE

Dexter is a town of hills and valleys and people whose lives circle about and connect in unexpected ways. Living in that small Maine town in the '50s and '60s shaped my expectations of people. It also shaped my perceptions of the world and my place in it. Living in Dexter gave me a tapestry of memories that I could compare to new people I met or new situations I encountered in literature, and in life.

Main Street in Dexter was the thread that connected most of the places in my childhood. This book is an attempt to weave together memories to create stories that come full circle illuminating lives and experiences.

When I made a map of Main Street, it became clear how my memories spanned the generations, linking me with the lives of many people who are now gone, but whose influences are never ending.

My great-grandmother, Nanny Hatch, lived at the top of Main Street Hill, with her boarders and the lingering, unpleasant odor of greasy meat and cooked cabbage. At the other end of town, a mile away, on lower Main Street, Papa and Nanny Hill, my other great-grandparents, resided. Here they helped their three daughters raise six children, one of whom was my father. The house I lived in for nineteen years was situated about half way between the homes of my great-grandparents. Next door to our house was the hockey rink, where I learned the ways of boys, as we played cowboys and cowgirls, baseball, football, sledded, skated, and talked into the night in the teenage years.

A building near the rink site once housed my grandfather's preparatory school for boys. Grampy's ideas propelled him to the pinnacle of success in Newport, Rhode Island. Eight years later his extravagances sent him plummeting to ignominy back in Dexter. After the financial debacle at the Newport school, and my grandparents' return to Maine for year round living, their big house on High Street became a place for me to visit with my friends.

The business section of a once thriving community sits at the bottom of Main Street Hill. Dexter is like so many other small towns that peaked in the 1950s and have been on the decline ever since—all victims of time, change, catalogue shopping, and sprawling malls.

For forty-seven years, my father's business was on Main Street. His insurance and real estate office was up over the Ben Franklin Five and Ten Cent Store until he had to move in the 1970s so the building could be torn down to make room for a bank with a drive up window.

Townspeople, after a week of work in the mills or factories, came trudging up the creaky, dusty stairs on Friday to pay five dollars toward their insurance bill and cash their paychecks. My father, or his secretary, would say, "Five dollars on account," pulling the crank on the receipt maker. And I heard one man say, "Yep, on account—that's all I got," and they chuckled. People would say with their Yankee accents, "Go see Hahvey Hatch; he'll help you out."

Children tiptoed timidly up the stairs after school, and we could hear their whispers in the hall as they looked at the huge bulletin board with 8x10 photographs of smashed vehicles, burned houses, and accident scenes of claims paid by the Hatch Agency. We waited until the children mustered the courage to open the door and come in to ask for a pencil, a pen, or a ruler. They usually got all three, if my father was in a magnanimous mood, and a few years later, some of them climbed the stairs with their paychecks from the shoe shop to be cashed and money paid on account. The cycles and rhythms of the town flowed on, weaving a pattern of familiarity.

Over the past forty years, the fabric of the community has changed. Dexter's woolen mills are gone, as are the men who once worked at the desks and looms. Many Main Street buildings have fallen victim to fire or demolition. The three elementary schools—schools my father, grandparents, and I attended—are all gone now.

About halfway up Main Street Hill, two houses beyond the one where I lived, is the Bryant Hill Road, which leads to the old reservoir and Dexter's cemetery. It's a beautiful, quiet, secluded place on a hilltop overlooking the road that comes into and leaves the town. The pristine view of a small pond, trees and an expanse of landscape and sky is serene and comforting.

As a child, I went to the cemetery with my mother and great-aunts just before Memorial Day, putting jars of lavender lilacs at the headstones of deceased relatives I hardly knew or remembered. During my teen years, the cemetery was a private place for parking with boyfriends. It was a sophisticated and mysterious place to go on a summer's night with my friend Carol and boys we knew, to lie on the grass, look at the sparkling stars in the dark dome of sky above us and philosophize about the present, the future, and the immensity of the universe. The cemetery was a place to be alone, to feel connected to the past. This was in a time before vandals destroyed and desecrated cemeteries, before gates were locked.

It was also a time when I didn't really know the people who were dead, reposing under the grass and the starlight. They were like characters in the novels we read in English class—born in the 1800s, old people whose time had come and gone. Not loved ones of my childhood.

Now, most of the older members of my family are buried at Mount Pleasant Cemetery. After each funeral, I have looked out at the panorama before me under the expanse of blue sky. The landscape has changed. Some trees are taller, others, new, are shorter; the band pavilion is gone, a victim of decay and the elements. Shabby houses and trailers crowd the sides of the Bryant Hill access road, and the old reservoir, having outlived its purpose is empty now and covered over. The well of wisdom, the stories, and experiences of the elders can't be allowed to dry up and pass by and be forgotten after their burial. For that reason, I take it upon myself to tell their stories and mine.

THE ERRAND

The year was 1954, and I was seven years old when my father sent me on an errand to Marvin Salisbury's fish market while Daddy discussed real estate and insurance matters with a customer. "Tell Marvin I want five pounds of filleted haddock."

I dutifully skipped off to the nearby market.

The pungent odor of aging fish and wet sawdust pervaded the air as I entered the small store. Mr. Salisbury, bald, with a fringe of gray hair, wiped his hands on the soiled white apron tied about his waist, peered over the glass case through rimless spectacles and asked, "May I help you."

"My father wants five pounds of filleted haddock."

He pulled out the fish, ready to weigh it and asked, "Who is your father?"

I was used to this game. Why, everyone in Dexter knew my father. His name and business, Lloyd Harvey Hatch Jr. Real Estate and Insurance, were printed on every matchbook, pencil, pen, ruler, calendar, key chain, fire alarm card, bridge tally, pot holder, desk blotter, note pad, and envelope I had ever seen. (My father was a man who believed in advertising and who liked, even needed, to give things to people.)

Yes, I knew how to play the game Mr. Salisbury wanted to play. It was an odd, teasing game that my sisters and I obligingly played along with whenever we saw Max Glazier at Koritsky's department store, or the brothers, known as Nig and Nummy, at Mountain Motors, or Mr. Landry at the gas station. Mr. Salisbury's question triggered the usual response, and I replied, "You know." He asked again and again and again and each time I repeated my line, "You know," with the saucy, coquettish little inflection that I was supposed to use.

Finally, becoming thoroughly exasperated he snapped, "No, little girl, I don't know who your father is."

A wave of painful, humiliating realization came over me. He didn't know who I was, that Harvey Hatch was my father. Mortified by my coyness and naiveté, ashamed to let him know now who my father was after that performance, I unglued my feet from the floor, turned on my heels, and hurried out of the store fighting back tears, with my throat aching.

As I mounted the steep stairs to my father's office, I struggled to compose myself. When I walked into the office empty handed my father asked, "Where's the haddock?"

"He didn't have any," I replied as I sat in the chair to wait quietly until Daddy was ready to go home.

As I sat there with my neck and ears still burning from the embarrassment of making a fool of myself, I prayed that Mr. Salisbury would never find out who I was, and I vowed never to go in his store again.

In those days, I defined myself as Harvey Hatch's daughter. Usually, the good-natured teasing, and the extra attention that went with it, made me feel special, with a sense of pride in being the daughter of a well known man, even though the sphere of influence was a town of four thousand. It was a big world to me.

When Marvin Salisbury didn't know who I was, it began a tiny stirring of knowledge that, when I was by myself, where no one knew me, I didn't have an identity, I wasn't as special as I had thought I was.

That night as I sat thinking and waiting for my father to take me home, it didn't occur to me that being my father's daughter wasn't enough. It took decades of living and learning for me to come to a realization that I had to forge my own identity.

I spent a lot of years defining myself by the men in my life—Harvey Hatch's daughter, Lloyd Hatch's granddaughter, Brian McMann's girlfriend, Brian McMann's wife, Chris' and Andy's mother—and I let their accomplishments be mine. It wasn't until I was in my thirties that I began to define myself with my own achievement, and then I was able to put together all of the pieces of my identity into a whole that includes my relationship to the men in my life, but isn't overshadowed by it. I think, somehow, that relatively insignificant incident at Marvin Salisbury's market was the start of it all.

THE LITTLE RED BOOT

Philip Ramsay was my friend. In the early 1950s, when Saturday arrived, I gathered up my Roy Rogers double holster, my matched six shooters, rolls of new red caps, my bandanna, my Annie Oakley rifle, my Dale Evans cowgirl hat, and headed across the back yards to Philip's house.

Philip and his parents lived on the first floor of his grandmother's big old house, and she lived upstairs. Philip's neat, organized bedroom was off the new pink and gray Youngstown kitchen, and his room was filled with toys. Philip was an only child. His mother had been a teacher. Philip was smart and his mother worked with him to make him even smarter. He was a year and a half younger than I was, but Phillip was in my grade. In first grade Phillip could spell hippopotamus and Mississippi and I dutifully practiced and memorized the sequence of i's and s's and p's.

On Saturday, Phillip and I played cowboys and cowgirls in the cellar. We galloped around the supporting poles on our imaginary steeds, shooting at the bad guys, pretending it was an ambush. The noise of cap guns and a smoky smell filled the basement. When we tired of chasing the outlaws, we went upstairs to Philip's room to play school at his little roll-top desk or to play with the Lincoln Logs or the farm set.

The farm set was my favorite toy, because it had so many pieces and we could pretend. We both learned a lot about farms in Mrs. Gordon's first grade. Besides that, my Great-Grammy Ellms lived on a farm in near by Ripley, and Philip's Grampa Addington had a farm in Ripley, too, so we could play in real barns when we visited. At Philip's, we played for hours, setting up the yellow plastic bales of hay and the gray plastic bags of grain in the loft and placing the silo beside the metal barn with its realistically

8

painted interior. We snapped white plastic fences together and arranged them around the pond with multitudes of rubbery pigs, cows, chickens, ducks, and horses grazing on the gray linoleum floor.

Sometimes we were brave enough to venture into the Ramsay's living room, which was usually off limits to us. We sneaked in to turn on the TV for a Gene Autry western, Johnny Jupiter, or Sky King, and if we lingered unnoticed (or perhaps with permission) we sat on the floor—not the new sofa—remembering the rules.

The living room was perfect at Philip's house. The furniture wasn't spoiled or soiled, scratched or stained as it was at my house. At home we four girls carelessly, unrestrainedly ate as we sat on the couch, built cabins with the cushions or jumped and bounced on Saturday mornings as we watched Gerald McBoing Boing or Mickey Mouse.

At Philip's, the chairs, couch, tables, and lamps were brand new, because Philip's father owned Ramsay and Gate's Furniture Store. In the living room, they also had a beautiful, beige, vinyl hassock with matching ten inch, slim, shiny nylon fringe hanging down the sides from piping around the upper half. The soft silky strands swung, twisted, undulated like a hula skirt when I twirled and swirled the hassock on its edge as we talked and watched TV. I loved the slipperiness of the long fringe as it slithered through my fingers and we twisted, braided, and untangled the knots. I couldn't keep my hands off it, until I heard those sharp edged words, "Phil-LIP be careful with the furniture in there. I hope you are not playing with that hassock. Turn off that TV and go outside and play now." Mrs. Ramsay wanted us to get some fresh air and exercise. She didn't allow raucous play in her house, and we needed to work off our energy. So we went sliding, or made cabins, or tunnels, or angels in the fresh snow.

One winter afternoon, Philip and I went wandering up over the back hill looking for an adventure, wondering where the woods led. We continued on our walk until we arrived at the top of cemetery hill.

Dexter's cemetery was familiar to me, because on Memorial Day my mother gave Auntie and Aunt Teddy a ride to decorate the graves of Sharp,

Hill, and Tate family members who came from Scotland long ago. We helped carry water from roadside spigots, filling jars of lavender and purple lilacs to place in front of the monuments.

When we drove up Bryant Hill in May, I loved the feeling as we came up over the crest of the hill, drove between the iron gates and looked out at the panorama that suddenly appeared before us. Rows of gravestones jutted from the green grass surrounding the wooden pavilion. Beyond that there was a backdrop of trees, distant mountains, and Puffers Pond below, far to the left of the road to Corinna.

In January, the still whiteness of the cemetery was a different world. At first, Philip and I felt curious and brave, but as we wandered on past the century-old, lichen-flecked tomb stones, we began to feel a bit timid. At the top of the hill, the wind drifted and packed the snow as winter gales whipped up over the hill from Puffer's Pond below. It seemed as if we had wandered miles away from home.

Cold tree branches clattered against each other like my grandmother's knitting needles, and ancient trunks creaked and groaned in the frozen winter stillness as the wind swept by and the sun sank lower behind the skeleton-like trees. The sounds of the wind, the crunch plod, crunch plod of our boots in the crusty snow were the only noises besides our puffing as we struggled closer to the little granite house with its jail-like, iron grate door. Inside, we saw a little room with high granite benches built into the wall on each side of the building. Etched upon the high bench tops were the names of the dead people who lay beneath.

I had begun to feel an eerie discomfort as we inched closer. The sky, stratified pink and grayish blue from the setting January sun, was a signal that it was time to be home. I didn't like walking home after dark in the winter. I didn't like being away from home at that time of night when boogie men or bad men might get me, and I liked it even less in the cemetery.

Philip and I stepped closer to the mausoleum so we could read the inscription on the stone interior: Stanley Plummer. We recognized the name of the building he left to the town after he died. Plummer

Memorial Hospital was just up the street from Philip's house, and we were both born there.

As we peered inside the tomb, we talked of our discovery, covering the stillness with questions as our imaginations began to get away from us. What if the dead people came out to get us? What if they captured us and kept us in the little jail house and wouldn't let us go? My thoughts were even wilder than those I voiced. "Let's go home," I suggested. "It's getting late." We turned hurriedly away from the granite home of Stanley Plummer's bones and ghost and started on our way, our boots plunking and sinking deep into the snow in our haste to hurry home.

Suddenly, I heard a gasp, followed by a strangled cry for help and turned around to see a terrified look on Philip's face and his right leg covered above the knee in a huge white drift.

For a minute, Phillip looked as if a voice from the depths had called to him or a hand from below had reached up from a frozen grave to clutch his foot and pull him down under.

Stricken with fear, I called out, "What's wrong?" hoping for a reassuring answer, fearing we were done for, that they were going to get us now.

"I'm stuck. Something's holding me." Philip cried.

In my run away imagination, I had a vision of bony fingers grasping Philip's foot, but common sense told me the snowdrift held him fast.

"Can't you pull your foot out?" I asked.

"No, it won't come out!" Philip said, his voice quavering.

"Pull harder," I said.

"I am," he said, stifling a sob. "It won't come out."

"Can you wiggle your foot around?" I asked.

I struggled to help Philip free his boot from the packed drift, but Philip was stuck. His little red boot was wedged deep in the snow.

Once again we tugged, we pulled, then we panicked. Philip snuffled back the tears. I was close to tears myself as I thought about our predicament. My fingers, inside Grammy Ellms' hand knitted wool mittens, tingled with the cold; my toes ached with numbness. I was hungry. It was so cold. It was getting dark and scary. The noise of the wind and trees seemed louder. Maybe we would never get home. We might freeze in the cemetery, and no one would ever find us. Why did we ever wander off? Our mothers would be so upset.

We decided that I had to leave Philip and go for help. I hated to abandon him alone in the cemetery, but there was nothing else to do. Maybe his mother could bring a shovel and help us. Bravely, with a sense of mission, I thumped my way back down the hill following the holes left by our feet hours before, hoping that I too wouldn't become trapped in the snow.

Breathlessly, I plunged on, until at last, with a sigh of relief, I emerged through the trees to the top banking behind Philip's garage. In the distance I heard Mrs. Ramsay tweeting on her trusty metal whistle, followed by the familiar "Phil-Lip Phil-Lip," her high-pitched, nasal voice accenting the last syllable and a note of panic echoing.

I called out in answer, hurried down over the banking, and poured out the jumbled details of our misadventure and Philip's plight. Mrs. Ramsay, anxious and overwrought, rushed inside to put on a coat and boots for the trek up over the hill, through the drifts. Just as we emerged from the house, on our way to the garage for the shovel, we heard a shout. Recognizing Philip's voice, we looked up and saw him trudging down the hill muttering and dragging his little red boot, with his right foot clad only in his gray wool sock. Philip was home, and he was safe from the terrors of the cemetery.

Our adventure at that place of death was over, but our journey in life was only beginning. For two more years I was Phillip's Saturday morning cowgirl companion, but before long I outgrew him and switched my allegiance to girls. Carol and other girl friends became my more constant companions. Phillip spent his spare time in useful ways, reading the encyclopedia, because he was Ethelyn Ramsey's son and he was a very smart boy.

THE SCHOLAR

My grandfather, Lloyd Harvey Hatch, was born December 25, the day we celebrate the birth of the man who became a great prophet, a savior, and a teacher. My grandfather became a teacher also, but that is where the similarity to Jesus ends. Grampy certainly was no prophet, for if he had seen where he was headed on the roller coaster ride of life, he might have rethought some of his choices and saved himself.

Grampy moved to Dexter from Massachusetts at the age of thirteen, sometime before his father died and left his mother with two sons to raise. Later, Helen Hatch adopted an orphaned boy and raised the three as brothers.

I know little of my grandfather's childhood in Dexter. My knowledge of Grampy's life begins in his eighteenth year, when he and my grandmother were courting and his hormones over ruled his logic.

Grampy, Winnie, Grampy Ellms (my mother's father), Jere Abbott, and twenty-five others made up the 1916 graduating class at Dexter High School. I should say, would have made up, for during the July before their senior year, my grandmother became pregnant and could not finish high school.

In October, Mr. Bucknam, the principal, came to the house on Lower Main Street to talk over the situation and let Winnie's parents know that their daughter Winnefred would not be able to return to the high school. However, Winnie and Grampy were not married until April 12th, eighteen days before baby Barbara was born. I learned of my grandparents' pregnancy precipitated marriage when I was a senior in high school, but just recently learned that they were married so close to my aunt's birth. I can only imagine the emotional upheaval and discussions that ensued between October and April.

Grampy finished high school with the rest of his classmates. Someone saved the original graduation program, which listed the graduation speakers and honor students. Superintendent Ross made the decision that Lloyd Hatch shouldn't speak at the ceremony.

Grampy's name had an asterisk beside it to indicate that he lost the privilege of being a Valedictory speaker even though he had the highest grades. My father showed me the program one summer and I thought of the humiliation Grampy must have felt to be eliminated, labeled, and ostracized for the fact that he was recently married and had a child. I wondered if it had influenced his continual quest for recognition and acclaim in later years.

After graduation, Grampy worked for Mr. Maigs at his clothing store, taught math at Dexter High School, and postponed college for a year. In the fall of 1917, Grampy joined his former Dexter High School classmates at Bowdoin, destined to graduate a year behind them. Winnie stayed home with her parents awaiting the birth of their second baby (my father) in December. Mr. Maigs helped with the $500.00 tuition, and Grampy worked as the steward of Chi Psi fraternity house, which paid for his room and board. His job as steward meant that he ordered all the food and items needed by the fraternity house. His fraternity brothers prepaid a fixed amount. If the wholesaler offered a lower price Grampy earned a little money for the services he rendered as steward.

The biggest help came from my grandmother's parents. Papa Hill worked to support the growing family of Hatches. Nanny Hill cooked, cleaned, budgeted, sewed, and made do, so they could care for Lloyd Hatch's children while he had the privilege of attending Bowdoin.

Decades later, my sisters and I regularly visited the house where our father was born. In the 1950s, after her parents' death, the house belonged to my grandmother's unmarried sister, Estelle, whom we called Aunt Teddy. My three sisters and I gathered in Aunt Teddy's bed on cold winter mornings and she told us about the times when Dr. Foss came in a horse and buggy or sleigh to attend the deliveries when her nieces and nephews were born.

In the 1960s and 1970s, as a young adult, I heard and saw more references to the nickname "Pop" given Grampy in 1917 by his Bowdoin classmates. The significance of the name hadn't registered with me as a child. I never really understood until I was older how Grampy came to be called "Pop Hatch." The word pop went with weasel, stood for soda or lollipops, or was the sound of a balloon breaking. I didn't realize it was a synonym for father. There was no secret, but as children, my sisters and I never gave much thought to the details.

We knew that Daddy, our Aunt Barbara, and their brother Mac were born in the house on Lower Main Street and lived there with their mother in her parents' house while Grampy was away at Bowdoin. We knew that Aunt Teddy had lived there with them and that she helped her parents and sister Winnifred take care of those children in addition to her widowed sister Elsie's three children who lived next door. The cousins—Barbara, Harvey, Mac, Jimmy, Bunny and Margaret—grew up in one extended family.

I was a teenager when I learned the complete details and history of my grandparents' earlier lives, but I was an adult before I put the pieces together and reflected upon the effect this all had on my father, aunt, uncle, and their cousins, as well as on the lives of my grandparents.

Someone once said that whenever Grampy came home for college vacation, Winnie became pregnant. By December of his sophomore year, there were three little Hatches living in their grandparents' home on Lower Main Street.

With six children born between 1916 and 1921 in the two families, Papa and Nanny Hill had a big responsibility just feeding and clothing the children. Winnie found work cleaning houses when she could. Aunt Teddy sewed clothes for her nieces and nephews and paid room and board from her wages. Lloyd Hatch's contribution was to earn all As and to issue unreasonable, authoritarian commands to the preschoolers when he was home from Bowdoin or from Cornell where he later studied and taught.

My Aunt Barbara had vivid recollections of the times she visited her father at Bowdoin when he was an undergraduate student, and later in 1924 to 1926 when he returned to teach history at the college. She cherished the kaleidoscope of memories of being at Bowdoin from ages four to nine. "When I visited, I went to watch a track meet, had lunch with the faculty who treated me like royalty, and I attended commencement exercises. The faculty, President Sills, and his wife were friendly and accessible," Aunt Barbara said.

"I had lunch at the Moulton Union with six or seven faculty members. I was impressed by several young, handsome professors who paid attention to me and asked me questions as if I were a young protégé coed. I watched my first Shakespearean play (*The Merchant of Venice*) performed on the expansive stairs and in the courtyard in front of the lion-flanked art museum."

She was there in 1920 when Jere Abbott, Lawrence Weymouth, and my other grandfather, Ed Ellms, graduated. Posing for a picture, she stood beside her father, wearing her new dress and a huge stiff bow that rose from the back of her head like a pair of angel wings.

Aunt Barbara watched their procession through the campus, her eyes huge at the grandeur of it all. Thrilled by the winks and waves of recognition from the professors and Dexter scholars who knew her, she felt a warm glow of acceptance.

From conversations with my aunt, I knew she had an almost mystical feeling about being on the Bowdoin campus with all the scholars, for she was the only child present and she was the daughter of a "brilliant man."

Seven decades later she told me that once when she met with her younger son's teacher in the 1960s, she asked about her son's academic progress. The teacher responded, "David is very bright, not brilliant, but bright."

"Good." Aunt Barbara responded forthrightly. "We've had enough of brilliance."

It had not been easy being the daughter of a man whose ego and intelligence were matched.

I had often heard that back in his college days at Bowdoin, Grampy's erudition, athletic prowess, and intelligence were recognized and rewarded over and over. He won trophies as a formidable member of the debate team as well as for track, and graduated Phi Beta Kappa.

According to Aunt Barbara, Professor Mitchell once remarked that it nearly killed him to give Lloyd Hatch an A in advanced mathematics because he had only attended a few classes. Grampy was busy with his duties as steward, teacher, track star, or debater.

My Grandfather Ellms, who was also a top student at Bowdoin, told me, "Lloyd only studied the night before an exam. He didn't go to class, because he had so many jobs. He'd bone up for exams, put a towel filled with ice on his head, and cram into the early hours of the next morning. Then he'd have breakfast, take the test and get another A. He had a photographic memory."

In the 1940s, when my father was a less than shining student at Bowdoin, his professors often compared him unfavorably to his namesake father. Lloyd Harvey Hatch Jr. never forgot the words of the professor who said, "Your father was the most brilliant scholar ever at this institution. He was the only student, other than President Sills, to earn A or A+ in every class for all four years."

Daddy didn't need more reminders of his father's genius, or his own inferiority. He knew his father was "so brilliant" that he was chosen in 1920 to teach a history class during his junior year of college. Grampy was better suited for the role of teacher than he was for father, in spite of the fact that he was called "Pop Hatch" by everyone at Bowdoin. That was the irony.

Aunt Barbara remembers being at a Bowdoin track meet, seeing her father in his white uniform with the black "B" and trim, his bowed legs exposed beneath his baggy running shorts. She heard people say, "That Pop Hatch runs like a rabbit." One spring day, little Barbara stood near

President and Mrs. Sills and overheard Mrs. Sills marvel aloud, "How DOES that young man do so well at everything, in addition to having three little children?"

When Aunt Barbara was older, looking back on her childhood, she understood that the unsung heroes were her grandparents who made many sacrifices caring for Lloyd H. Hatch's children so he could earn the glory, honors, and awards at Bowdoin.

"Father was also in the Naval Reserve because WW I had begun. That was another reason why he taught. There was a shortage of teachers because of the war." Aunt Barbara told me. "He and the other young WW I volunteers at Bowdoin lived in a hall that became known as the 'S.S. Hyde.' Although most of them—and Father—never served in any capacity other than campus drills and marching, he received a letter recognizing his 'service to his country,' and his obituary listed his military service," Aunt Barbara said reminding me of the photo albums showing Lloyd Hatch in his Navy wool middy blouse, bell bottoms, and beret.

The photos Aunt Teddy developed in the pantry area of the kitchen show the story of those times. In one, Winnie and Grampy stand together, with Grampy sporting a straw boater. In another, they pose in their Sunday best, pushing a wicker carriage with baby Barbara. The most telling picture is of Winnie and Grampy with their three little children, standing behind the house on Lower Main Street, waiting for the train to come by and take Lloyd back to Bowdoin. Mac is a babe in Winnie's arms, little Harvey and Barbara are at her side. Grampy, wearing a crew cut, white shirt and tie, and tweed pants, looks at his family as he holds his college ukulele rather than one of his children.

In some photos, Grampy has on his raccoon coat, the talisman of a collegian in the Roaring 20s. It's the same fur coat he wore fifty years later when he hobbled along Dexter's downtown snowy sidewalks in his old galoshes, making partial payments to creditors.

In one photo, Grampy is on cross-country skis, wearing a wool sweater emblazoned with a capital "B." In another photo, Grampy, in shorts and track shoes, assumes the crouch of a runner about to sprint from the starting line, only he is in the dirt driveway on Lower Main Street. I have an engraved gold watch that he was awarded at the Penn Relays in 1920. I thought of his running days many years later, in the late 1970s, as Grampy shuffled weakly along the nursing home corridor, angry, snappish, discouraged, depressed, and ready to die, with nary a trace of the determination, agility, and fervor that once defined him.

In the old photographs, Grampy is dapper in a high collar white shirt and a tie, perhaps wearing clothes from Mr. Maigs store, a precursor to his shopping sprees on Boylston Street at Louis of Boston. Grampy was always a "snappy dresser." His visits at the Abbott home and his years at Bowdoin helped Grampy develop "cultivated tastes."

Those years also helped him realize that he wanted to be a teacher.

My collection of articles, pictures, Wassookeag school bulletins, and Grampy's obituary tell part of the story of how he became "an educator of vision." Conversations with my father and Aunt Barbara over the years have given me many details to weave together, but some specifics are missing.

I've pieced together some of the dates and events that followed Grampy's graduation in 1921 and most of the milestones that occurred following his return to Dexter in 1926 when he started Wassookeag Summer School, but it is the years in between that hold some mystery.

Grampy returned to Dexter for a while after he was graduated from Bowdoin. Until then he had been only a visitor in his children's lives. He was an intruder, castigating, commanding, never really close to them, never understanding their feelings, needs, or the ways of children. Papa and Nanny Hill, his in-laws, and his wife made up for Lloyd Hatch's lack of nurturance, but his authoritarian, pedantic personality took its psychological toll on the children in the middle and teen years. My father and Mac especially felt the sting of his words, the wrath of his reprimands, and the lack of recognition and acceptance for who they really were and how they felt.

Lloyd hadn't let his family get in the way of his ambitions and aspirations. He had parents-in-law who helped make his education possible, though he might not have fully appreciated their sacrifice and sense of duty. Those sacrifices didn't end after his graduation, for it was his father-in-law who later loaned Grampy $1,000 to start The Wassookeag School after his post graduate study at Cornell. When Daddy told me that, I asked if Grampy ever paid Papa Hill back.

"Probably not," was my father's terse, rueful reply.

That was Grampy's way.

Aunt Bunny, my father's cousin told me, "I remember Mother once telling me how cross your grandfather was with Papa. After Papa had helped him money wise for years, Uncle Lloyd wanted more money. Papa Hill said 'Lloyd, I have helped you all along financially and taken care of your wife and all the children, whom I love, but will no longer give you any more money, as I have them to take care of and think about.'"

After Grampy was graduated from Bowdoin, he returned to Dexter for the summer. That fall, Ed Ellms (my mother's father) went to The Sloan School at M.I.T. with Lawrence Weymouth; Jere Abbott went to Harvard after touring Europe and the art museums with his mother; and Grampy went to Cornell to teach and continue his studies. He was there for four semesters from the fall of 1921 to the spring of 1924.

I'm not certain what Grampy did for work that summer of 1921, but I do know that in the fall when he went to Cornell, he taught and continued further study in history.

"Father was a President White Fellow in Modern European History," Aunt Barbara explained. At Cornell, he met Katherine Young, who was affiliated with the college. For some reason, she gave him an endowment of $200 a month for the rest of his life."

Perhaps it was because Katherine Young favored his brilliance and believed in his dreams.

Aunt Barbara remembered the summers of 1922 and 1923 when she visited her father in Ithaca. She went to picnics and faculty gatherings when, as the eldest, she traveled alone by train or with her mother while her brothers stayed home with Papa and Nanny Hill.

"I met Professor Heinrick Van Loon. He wrote a history book for young people. His teenage son dressed as any young man at Eaton would—in wool shorts, a blazer, and knee socks. I was amazed to see someone his age wear such an outfit. The boys I knew usually wore knickers or long pants," Aunt Barbara said, as the memories poured forth.

"We never knew much about what father did, but we KNEW when he came home," Aunt Barbara said with a trace of resentment.

It wasn't a warm welcoming.

Aunt Barbara also remembered, as did my father, a darker summer a few years later in 1924 or 1925 when Grampy had a mental breakdown or suffered from severe depression.

"Harv overheard Nanny tell someone that 'Lloyd's lost his head.' Those words weighed heavy upon Harv, because as a boy of about six, he took them literally, picturing Father's head rolling around in the dust. Harv was so worried," Aunt Barbara said, still the big sister.

The summer of Grampy's breakdown, he just sat on the front porch, caught in a miasma of despair and depression. He was irascible and autocratic. The children were not excited about a reunion with the father who had been only a visitor in their lives. Living with the moody morose man who sat on the porch drinking cast a pall over their days. They avoided him as much as possible and wondered when Father was going to go away again. Mac for one, hoped it would be soon. They also wondered what was wrong.

I can only speculate that after all of his brilliance, recognition, academic achievement, and awards, Grampy had come face-to-face with the reality and the responsibility of earning a living for his wife and three children. World War I was over, college was over, and he was stuck in Dexter with no job and a family to support. He was somber, silent, but not sober, isolating himself from the children, scolding, and reprimanding them for seemingly insignificant transgressions. Grampy's drinking in the face of adversity was a harbinger of the coming years.

Perhaps his dreams of financing a school to prepare young men for college had begun to flounder. He owed money to people. His father-in law continued to help with expenses, even though Papa Hill's pay was small.

Papa Hill paid the bulk of the rental of Honeymoon Cottage. My aunt and my father remembered those summers fondly. Honeymoon was located across the lake from Moosehorn Camp, which was to become The Wassookeag Summer School a few years later. It was a treat to be at Honeymoon. The children swam and played on the water's edge all day. At night, they lay in their cots in the partitioned rooms and listened to the adult voices drift over the wall dividers.

"We never really had our own home as a family," my father once said. "Being at Honeymoon was the first time we were all together. We thought he bought Honeymoon, but it was like everything else—Father finagled it."

In 1926 Grampy came home from Bowdoin (where he had been teaching) with three boys who would be the first students of his school. Grampy lived with them, but his children lived with their mother and grandparents. As the school grew and developed a solid reputation, Grampy acquired the house on High Street. He became the headmaster and Winnie became his co-worker and the school's matron. Barbara, Harvey, and Mac still preferred to live "down home" as they called their grandparents' house on Lower Main Street, because Papa Hill was the man they loved as a father. Lloyd Hatch was the scholar, teacher, headmaster— a man who inspired many feelings, none of which were filial love.

The Wassookeag Summer School

Barbara Hatch with Grampa Hill—1917

Mac, Harvey and Barbara—1919

Mac, Barbara and Harvey—1922

LLOYD HARVEY HATCH, SR. THE MAN, THE MYTH

"The great use of life is to spend it for something that will outlast it." William James's maxim is on the first page of *Friendly Lines*, a little booklet of wisdom that Grampy mailed to families of students and other people on the Hatch Preparatory School mailing list. Grampy subscribed to the privately published editions and no doubt read them for pearls of wisdom. I wonder if he ever guessed, as a teacher of history, how short lived his empire would be. Maybe that is why pictures and printed brochures of his schools and camp were so important to him.

There is another bit of wisdom in the April-May 1959 edition of *Friendly Lines* that Grampy believed in. "People ought to dress as well as they can. It's short sighted economy not to. Clothes do something for one's self-respect. Clothes are eloquent testimony of—not only good taste—but also of what you think of yourself…There's therapeutic value in a new hat!"

In 1943 Grampy returned from a shopping spree at a New York haberdasher. My father told me disdainfully, "I'll never forget seeing him standing in the bedroom trying on new purchases—a $40.00 derby and a $200.00 top coat—very expensive in '43—that he had charged with some other clothes. Father had been cavorting around the city in his new duds."

Whenever he was in the city for recruiting and for a reunion of former students at the Waldorf Astoria, Grampy outfitted himself in the latest fashion. There is a framed photograph of one soiree at the Waldorf Astoria with male guests, including Grampy, dressed in tuxedos and women in long gowns. For other school functions, Grampy dressed the part of headmaster in his three piece tweed suit with his Phi Beta Kappa pin on the lapel.

Daddy felt embarrassed by his father's spendthrift ways, yet Daddy's voice had a tone of a rueful marveling about his father's ability to coolly finagle and juggle huge debts. In the mid 1950s Daddy walked into our house shaking his head in bafflement or consternation and said, "Well, L.H. is at it again…" or "L.H. always has to put on the dog…" or "L.H. will be satisfied with nothing but the best…whether he can afford it or not."

L.H. was the name my father and his brother Mac used when referring to Grampy, unless they called him "Father" in a formal way to distance themselves as he had distanced himself from them when they were little. They never called him Dad or Daddy or the ubiquitous Pop. When they said L.H. it sounded like one word—L-Laich. In 1958 I caught the undertones of annoyance and disapproval and overheard conversations with Daddy muttering and swearing because L.H. had called during business hours to say, "I need half an hour of your time for a conference." The half hour stretched into two hours, long distance from the Hatch Prep School in Rhode Island as Grampy went over item by item on his paper clipped list of notes.

Grampy patterned Hatch Prep and The Wassoookeag School and Camp after Bowdoin with the same school colors—black and white—in homage to the college where he was teaching when he got the idea for a summer school to prepare boys for academic success. Thus Grampy began the first summer school camp in the United States. That was Grampy's claim to fame—his original idea of combining academics with summer fun and athletics. The boys spent time at Moosehorn on Lake Wassookeag when they weren't under Grampy's tutelage.

For the next two years, Daddy, Mac, and Barbara lived together with their parents in several houses around Dexter, one of which was at 481 Main Street. Twenty years later, when I was a baby, my parents bought that house.

Grampy had some income in the summer of 1926, but in the winter, sometimes there wasn't enough money for food. Once my grandfather sent my father on an errand at Brewster's store. Daddy picked out the groceries on his list and, as he was instructed, told Mr. Brewster, "Put it on the slip."

Mr. Brewster responded, "Tell your father we are all out of slips."

Daddy left the store feeling puzzled for he didn't know what the grocer meant. Perhaps Daddy felt that he had done something wrong to leave empty-handed, just as I had that day at Marvin Salisbury's fish market.

In the winter 1927 or 1928, Daddy, Mac, and Aunt Barbara moved to the Bridgham house on Maple Street with their parents. Decades later, the Bridgham's daughter, who was then an elderly widow, lived there and turned the front parlor into a chapel for Messiah Mission Episcopal Church. I have a 1957 photo of myself in my white veil and Confirmation dress standing in the living room with a background of old-fashioned sepia-toned wallpaper—probably the same paper that was on the walls that winter my father and his family lived there. That is another of many syncronicities and connections woven into my life.

Grampy expanded the summer school to a winter school in 1928. Somehow he borrowed the money to rent or buy the stucco house on High Street. My father, who was ten years old then, said he would never forget the day two moving vans from Boston drove up to the school and drivers began unloading new furniture. In a matter of hours, the twenty room building went from empty to being fully furnished.

"No one knew where it all came from, how he could pay for it. The men just kept unloading the vans: a mahogany dining room table with sixteen chairs, the dark oak tables, sofas, green desks, beds, bureaus, chairs, lamps, bookcases...we couldn't believe it," my father said.

Later, they found out. Walter Whitehead, who owned Levin's of Boston, (which later became Payne's) sent the furniture in a barter arrangement with Grampy. Walter Whitehead Jr.'s tuition for a couple of years turned an empty house into an official school.

Walter Whitehead Jr. became Aunt Barbara's first boyfriend, when he was fifteen and she was twelve. By that time the three Hatch teenagers were spending more time at the "big house" on High Street as they visited or attended classes.

Because of his student's affluent backgrounds, Grampy felt that Wassookeag School should offer the comforts and atmosphere to which the boys were accustomed. To do that, he bought nothing but the best. However, he bought on credit and whim. Grampy was a spendthrift.

Daddy told me, "Father would travel to New York to line up students. He spent money on high and wild living, cavorting about New York City, but couldn't pay people when he came back. Money went through his hands like water through a sieve. He owed people months of pay. Aunt Teddy was the bursar. (Father had to use a British term because it sounded more elite.) There were times that he owed her (and others) months of pay, yet she kept working that job plus another where she actually received money regularly."

Grampy did everything with fanfare and flair. He had his photograph taken by Bacharach, placed in a wide brown leather frame embossed with gold leaf, it stood on the marble mantle in Newport, Rhode Island after he moved the school there in 1951. He wore his three-piece-suit with a pocket handkerchief and his Phi Beta Kappa pin. His hair, parted in the middle and slicked back made him look like the headmaster personified.

My father told me that at one time U.S. Postmaster General, James Farley, held a mortgage on Grampy's and Winnie's cottage at lake Wassookeag. Grampy had a double mortgage—two payments. He also borrowed from the bank to buy land and develop Moosehorn, which became The Wassookeag Camp. Grampy owed everyone. Other students' parents held mortgages on Grampy's buildings over the years, as he mortgaged three houses on High Street and four cars, and lived high on the hog.

Years later, on a day when my husband and I visited him at the nursing home, Grampy told us about all that he had done, and all that he had spent. I thought about something Aunt Teddy once told me.

After years of cooking at The Wassookeag School and the camp in Dexter, Auntie (my grandmother's sister) moved with Winnie and Grampy to the new school in Rhode Island. Day in, day out for seven years, Auntie quietly went about her business of cooking, going alone each night to her quarters in the back of the school like the hired help, instead of the head matron's sister. For years I've wondered why she didn't visit us in Winnie's and Grampy's suite, or if Auntie's feelings were hurt by the slight, or if my grandmother felt sorry or ashamed.

Grampy's secretary, Yolande, had a lavish suite just down the hall from Grampy's office, but Auntie in her sixties had only a cramped room with an old bed to rest her weary bones at the end of a long day on her feet. Daddy stewed about that often, and I caught bits and pieces of his comments about Grampy and Yolande when I was twelve or so. I also figured out, years later, that perhaps there was something going on between Grampy and Yolande, and that was why she had better accommodations than Auntie.

Never the complaining type, Auntie, as an observer of Grampy's successes and excesses over the years, remarked to Aunt Teddy, "When this thing blows, it's going to blow sky high."

It wasn't long afterward, that J.J. Newberry, Sr. and the school's board of trustees asked Grampy to retire, putting a stop to his runaway spending on mansions, antique furnishings, classroom alterations, house parties, sports teams and events, and the other luxurious ways of living.

Grampy summed it all up for us one day at the boarding home, as he sat in his worn, but still classic clothes from Louis of Boston. Grampy talked with me and my husband about the past and his profligate spending, and then he said with a sigh, and not a trace of regret, "I really knew how to make it fly."

*The Hatch Family (Winnie's dress was one of
our dress-up outfits in the 1950s)*

Lloyd H. Hatch and Mac—1925

Front L-R: Bunny, Mac, Pa Hill, Harvey and Margaret
Back: Barbara and Jimmy

Llyod Hatch instructing Mac—1940s

Lloyd Harvey Hatch, Sr. the Headmaster

"Your Grandfather had a million dollar mind, but not a nickel's worth of common sense. He was a genius, but he had no practical sense. He needed a business manager," Hector Hebert said one day as he and his wife Renee reminisced with me and my father about the years they spent at The Wassookeag School Camp and the winter school.

"Those were the best years of our lives," the Heberts exclaimed almost in unison. "Wonderful years…"

Hector Hebert in his eighties, white haired and bespectacled, resembled George Burns without the cigar. Even with the craggy looks of old age, the firm handsome jaw line was still present. Quite agile after six decades of tennis, he could no longer play, but he still had his jazz records, a library full of history books, memories of a lifetime of teaching, and his wife Renee, the love of his life, who had once been his student.

"It was love at first sight when I saw her, but I waited until she was graduated in 1932 before expressing my intentions, and we were married three years later," he said, fond memories moistening his eyes.

He continued, "The Wassookeag School Camp and the winter school had students whose fathers were the business leaders of America, and they wanted to get their sons into Ivy League colleges. Studying at Wassookeag enabled them to be better prepared. Your Grandfather used the tutorial method. During the first years, he had more teachers than students. Wassookeag was a school of national distinction and reputation," Mr. Hebert said with pride.

"Lloyd spent all of his time on academics. He was always available to talk about the academic program. He'd go over the files on each boy,

36

studying the individual program. Parents received a written report at the end of the summer. The boys received a report daily or weekly. They had six days of classes and study hall in small groups with only Saturday nights off," Mr. Hebert explained, warming to the topic.

"We had recommendations and connections with Poly Prep, Deerfield, Hotchkiss, Loomis, Hebron, Governor Dummer, The Hill School, St. Andrew's, Williams, Wesleyan, Bowdoin, Cornell—all the top schools."

The list of famous fathers who sent their sons was a litany of names from *Who's Who*. Mr. Hebert reeled off the names with a trace of pride in his voice to have played a part in educating young men about history so they could be business men and lawyers who realized that the past does repeat itself.

"Over the years we had U. S. Postmaster James Farley's son, young Jim. We had the son of the maker of Baldwin locomotives, the Brennard boys whose father was a big deal at Aetna Life, the son of the ambassador to the U.N. from Holland, the son of the Ambassador to Vietnam before the north and south divided."

Mr. Hebert paused, then continued. "We had Jim and George Roosevelt from Oyster Bay—the Republicans from Teddy's side. Ray Hellman from the mayonnaise company, J.J. Newberry, Frank Howard whose father was president of Standard Oil of New Jersey, Nelson Goodyear from the tire family, Mike Mulroney whose father was an Oklahoma millionaire and a U.S. Senator, Morton Downey, Jr., his brother, (their father was a singer), John Phillip Sousa's grandson, and the son of a Justice of the Supreme Court."

"We also had the McNally map people's son, Andrew Eiken whose father built the Empire State Building, your uncle, Don Rust, whose father started Rust Craft Cards, Ray Gram Swing whose father was a famous radio commentator, Monroe and Kip Dupont and a Rockefeller. Later when Mr. May owned the school, we had Johnny Carson's three sons, Gordon and Sheila McCrea's son, Lindberg's and Steinbeck's sons."

My father added, "Stirling Hayden, the movie actor, was a student for a year or so, but left owing the tuition after his father died. That was one of the few times that Father was the stiffee rather than the stiffer."

Grampy saved a portion of a page from Photoplay magazine that told about Stirling Hayden and his sailing adventures before he went to Hollywood. The article says, "Stirling was sent to the exclusive Wassookeag School in Dexter, Maine, which the young man describes as an institution of twenty-four students and twenty-eight automobiles...The death of his father cut short his education and the lad, then fifteen, took a job on a schooner for the princely sum of one dollar a month. Hayden later wrote *The Wanderer*, The *Wayfarer*, and *The Voyager*."

My father said, "The biggest years for the winter school were 1931, 1932, and 1933. We had around twenty boys each of those years. One of the other years we only had eleven. At the summer school we had forty to sixty boys, never more than that. Wassookeag catered to the super rich who wanted nothing but the best for their sons."

When Grampy had the school, the students were from ages fourteen to twenty-one. When Mr. May owned the school in the 1950s and 1960s, some students were shunted off to summer school as young as ten years old, so their parents could travel to Europe or have freedom from parenting while their sons had an enriching camp experience.

Mr. Hebert said, "Some of the boys would flaunt their wealth. Many were ordinary people who made it and moved to Scarsdale, putting on the dog because they made money on a big deal. They were the nouveau riche, bragging about their fleet of cars. I could spot a phony in five minutes. The real rich never told who they were or what they had."

My father added, "L.H. ran the school like a country club, with coaches for tennis, golf, swimming, sailing, and two instructors for horseback riding lessons. The boys arrived in their fancy cars and had privileges to drive the roadsters. Meals were served at small round tables on white linen table cloths with matching napkins and Blue Willow dishes. Breakfast was a la carte—the boys wishes were the command of Auntie, Bertha Hall, Althea

Littlefield, and the other kitchen help. Waitresses served the food to the boys, because Father wanted them to feel at home. Any other camp had picnic tables and a tin cup, but not Father's."

"Lloyd hired only the best staff to teach," Hector Hebert interjected with admiration, remembering his esteemed colleagues. "Stan Ross from M.I.T. taught math, Jim Stonier taught five classes and coached four teams. Prep school and college teachers from across New England welcomed the chance to summer in Maine at Wassookeag, with Elsie Sharpes' cooking, a country club atmosphere, and strict academic standards. Other teachers were Dr. Jepson and Bob Ashley from Bowdoin, Roy Howland from Belmont Hill, Walter Metcalf from the Horace Mann School, and George Freidy from Hebron Academy. George and Rose Adams from The Hill School taught with us also."

"One summer, a boy needed Latin IV, and no one was qualified to teach it. Lloyd sent to Bowdoin for a professor and hired him to teach for the summer. Lloyd knew what every boy needed and what they had to accomplish. He was very fussy about his boys," explained Mrs. Hebert with obvious respect in her voice.

"Boy, I'm telling you," Mr. Hebert repeated, "when Lloyd ran the school he knew what every boy needed and what every teacher was going to do."

I remember hearing my grandparents lament that when Mr. May took over, it wasn't like the old days. One year he had 120 boys. I over heard Grampy say, "Les is so busy counting his money, academics are suffering." Les May ran the camp like a business. Grampy also found the fancy new entrance signs ostentatious. As a teenager, I liked the paintings of a boy leaning over a desk studying and of another boy sailing. It was a reminder that BOYS were at The Wassookeag School Camp, just down the road from our cottage.

Mr. Hebert said, "Lester and Lloyd were so different. Lloyd was going to help Lester the first year after Mr. May bought the camp. You can imagine how that went. Your grandfather went overboard one way and Les May went the other. It didn't work out."

"L.H. never had more than sixty boys. He had as many people working there as he had boys. You don't make money THAT way, do you?," my father asked rhetorically. "Look at this picture; the back row is all faculty, and it looks like two or three counselors."

I asked the Heberts and my father to tell me about the house parties. I had heard about them over the years and they sounded like magical, glorious events. I could picture the people's hair styles and clothes and the dancing of the 30s and 40s from the old movies I saw on TV as a teenager.

"We had SOME house parties then," Mrs. Hebert said with a sigh, her emphasis on the word "some" saying more than a string of adjectives could. "The boys came from away so they imported girls from Dexter and Guilford. Peg, your grandmother, would ask people for nice girls to invite as guests. In the winter they'd invite girls from away to the house parties. They'd move all the boys out of the big house and move them over to the Lodge, the Edes' house, which later became Dr. Taylor's."

I have a bracelet that an antique dealer brought to my father's office one day in the 1980s. It was given to one of the local girls from Guilford or Dexter or Dover as a party favor. The dealer knew my father would like to have it and he would take no money for it. The seven silver filigreed shapes have black and green enamel insets. The middle shape has an oval with a large "W" in the middle, and "The Wassookeag School" written around the edge. It is tangible testimony of something that is only a distant memory for a dwindling number of people.

"When the girls came in the winter, we'd have a sleigh ride to the North Dexter Grange Hall on Friday night," my father explained. We had a fine oyster stew supper put on by the Grange ladies. Afterward we had a dance with Jim Boyington's orchestra. Of course, the boys all made fun of the thing, but then they decided they liked it."

"One Saturday night, we had a house party dance at the school. Father hired the best band in the state—Lloyd Rafnell or the Fenton brothers.

Father wouldn't have a cheap band," my father said, his voice dripping with sarcasm

"Oh, Geez,"…interjected Mr. Hebert his voice sounding dreamy, "Lloyd Rafnell…I was chairman of the commencement ball at the University of Maine and it 'twas my job to get a band, and I got Lloyd Rafnell."

"We had Lloyd Rafnell at the summer school one year, …boy, what a house party THAT was," my father said, his voice trailing off at the memory of his teenage years dancing to a live band on a starlit night by Lake Wassookeag.

My father continued, "After one of the house parties, I had to take Katherine Hepburn's sister Peggy to Newport in the late evening to meet the eleven o'clock train. Her date, John Avery Ingersol, was a drip, but his family had connections in Hartford so he brought her to the house party. She didn't care anymore about him than nothing."

My father and Mac had attended the school and camp from the ninth grade on. Aunt Barbara went to Westbrook Seminary for Girls in 1930 and 1931 for her freshman and sophomore years, then chose to return to the all male Wassookeag School because she could get a better education with less restrictive rules. Aunt Barbara and J.J. Newberry took classes together at the winter school. She and another boy studied German for six weeks one summer, covering a whole year of material. When Aunt Barbara arrived at Wheaton as a freshman, she was way ahead of everyone in her German class.

"My teachers at Wassookeag were Charlie Berry, Art Owen, Eddie Buxton, Stan Ross, Rose and George Adams. Boy,…did I have an education with Rose Adams," Aunt Barbara said, speaking with such emphasis that I knew she had received something more precious than jewels, something she would always have with her.

I was struck by the sad irony that Rose Adams couldn't keep her genius with her, because she ended up with Alzheimers.

I last remember seeing her in 1987 at a funeral in Dexter. Rose Adams, in the early stages of her illness, sat staring near the casket. I wondered if she was thinking of the old days when she and her husband's niece (who lay in the casket) were all younger, dancing the night away at a Wassookeag house party. I thought she might also have been thinking that in the not too distant future she would be in a casket like the one before her. Rose lived on for more years than she would have wanted, a shell of the vital, intelligent woman she had been.

As a child, I listened when Rose Adams visited Winnie and Grampy at their cottage. She reminisced about Wassookeag comparing the difference between working for Grampy and Mr. May at the summer camp. In those days, Rose Adams had a bosom like a ship's prow and a prominent, hawkish nose. Her voice was deep and throaty from cigarettes. She spoke of The Hill School. Decades later when I read Tobias Wolff's book *This Boy's Life*, I wondered if Rose's brother was still teaching at The Hill School when Wolff finagled his way in by forging letters of recommendation and having a friend alter his academic record.

Rose Adams wasn't teaching at The Hill School then because, in 1960 when she was in her mid sixties, she married her former fiancee, Norman Plouf. Norman's wife Judy had been dead less than a year, and some people thought it was too soon for him to marry. My friend Carol and I tried to imagine what had broken Rose and Norman's engagement and thought it romantic that the star-crossed lovers had another chance in old age.

Winnie and Grampy gave a gala dinner party for the Ploufs at the house on High Street that fall when Carol and I were in the seventh grade. We acted as waitresses, serving food to the guests and doing the dishes afterward. We had a grand time and were excited to be a part of it all. I didn't know as much about the history of the Wassookeag School then or how quickly the decades of adulthood slip by, so I never imagined what it was like for them with the ghosts and memories of the grand days of the 1930s and 1940s when they had all been in their prime attending house parties at the school.

The grass cloth wallpaper had darkened with age, the ivory colored staircase with raised panels was perhaps more yellowed, and the guests were approaching the infirmities of old age, but the house was full of life once more after eight years of being empty while Winnie and Grampy were in Rhode Island.

The elderly guests all sat at the mahogany table for sixteen and at cloth-covered card tables in the adjoining music room. Auntie, whose feet and back bothered her from all those decades of cooking, fixed a sumptuous meal. One of the deserts was a dark tapioca, called Indian Pudding. Auntie and Daddy joked that the boys had called it "fish eyes and glue" when she served it at school and camp years ago.

Mrs. Hebert told me, "The Wassookeag Camp also had dances at the Lakewood Theatre Country Club and at the small country club in Guilford before it burned. The piazza was screened in and the boys and their dates danced away the evening to a three-piece band. Going to the theater at Lakewood each Saturday was also a tradition. The teachers took turns driving two or three busses of students to the plays or dances held there as a break from studying."

Hector Hebert explained, "We had a combination of goals at Wassookeag—to help the boys stay in a good prep school and to help them make up a failed grade. (St. Andrew's Prep School in Delaware sent the Dupont boys to Wassookeag to do course work if they wanted to return to the school.) People sent their sons for remedial help, to make up a deficiency, to pass a course, or to get credit for a course by intensive study of new material. Sometimes a senior was prepping for an Ivy League college."

"We had boys from Central and South America and Cuba who would brush up on English or Math before going to M.I.T. They had provisional approval, but needed the extra boost," Mr. Hebert explained.

"We had rugged academics, and I mean rugged," emphasized Hector rolling his RRs in his distinctive enunciation. "The boys had essay tests every week. The questions were on the blackboard and the final exams lasted two to three hours. Credits were accepted at all the Ivy League colleges and prep schools. Wassookeag's reputation was excellent, no question about it, even Harvard."

"We might have four boys in a math class. Two boys might be way ahead. Rather than hold them back, Lloyd hired another teacher or Mr. Patterson rearranged schedules to split the class. The slower boys would receive intense instruction twice a day with time in between to do the work. No class was larger than four," Mr. Hebert proclaimed proudly.

"Most of the boys came to Wassookeag for two or three courses. We had the double-up program. That was quite a feature. If a boy flunked U.S. History at his school, he came to Wassookeag to take it over. He had to do a year's work in eight weeks. If we felt a boy simply couldn't do it, after a few weeks went by, I'd go to see your grandfather. I'd say, 'Mr. Hatch this course is too much for this boy. He just can't do it. He has to have a double-up.' Your grandfather had such confidence in us that he'd take our word for it. He never argued the point. He'd say, 'All right, you go see Mr. Patterson right now and arrange for it. (Mr. Patterson was the director of studies.) Tell him you want a double-up starting tomorrow with this boy.' He'd always follow your recommendation. He never crossed me on anything," Mr. Hebert added.

"So you had this boy from a single course. The kid was just licked and knew he couldn't do it. It was too much, too heavy assignments, but the next morning he'd come in with this double-up program and he'd have a different attitude. I'd try to explain to him, 'You couldn't do this course in one class a day, Bill. It's too much for you, but you can DO this course if you meet twice a day, period one and three," Hector Hebert said, his voice falling automatically into that of the encouraging, inspiring teacher. "And the boy said, 'Oh, I think so, sir.' And it worked fine."

"We had a double-up in physics; a rugged course…my gosh…" Mr. Hebert paused to measure his words, and his distinctive enunciation of SH like a whistle stretched out in the seconds. "They used to go down to the lab at the high school for physics and chemistry too. That double-up program was quite a feature."

"Sometimes a boy would start a year of math and a year of U.S. History and English, and couldn't afford a double-up program," Mr. Hebert explained.

"After a few years, we had double-up for all U.S. History, Modern European History, and Algebra II, ...a tough course Algebra II...They were double-up. It t'would take an outstanding boy to do a year's work in one session a day—a whole year's work. We had Advanced English History, the toughest course I ever taught, and every year, St. Andrew's in Delaware sent students to study it."

The first evening of camp the staff had their meeting in the faculty lodge; everything had to be just right. The meeting began at 7:00 P.M. and Grampy, the orator, went through the night speaking about each boy's program to the entire group, heedless of the teachers' fatigue or feelings that most of what he spoke of didn't pertain to them.

Hector Hebert said, "Now what we thought was a great waste of time was that Lloyd would start in with Robert Allen and give the kid's whole life history, every problem he had. My God, he'd go on and on...and then tell us about the next boy for half an hour, and then the next, for all fifty or sixty boys. How the boy had to get back to this very fine prep school, and each subject he needed help in, and what his program would be."

"We're 'sposed to take notes, see, but by that time we each knew which boys we had. So why should I have to sit there and listen to this kid's mathematics problems? It was irrelevant to me. I had nothing to do with his mathematics or English problem," Hector said, vestiges of old annoyance creeping into his voice.

"We used to talk about it. My God! He should have a different way of doing that. We'd be there 'till three, four, or five A.M. and have to teach at 8:00. One night Bob Hanscom fell asleep and keeled right over onto the floor."

And I presume Grampy kept right on talking, oblivious to Bob or his staff's fatigue or lack of interest in each boy's profile. Perhaps that is the

year that one of the teachers or students composed a poem that I found in
a box with Grampy's school papers, catalogs, and brochures.

The Headmaster or Highwayman of Wassookeag, A Ballad

The wind was a torrent of darkness among the gusty trees,
The moon was a ghostly galleon tossed upon cloudy seas,
The road was a ribbon of moonlight over the purple moor,
And the headmaster began talking—
      Talking—Talking
The headmaster began talking, all over the schoolhouse floor.
He'd a huge fur coat for his shoulders, a bow tie under his chin,
A handful of notes in his fingers, as we waited for him to begin;
He started with never a tremor; his voice rose up to the sky,
And his endless words began pouring—
      Pouring—Pouring
His endless words began pouring forth, telling us how and why.

Rules, regulations, restrictions, he explained them to all the
throng,
Punishments, grades, rewardings; —Lord! (How can he speak so
long?)
He told where we might go to, and he told us where we might not;
And he kept up his ceaseless lecture—
    Windy, drawn-out lecture
We heard more, more and more of this lecture, and most of it we
forgot.

Blah-blah in the frosty silence! Blah-blah in the echoing night!
Onward he talked and onward! His face was a light!

His eyes grew wide for a moment; he drew one last deep breath,
Then his throat burst from his talking—
He pitched on his face from his talking, and was silenced at last—by
death!

And still of a winter's night, they say, when the wind is in the
trees,
And the moon is a ghostly galleon tossed upon cloudy seas,
And the moon is a ribbon of moonlight, over the purple moor,
The headmaster starts talking—
    Talking—Talking
The headmaster keeps on talking, and is silent never more.

Grampy must have been flattered to have been featured in a poem, but
he never changed his ways or fully understood that his long winded lectures were a source of annoyance rather than inspiration.

Bob Hanscom, who keeled over during that one opening night lecture, brought his wife Maude along for the summer. Bob, a Bowdoin
grad, was head of the English department at Cushing Academy, and
Maude said she came to Wassookeag just to get Elsie Sharpe's cooking,
especially the iced coffee with a dollop of whipped cream containing a
drop of almond extract.

When Roy Howland arrived, he went right to the kitchen to see Elsie,
to chat and get a bite to eat. His first wife, a city girl, said, "You don't frat-
ernize with the cooks," her disdain clearly evident.

"Gretchen," Roy said with equal disdain, "this is not New Rochelle."
He proceeded with his plan to see Elsie, Bertha Hall, Althea Littlefield,
and others who worked in the kitchen.

"Everyone loved the food at Wassookeag. Every meal tasted homemade, not institutional. Elsie Sharpe was an artist as a cook," Hector
Hebert said with such pronouncement.

One day Auntie didn't know what she would fix for desert. She ended up making white cup cakes from her favorite recipe. Then she made chocolate sauce, poured it over the warm cupcakes, and served them with a dash of whipped cream on top. It was an instant success. Everyone commented on it and it became known as Aunt Elsie's Wassookeag Special.

When Mrs. Hebert gave me the recipe, she said, "Hector HAS to have his Wassookeag Special. My grandsons want it whenever they visit. I make it every few weeks."

One spring, Auntie served dandelion greens at a house party, but no one would eat them. Winnie and Auntie planned the menu and thought the greens would be a treat. One of the boys said he felt as if he were eating angle worms. The boys also didn't like the New England boiled dinner with fresh carrots, onions, potatoes, and turnip cooked in the broth with corned beef brisket and served with beets cooked separately. My father had grown up with it and couldn't understand why they didn't like it. His favorite was red flannel hash made with the left-over beets and corned beef ground up together then heated in a frying pan.

In the 1970s and 1980s, my father regularly ordered chicken pies from Frank's Bake Shop in Bangor. One day a man came out of the kitchen where he was baking and introduced himself.

"Are you Mr. Hatch from Dexter?" the baker asked.

When my father responded that he was, the man whose last name was Frazer, told my father of his appreciation and fond memories.

"I've been wanting to meet you and say thanks. Hell, I used to go up to The Wassookeag School when your brother or father ran it. I lived in Hartland and we'd go up to Dexter to play basketball with the students. I wasn't much of a player. Everyone wanted to be on the team. We knew if we went there to play, we'd get food. We'd take forty people to play and watch the basketball games. We didn't have much to eat in those days during the Depression. They fed everyone, invited everyone to eat. There would be boys from Hartland, Dover, and Guilford. What a feed we had!"

Auntie's cooking was her legacy. Widowed at a young age with three little children, she had no means of support other than her cooking. At Wassookeag, she and her staff, with Winnie's help, made mounds of sandwiches and covered them with clean damp dish towels to keep the bread fresh and not dried out in the refrigerator. Auntie fixed a large kettle of homemade hot chocolate each morning for breakfast served with a topping of whipped cream.

My grandmother and Auntie were an integral part of the Wassookeag School Camp and the winter school. If it were not for Winnie's day to day-to-day handling of situations and planning of meals, parties, and entertainment, the Wassookeag School would never have been as successful. Winnie and Auntie were the people who added the human dimension and the family atmosphere to the winter school and school camp. Winnie was a mother figure as well as the matron.

"Elsie and her crew prepared lunch for the crowd when Lakewood Colony's tennis players came to play at Wassookeag. It was quite an event. They even fed all the spectators. Peg and Elsie made bundles of sandwiches," Mr. Hebert said, in awe at the memory of the work and generosity.

Breakfast, lunch, and dinner were served at the camp to the teachers and the boys visiting parents. Grampy encouraged parents to visit. They were treated royally, given accommodations in town at the winter school, and fed at the camp with their sons. They could go into the kitchen, meet Elsie Sharp and her staff and see that they didn't use powered eggs, that everything was fresh from the Wassookeag Farm.

When the parents visited, my Aunt Barbara, who was about sixteen, had the honor of entertaining them at her table. She wasn't impressed with the Republican Roosevelts from Oyster Bay. "Heaven deliver me from them!" she said emphatically. According to Aunt Barbara, George senior was an obnoxious man, especially when he was drunk, which was often. "Every night he'd get plastered," she said in disgust, "and I had to sit with them at dinner."

Another parent, Mrs. Spear, who wore flowered chiffon dresses and big hats, also drank excessively. Grampy and Winnie discreetly chose other parents to host at their table. Aunt Barbara quickly learned that it was no fun to be around Mrs. Spear. Aunt Barbara resorted to sneaking into Mrs. Spear's bedroom at the house on High Street and taking her bottles of liquor to hide. Maudie Hanscom was appalled and feared Aunt Barbara would be caught. After those years of meals with parents, Aunt Barbara could carry on a conversation and deal with any situation, even though she was only a teenager. Sadly, Aunt Barbara later saw the effects of alcohol on her father, husband, and brothers.

Like everything in life, things at Wassookeag were not just wonderful memories. One summer, a student named Paul Weadlock drowned in a terrible sailing accident when the mast of the boat hit a high tension wire stretched across the lake. The wire hadn't been properly cared for and was sagging lower than usual from the wind.

"It was a horrible afternoon," Aunt Barbara said. "Don (whom she later married) was there with the boys diving, trying to find the body. Bob Marison, from South America, was with Paul in the boat, but he was thrown out and was okay. I sat in the car on the Float Bridge with Paul's older brother, Barney. I was fifteen or sixteen, and I'll never forget that afternoon."

"The boys, who were good swimmers and divers, had no success in finding Paul in the water. Father called Waterville, and they sent an airplane up to fly above the lake to try and locate the body. After they sighted the body, Father hired the best divers in the state to swim the depths of Wassookeag and recover the body," Aunt Barbara told me.

That afternoon left a gloom on the summer. Paul was well liked and everyone was stunned.

"The family was nice about it. They were wonderful people. Today people would sue, even though it was an accident," Aunt Barbara said, reflecting on the tragedy. Ironically, Mr. Weadlock was an owner of a utilities specialty company in New York that was responsible for taking care of sagging wires in need of repair. Aunt Barbara wasn't sure if his company directly or indirectly had something to do with the utility in Maine, but it was a tragic coincidence that the Weadlocks lost their son in a sailing accident involving an electrical wire.

A summer or two later, Barney Weadlock, Paul's brother, was in a car accident with another boy from camp and Ed and Steve Merrill from Skowhegan. The four of them were all on the way to Canada. There was a terrible car crash, and the other Wassookeag boy was killed. Barney Weadlock was driving, and was injured, but survived. Aunt Barbara said, "The boy who was killed was the nicest boy, and his family was just wonderful. Having double tragedies involving the Weadlock family added to their grief."

The boys still brought their autos to the school and camp, but the accidents had a sobering effect.

Lakewood Theatre, as well as Bowdoin, brought together Skowhegan families and the Hatches. Every Saturday night, Winnie, Grampy, the faculty, all the boys, and their visiting parents attended the plays. That must have been quite a financial boost to the owners to have such a crowd from Dexter every weekend.

Wassookeag School Camp had an economic ripple effect in several central Maine communities. Teachers, coaches, gardeners, cooks, laundry and ironing services for students' clothes and table and bed linens were some of the jobs necessary for running a camp for young men used to amenities. Indirectly, Grampy created many jobs in Dexter during times when it was difficult for people to find work. That fact could engender a feeling of pride.

This fact would not. Another summer in the 1930s an African American boy arrived. He was admitted because they had not seen a picture of him, and his parents had enough money for the tuition. My father said, "L.H. had to send him back home, because we had too many southern boys, and we would have lost them all. Mac took the boy back to Newport and put him on the train."

I wonder what Mac, the black sheep of the family, had to say to the black boy who was on his way home, rejected because of the color of his skin. The whole incident was a shameful commentary on the era and on my Grandfather's handling of the situation.

When I asked how the Depression affected the school, Daddy said, "Some people always have money. They could afford the two thousand dollar tuition, even during the thirties. If they couldn't, Grampy did some bartering. Mother and Barbara got clothes from Porteous Mitchell and Braun in Portland and Cliff Venard's in New York City. The furniture came from Levinson's, and he no doubt made other deals of bartering."

At the summer school, Grampy hired carpenters to build study cabins with fancy lettered signs giving each cabin the name of a famous prep school or Ivy League college. He had carpenters add a second story to a building for junior dorms. In 1937, Wassookeag School Camp had thirty-five or forty boys; three years later, Grampy enrolled sixty boys because of the additions. My Uncle Mac helped with the carpentry, did odd jobs, and was a chaperon and informal counselor to the young boys in the 1940s after his years as a camper.

In addition to the camp property and the three buildings on High Street, Grampy bought a house, barn, and acreage on the Ripley Road, a mile away from camp. He called it Wassookeag Farm. The horses were stabled there or at the camp, and caretakers grew vegetables at the farm for camp meals. Faculty and visiting families stayed there, too.

"The farm was sold sometime before we arrived in 1937," Mr. Hebert said, "but I always heard about the big garden and the fresh vegetables. Lloyd had to do everything just right."

"Lloyd was a perfectionist," Mrs. Hebert interjected with a shake of her head. "He had to supervise everything. He seemed to know about everything. He'd come and boss the workers—the carpenters, the kitchen help, and office help—and tell them how they should do it."

"Yes, Father ran a good school, my father said, "but he over-hired, over-spent, and over-borrowed. Money flew through L.H.'s fingers like scraps of paper in the wind. Jesus, that man could go through money."

The Wassookeag School, High Street, Dexter, Maine

Hector Hebert and students from the Wassookeag School

Harvey Hatch, Renee and Hector Hebert in front of a former study cabin—1989

THE NEW YORK TRIP

Three stern visaged young men in fedoras flank a serious older man and a smiling young woman, all staring directly into the camera lens. The handwriting on the bottom white border says, "The New York Crowd 1934." Aunt Teddy's familiar script on the top of the border says—Mac, Lloyd, Barb, Harvey, and Jimmy. The photo recorded her nephews and niece embarking with Lloyd Hatch on a trip to the city.

Mac and Harv, with their cousin Jimmy, identically dressed in bulky, belted, wool topcoats and fedoras that almost disguise their youth, stand erect and serious beside their father and sister in the December snow outside the screened piazza. They lined up at the edge of the driveway where my grandfather once posed in his Bowdoin track uniform and where the children posed through the years with tricycles, wagons, and long runnered kick sleds.

Years later when I asked my father about the trip, he told me that Jimmy was ill at ease in his grandfather's old hat and too large coat. Jimmy's top coat is not buttoned, but is wrapped across the front unevenly with the wool belt's extra length wrapped around and looped to take up the slack. Aunt Barbara wears a fur coat with diagonal lines and a perky black hat. "Yes, I felt pretty snappy in that hat and fur coat," she told me.

My father said that he felt rather special that day, too, in his new spats, which are barely visible on top of his shoes, beneath the cuffs of his creased wool pants. All of the teenagers were excited about the trip. They were on their way to the city, leaving Dexter behind, but still feeling as if the aura of country hick clung to them like hay chaff.

For eight years, sons of the rich and famous had come to Dexter to The Wassookeag School. Barbara, Harvey, and Mac were used to being around young men who dressed well, drove fancy cars, and knew their way around a city. On that spring day, it was Barb's, Harv's, Mac's and Jimmy's turn to visit a different environment.

The Hatch teenagers lived in two worlds—the frugal world of their grandparents, Papa and Nanny Hill, and the spendthrift world of their father and his wealthy students.

In their younger days, life held simple pleasures and strong bonds for the six Hatch and Sharpe cousins growing up together with their mothers, their aunts, and their grandparents. The teen years proved more problematic for my father and Mac with the autocratic rule of their father, the headmaster. When Mac, Harv, and their cousin Jimmy were old enough, they became students at The Wassookeag School and their father and Uncle Lloyd, as headmaster, lectured to them about grades and conduct. There was always that distance and formality with the man who never really learned how to be a father, but remained always the headmaster.

Daddy told me, "We were treated just like the other students in the same across-the-table interview setting. When it came time for a report card conference, we were called into the office for a formal discussion of our grades and academic progress."

Mac and Harv, dressed in itchy wool suits with starched shirts and silk ties, stood in turn awaiting the verdict on their grades. They didn't have an informal chat in the evening with Dad. Needless to say, this meeting didn't engender fond memories.

Although Grampy was a stern man, the Hatch children and their cousins Jimmy, Bunny, and Margaret Sharpe had many opportunities for fun as youngsters and as teenagers. They visited at the summer school camp and the winter school. As a boy of ten, my father posed in a uniform as the team mascot, holding the ball, suited like the other members of The Wassookeag School basketball team in the school brochure. The Hatch and Sharpe children participated in activities with the boys and posed for group pictures with faculty and students at the winter and summer schools.

On that day in 1934 when they stood by the piazza, Mac, Harv, Barb, and Jimmy were eager not only for sightseeing, but also for a chance to see former students. Lloyd Hatch had planned meetings with alumni and families of potential students.

When they left Dexter, Lloyd Harvey Hatch, Sr. let Harvey, drive the 1933 Hudson. They drove first to Fairfield, Maine to see their mother, who was at the Tuberculosis sanitorium that year. Malcom posed beside his mother's bed for a picture. She looks weak and thin in the photographs.

Aunt Barbara told me, "That year of 1934, when Mother was confined at the sanitorium, was difficult for everyone, especially the boys. I was away at Westbrook Seminary for Girls then, so I didn't have to deal with father. I was the only one who could stand up to him. One weekend, I was home from school, and the boys wanted to go to a movie. Father thought they should stay home and read a book. I spoke up to him and they finally went to the movies, but what a row."

After they left Fairfield, Daddy drove the Hudson to Connecticut. Just before they reached New Haven, Grampy told Harvey to pull over to the road's edge, stop the car, and take off the gray spats that covered the tops of his shoes.

"Spats aren't proper attire after five o'clock," advised Grampy. Once the offending spats were removed, Daddy, Mac, Jimmy, Aunt Barbara, and Grampy were on their way to meet the train to New York. After they boarded the train, the conductor announced the upcoming stops, and the teenagers' anticipation built as the train clickety-clacked closer to the city.

When they emerged from Grand Central Station, the four teenagers stood in awe of the sights and sounds of the city. They checked into the McAlpin, "a splendid place," according to my father.

Grampy Hatch spared no cost on their trip. He felt a sense of pride and importance to have arrived at this stage in life—a long way from the poor boy who had grown up on a farm.

He took his sons, daughter, and nephew to see a Rangers' hockey game, to Jack Dempsey's nearby restaurant, and to a Broadway show. Everyday they had lunch in a cafe, or in a restaurant, or at the McAlpin. Each night they had dinner in a different restaurant. The Kretchma, an exotic, expensive, authentic Russian tea room was their favorite, although Daddy told me he didn't like the food. Aunt Barbara said, "On the first night at the Kretchma, the boys nearly split themselves laughing to see the men in costumes dancing, twirling about, then squatting and kicking out their legs and feet to the fast paced music."

While my father, his siblings, and cousin were dining around the city, they met with alumni of The Wassookeag School, boys a few years older than they were. Jack Fink, a former student was eager to show them around. Jack took my father to a bar for his first drink. "I was feeling pretty sophisticated, so I ordered a whiskey highball. It had ginger ale in it and spoiled the taste for me," Daddy told me when I asked him for details about the infamous New York trip.

"We had a wonderful time seeing the sights for three or four days," Daddy said. "Then Father said, 'It's time to go home. The money's all gone. We have just enough for the train ride back to New Haven.'"

Daddy continued, "That was when Mac surprised us all by announcing, 'I've got some money,' as he reached into his pocket and pulled out a fistful of ones—$43.00."

"Where did you get that?" his father asked.

"You left it on the tables at the restaurants, so I picked it up."

"Well," responded my grandfather, "we'll stay another day then."

And so they had one more fun-filled day in the city, compliments of Mac's light fingeredness. What was done, was done. The currency was in hand, and when it came to money, Grampy's scruples were a bit skewed.

As the story was repeated over the years, it was never clear to me whether Mac, the teenager from rural Maine, knew he was taking tips from waitresses and waiters, or if he was just scooping up money he thought his father had left in haste. I have often wondered if Mac might have become a different person if his father had escorted him back to each restaurant and cafe to return the money to waitresses and waiters. Instead, the episode gave Mac notoriety and a certain measure of respect for his resourcefulness.

There is more than a little irony that just before getting on the train in New Haven, my father was admonished to remove his spats because they weren't proper attire, yet as far as I know, Mac was not reprimanded for confiscating tips.

Mac and my father were different. From earliest childhood on, it was clear that Mac was the mischievous son. Mac was the child whose charm and disarming smile helped others overlook his transgressions. Both my father and Mac were gregarious, ebullient storytellers. Each could entrance a room full of people. Having an appreciative, laughing audience spurred them on to embellish the tales.

Money, as well as adulation and acclaim, was something else that spurred them on. Daddy once told a story about how, when he was a little boy in knickers, he earned money for the movies: "I went to Fossa's store and bought a candy bar for a nickel. Then I went over to the Amos Abbott Mill and hollered up to the open windows, above the noise of the looms, to see if one of the men wanted a candy bar for six cents. One of them threw down the money and I threw the candy up into the window. Then I went back to the store for another candy bar, then back to the mill, and tossed it up to another man and he threw down six cents. I kept it up until I had ten cents, enough money for the movie."

Daddy also regularly helped an old widow with some chores. After he had finished hauling firewood inside for her, which he thought he was doing as a favor, she gave him a five dollar gold piece.

When Daddy was a man, trying to establish an insurance and real estate business in Dexter, his generosity, hard work, and his anticipation of other's needs and wants helped the business grow. Daddy and Mac needed to be liked, needed to do things for, and give things to people. Daddy gave away rulers, pens, pencils, and other advertising gimmicks with his name printed on them. Mac gave away vegetables from his garden at Aunt Teddy's, including pumpkins for his great-nephews with their names carved into the pumpkin skin and the letters healed over with a raised scab of an orange scar.

In many ways both Mac and my father were gamblers. Daddy gambled that he'd sell houses and that not too many of the ones he insured would burn down. He gambled at the horse races, telling us of the big win of $500.00 or $1,000.00, but he never mentioned his losses. He gambled with his health with all the expensive cuts of roast of beef, the sweets, the cigarettes, and the liquor he secretly consumed. He gambled that the people who owed him hundreds or thousands of dollars would eventually pay him.

Mac also gambled away his health on cigarettes and liquor which he drank openly. He gambled that when he sold or pawned his tools to Roland Goulette for the price of a few six packs, he'd be able to get the tools back when the next carpentry or painting job came along. Mac gambled that each of his two failed marriages would last, and gambled that he wouldn't get caught taking lanterns or lawnmowers from family members.

Over the years, Mac and my father played out their roles, and near the end they couldn't spend any length of time in each other's company without harsh words, thinly veiled put-downs, and the hint of unresolved conflicts.

Mac learned to finagle like his father, and glibly accept whatever came his way. Mac made his way in the world, or at least he made it in Dexter where he spent most of his life. From his earliest childhood on, Mac was the subject of stories, and they all centered around his antics. I suspect that his trip to New York, with the extended stay because of pilfered money, affected Mac and became his *modus operandi* in life.

The "New York" Crowd   1934.

A LOSER OR A HELL OF A NICE GUY

As I got dressed that August day in 1980, I reminded myself that today was my Uncle Mac's funeral. Those words did not have real meaning until I entered the funeral home and heard the eerie strains of recorded organ music that I have come to hate. Until that moment, it could just as well have been a wedding or some other occasion drawing the family together. Five months had passed since Mac was one of the mourners in the same room at his father's funeral. One month ago, he had attended a celebration and family reunion in honor of Aunt Teddy's ninetieth birthday. Today he lay in a casket in the next room.

Quietly, the family filed into that room and sat waiting for the services to begin, talking in hushed tones, identifying floral arrangements in vain attempts to dispel their uneasiness. Among the dozen or so bouquets with their colorful, puffy, satin bows, one lone bud vase with a single red rose stood out. I thought of Becky Salisbury, Mac's friend, and wondered if the rose symbolized her tribute to their relationship. She knew him to be thoughtful and sentimental, but also irritable and intolerant.

They were an unusual pair, both doomed by fate and life circumstances as they came together in a late life affair. Becky lived with her elderly father, who had owned the local fish market in the 1950s. She waged a daily battle with a terminal brain tumor, while Mac regularly administered his own death potion—alcohol. The words romantic and intimate did not seem to describe their relationship, yet how was I to know? I was never with Becky and Mac when they were together, and only heard about them from Aunt Teddy.

62

To the left, in front of Becky, I noticed two unfamiliar young women who must have been friends, sobbing uncontrollably, dabbing their eyes with white tissues. Across the room sat dry-eyed family members, each immersed in personal thoughts and reminiscences. I whispered to my sister that it was ironic to see Mac's friends, whom few of us knew, more visibly upset than his family.

My eyes and thoughts turned to my great-aunt, and I wondered how she was bearing up under the emotional stress of his sudden death. Aunt Teddy had helped raise him from infancy through boyhood, and it occurred to me that she still thought of him as that little boy. He had returned to live in her house even as a grown man until 1976, when she moved to a senior citizens' apartment.

With feelings of resentment, I recalled that she had endured his drunken rages when he hurled vulgar insults as well as plates of food. Yet she forgave him long before any of the other relatives. Aunt Teddy had told my father that the last time she saw Mac, he had left his customary spot on the steps of a Main Street apartment to help her cross the busy street. Afterward, when he asked if she had five dollars he could have, she gave it to him with no admonition. For six decades, she cared for and worried about this man who lay dead. Her sister's son was more hers to worry about than were the other nieces and nephews. Now she would rest easier, no longer wondering, worrying who would care for him if she died first.

As I sat facing the casket, I thought about the little boy he had been and the man he had become. I remembered the photographs of a mischievous preschooler in his sailor suit, perched on top of a mailbox, and the dare-devil boy of seven clinging to the top of a flag pole. He had seemed to always be climbing, reaching. I wondered what had happened to those boyhood aspirations. Somewhere along the way he became mired down by failure and a sense of loss for what he once had.

I thought of Patty, the daughter of the first of Mac's two failed marriages. Until recently, he had never discussed Patty with me, even though he knew I had met her in 1957 while visiting my grandparents in Rhode

Island. He had not seen, communicated with, or supported her financially since shortly after she was born in 1943. Yet, out of sentimentality, guilt, or both, he secretly kept a small wooden box, like a treasure chest, with her baby pictures and tiny, pink kid baby shoes. They were found after he died.

A year after he had a coronary bypass, fortified by a bottle of cheap wine, Mac gathered the courage to telephone the daughter he had never known. He realized he would not live many more years and the separation was a loose end in his life. Patty and Mac communicated by telephone and letter for six months until his death.

Although he was never a true father to his own daughter, Mac was, in some ways, like a father or pal to several young adults present at the funeral—Doug Pooler, the unknown young women, my sisters and me. I remembered the summer Sundays when he took my sisters and me for rides in his battered old car to purchase the forbidden treat of bags of penny candy. We drove back to the cottage chomping on chewy Mary Janes or sucking on sweet root beer barrels while Mac sipped on a bottle of cold Budweiser which he kept between his legs. He had bought it illegally on the Sabbath at Snyder Provost's store while we picked out our candy. We sanctimoniously reminded him that he should not drink and drive, but begrudgingly accepted his joking, rationalizing excuses.

I looked at the casket, trying not to imagine Mac as he looked now, but remembering the way he looked twenty-six years ago, driving the car in his rumpled, faded green cotton bathing trunks with a bottle of beer between his legs.

Mac's back, chest, and muscled arms were burnished reddish bronze from painting houses shirtless in the sun. A large cyst, which sometimes twitched, protruded on his right cheek, as if he held a candy Hot Ball in his cheek.

As he puffed on his cigarette, we pleaded with him to show us his trick. When the cigarette was smoked to an inch and a half stub, he expertly flipped the lighted end back into his mouth using only his lips and teeth.

We didn't believe that the smoke would come out of his ears, as he told us it would, but we were nevertheless awed by his deftly perfected trick and had him show all of our friends.

We scoffed at the stories Mac told.

"You don't believe me?" he'd ask. "I wouldn't tell a lie. I might prevaricate; but I wouldn't tell a lie," Mac said it in such a way that I figured out the words meant the same thing.

I thought of the occasions when Mac let us dive from his broad shoulders into the waters of Lake Wassookeag, or aided us in flips and other acrobatics, or flexed his arm muscles and make them dance to music. One Sunday afternoon in October of 1957 he arrived with a black Labrador Retriever puppy and a dog house he had built, while we pleaded with our parents to keep the puppy. We had many years of enjoyment with Cindy, because Mac thought kids needed a dog …and because my father paid the bills. That was the way it was—Mac got the glory and my father paid the bills.

I glanced at my father sitting stiffly in his seldom worn seersucker sport coat, knowing what he and many family members thought about Mac's lifestyle. Echoes of the past came into my mind as I recalled one Sunday when we returned with Mac from the ride to Snider Provost's market. The delight I had felt only moments before evaporated as I overheard my father ranting and raving to my mother in what seemed to be angry, jealous resentment over the attention we gave to Mac and the attention he gave us. As the last sliver of root beer barrel dissolved, I felt a puckerish, wrinkled feeling in my mouth, a knot in my stomach, and a bewildered feeling of sadness.

My father, and many others, saw Mac as a sponger, a man who thought the world owed him a living. How many times had I heard those words? In his role as his brother's keeper, my father had bailed Mac out of many financial scrapes over the years. Mac took money from his elderly aunt; he charged to my father's account personal items mixed in with materials needed for a repair or construction job at our house. Later in life, he actually stole a lawn mover from our camp and took an antique lantern of Aunt Teddy's and sold it for beer and wine. I remembered how Mac, much to my father's consternation, called the lot on the lake near our cottage, "his picnic grounds" and how he invited anyone and everyone to use it, when my father was the one who paid the taxes on it for twenty years. Mac had a penchant for deceiving himself about the reality of his actions and the reality of his life.

How irked my father and family members were to see Mac, who was a talented carpenter, an accomplished machinist, an expert painter, and a jack-of-all-trades, seldom hold a steady job even when he was physically able. The family knew Mac bought expensive tools or fishing and hunting equipment rather than basic necessities, and that he sold his tools for next to nothing at a local garage when he was down and out and needed a drink. Mac was like a child with a dollar at a candy store, with no thoughts of future needs—only instant gratification.

"Mac was just like L.H," my Father once remarked. "He never planned more than a week ahead."

As more mourners filed in, I saw the professional people of the town— teachers, doctors, lawyers, and businessmen (many of whom Mac probably owed money). These people had been friendly with Mac's parents and my father, and they genuinely liked Mac despite his failings. The teachers, one of whom was an author, were outdoor enthusiasts who had spent days and weeks hunting and fishing with Mac. They, like many of the people in the room, were recipients of an abundant supply of vegetables that Mac produced in his huge garden. These people also remembered Mac's generosity and the skilled labor he offered them as a favor.

On the other side of the room, I saw the street people, friends of Mac's from the lower strata of Dexter society. Some looked uncomfortable in ill-fitting, out-of-date suits, greasy hair slicked back, and bleary-eyed (whether from alcohol or tears I couldn't say). I noticed the contrast of friends and mourners, and it struck me as odd, but fitting, that such a diverse group would come to pay their last respects to Mac.

I remembered how life changed for Mac after his heart attacks. He was unable to do any strenuous activity or odd jobs, even though he wanted to. So he sat, idly, a bloated, pathetic fixture on the steps of a Main Street entrance with his Collie and a small, brown bag at his side, engaging in conversation with all passersby. Businessmen, family, or friends stopped to chat, if they had time, especially if he was sitting alone. Usually Mac's street friends—unemployed nare-do-wells—would join him for hours on end. It was a source of embarrassment for my father to see his brother sitting there day after day. The brothers spoke to each other, yet they were uncomfortable when together for any length of time.

When Mac failed to appear on those steps for two days in a row, my father became suspicious and went to check on him. He found Mac's ever faithful dog pacing nervously and his master sprawled on the bedroom floor where he had lain for two days.

Questions arose. Did Mac stagger, drunk, and trip over the stool, then fall and hit his head on the metal bed frame, or did he have a heart attack and fall? Did he die instantly, or was he alive for a while with only his dog at his side, nudging him, offering what little comfort and solace he could? Could someone have bludgeoned him after an altercation and staged the scene? The police saw no need for inquiry or an autopsy. He was an alcoholic with a bad heart. Case closed.

My thoughts were interrupted as the minister strode in, his black robe billowing after him, a book tucked under his arm. His eulogy was simple and forthright, not extolling Mac's virtues or lack of them, yet it was somehow fitting for a man who did not profess a belief in God. He concluded with a poem by Alfred Tennyson that Mac had heard at his grandfather's funeral many years before. Only his ninety-year-old aunt remembered that he had liked the poem.

CROSSING THE BAR

Alfred Lord Tennyson (1809-92)

Sunset and evening star,
   And one clear call for me!
And may there be no moaning of the bar,
   When I put out to sea,
But such a tide as moving seems asleep,
   Too full for sound and foam,
When that which drew from out the boundless deep
   Turns home again.
Twilight and evening bell,
   And after that the dark!
And may there be no sadness of farewell,
   When I embark:
For tho' from out our borne of Time and Place
   The flood may bear me far,
I hope to see my Pilot face to face
   When I have crost the bar.

As I listened to the unfamiliar poem, I cringed and a flush of embarrassment crept up my back and neck at first mention of the word bar, even though it had an entirely different connotation, that of a sand bar I guessed. I didn't look around the room as we filed out, but I met my sister's gaze. The poem and the reasons why Mac, the young man, liked it hit me. I thought about his life, the futility, the pain, the humor, and, for the first time, tears came.

*Mac and Harvey Hatch—1970s—standing in front of
a former study cabin converted to a tool storage shed.*

THE HOUSE ON RUFFLES AVENUE

For years after my last visit to Newport, Rhode Island I dreamed of returning to the house on Ruggles Avenue. I saw myself at the threshold of the arched doorway, knocking on paneled oak or introducing myself, hesitantly offering identification, photographs from the past that would allow me to enter the front hall. I would awaken, disappointed by the illusion, feeling so close yet so far from the ephemeral reality of what was once the Hatch Prep School for Boys.

Sometimes in my dreams I would find myself on the fifth floor in opulent rooms that didn't seem familiar, and I would awaken puzzled, trying to remember if the house had four floors or five. In other dreams, I climbed the grand staircase, hugging the wall, fearfully forcing myself to venture to the leafy wrought-iron-railed edge of those marble wonders, those stairs that jutted ten feet from the wall. Their attachment to the walls seemed even more tenuous, as if they could break away from the wall with the pressure of my stepping. I would climb on and on, up a stairway to the sky, gazing down deep, into the vast center, still seeing the fifty-foot chain and the huge bowl-shaped crystal chandelier with crumpled Necco Sky Bar wrappers caught in the prisms.

I am no longer taunted by the dreams, but the memories are still clear.

I was four and a half in 1951 when I made my first visit to the house on Ruggles Avenue. The whispery fronds of a large old weeping willow hung down like a giant green umbrella, providing a play house for me and my Ginny doll. Hearing my grandparents' call, I carefully folded the little Chinese paper parasol and the tiny pink plastic comb and mirror into Ginny's miniature gray cardboard suitcase and emerged from my leafy hideaway. My grandparents' talk with Mrs. Emerson, the building's owner was concluded. This would be the new home for Grampy's school.

Lloyd H. Hatch, Sr., my grandfather with the grandiose dreams, had decided to move his Wassookeag School from Dexter, Maine where it had prospered for twenty-five years, to Newport, Rhode Island, changing the school's name along the way. With his idiosyncrasies and egocentricities full blown by 1951, he renamed it Hatch Prep, hoping, perhaps, to immortalize himself in the process.

Grampy and Winnie moved from the twenty-room, Spanish style stucco house in Dexter, to a huge ivy-covered mansion that was the most magnificent building I had ever seen. The Newport house, built in 1925 for more than $2,000,000 and patterned after a French chateau of the Renaissance period, looked like a fairy tale castle to me. It was a grand building with turrets and chimneys, gothic gargoyles, balconies, balustrades, and floors of marble, Persian mosaic tile, flagstone, and parquet, and enough 16th century stained glass for a cathedral.

A veritable European palace, the house on Ruggles Avenue became Winnie's and Grampy's home from September until June when they returned to their summer cottage in Dexter. For eight years, Grampy (with his newly-formed board of trustees) leased that building from Mrs. Emerson. She had purchased it from the city in 1949 for less than its assessed value of $60,000, thus saving it from the wrecker's ball and subdivision of the land. In the summer, when my grandparents returned to Dexter, Mrs. Emerson ran a girls' school called Burnham By the Sea.

Small Maine mill towns can impoverish the senses aesthetically, if not spiritually. And Dexter was decidedly dull. To my three sisters and me, the opportunity to leave the town where we were born was exciting. Visiting the house on Ruggles Avenue felt like staying in a museum or stepping back in time and living in a palace; but most of all, we could visit our grandmother, Winnie, and her sister, Auntie, who ran the kitchen.

We didn't see much of Grampy. He was a very busy man. When we arrived, he greeted us with his odd, ritual purr, barely touching the tops of our heads as he bent over us before retreating to his office to dictate to his secretary, Yolande Veilleux. I don't ever remember a kiss or a hug, just the formality, the austere distance, and the distracted purring.

Grampy looked a bit like Fred Astaire, because he parted his hair in the middle and smoothed it straight back. His hairline resembled the flying birds I drew in my pictures, and his long ears lay flat to his head. Grampy was a fastidious dresser, who bought most of his clothes at Louis' of Boston. In the daytime he wore double-pocketed rayon or Viella shirts and pleated-front pants with nary a wrinkle. He smelled of Chesterfields and Canada peppermints, which were both ever present in his shirt pockets.

Winnie greeted us with embraces and the scent of Bologia perfume, hugging each of us in turn to her rotund, tightly corseted body, while the texture of her crepe dress brushed our cheeks. She was so glad to see us.

One year, when I was in the fourth grade, Randy, Sally, and I boarded the train in Newport, Maine and met Winnie in Providence at the station. I felt very responsible to be in charge even though the conductor kept an eye on us. I read my book about the Happy Hollister family, talked to my sisters, drank lots of water from flimsy, cone-shaped paper cups, and went to the adjoining car. I stepped gingerly over the coupled area from one lurching car to the next on my way to the bathroom. I was surprised when I stepped on the pedal and saw waste water flushed onto the railroad ties as we rumbled over them. Then I went back to my seat to listen for the stop in New Haven so we wouldn't miss Providence.

After the long trip from Maine, we usually went eagerly with Winnie to the kitchen to see Auntie and to have a snack. We sat for half an hour munching Auntie's molasses cookies and refilling our milk from the stainless steel machine in the unlocked pantry. Then it was time for us to go to Winnie's and Grampy's quarters, a second floor suite, to unpack and freshen up for dinner.

When we visited Newport, our attire and social conduct had to be appropriate for all occasions. We always dressed for dinner in our best party or church dresses with patent leather shoes and white anklets. Those were the days when we often wore matching dresses and were arranged like stairs for photographs. Later on, when I was twelve and in an awkward growth spurt, there was a discrepancy in the line up. My sister, Randy, at twenty months younger than I, was ten; Sally was nine; and Susie was six years old. They were still cute little girls, but in the 1959 photograph near the portico at Hatch Prep, I looked, and felt, like a pubescent Minnie Pearl with my wide-brim straw hat, pointed frame eye glasses, and my dress hanging an inch below last year's Easter church coat.

Shortly before that picture was taken, I acquired seamed nylons and a garter belt for dressy occasions. I was a lanky, flat-chested sixth grader with straight brown hair pulled back in barrettes on each side and my bangs styled with water still dripping. Sometimes I tried to set my hair with rubbery brown curlers that had a strap to snap onto the pointed end.

One morning my hair stuck out in sausage shaped clumps after I had rolled six or seven curlers from ear to ear around the back of my head. When I took the rollers out in the morning, hoping for a beautiful transformation, I was dismayed at the sight created by inept fingers. Winnie said the water in Newport was hard, with lots of iron in it, and that was the cause of my tight tube curls. So I watered my hair down in an attempt to train and tame it.

Then I stood for a while in the bathroom on the black and white tiled floor, leaning over the marble pedestal sink, gazing into the mirror, disliking my image. After fixing my hair with barrettes, I liked to use Dr. West's tooth powder from the blue and white can. Winnie used it to clean her dentures. I put some in my hand, dipped my wet toothbrush into it, and scrubbed the dry paste on my teeth.

My reflecting smile was different after one night's activity when I was ten. My sisters and I finished eating dinner and for some reason we were excused from the table early, perhaps while my grandfather intoned one of his infamous lectures to the boys and faculty assembled in the dining room. When my sister Randy and I went to the empty game room, we found amplifiers, guitars, and a microphone set up. Ever the actress, I began to mimic Elvis Presley. Unfortunately, when I grabbed the micro-phone, pulling it toward me, I smacked the device against my front tooth. I chipped a fair sized chunk off the bottom of my top tooth, giving myself a permanent reminder of Newport.

On Friday nights, everyone—students, faculty, visiting Hatch family members, and other guests—went to the spacious library after dinner, for the formal coffee / social hour. I always loved the ambiance of these evenings: the murmur of voices punctuated by occasional raucous laughter of some boys or sedate chuckles of those standing in a group with their teachers.

Winnie let me and my sisters use the silver tongs to grasp sugar cubes to plop into the coffee she poured from the silver service into delicate Haviland china demitasse cups. Sometimes we poured the cream and stirred it into the coffee with the miniature silver spoons. It was exciting to be part of these ministrations and to have such grown-up duties.

Gingerly, we carried each cup and saucer of coffee or tea across the ori-ental carpets and the parquet floor, or we just sat on the carved oak bench adding cream and lumps of sugar. When the boys left for the Friday night movie, the room became quiet. The shy, nervous French maid (Yoland Veilleux's cousin from Canada), scurried about in her burgundy, taffeta uniform with its lace collar, cuffs, and apron. While she gathered coffee cups, we went upstairs with Winnie and Grampy to their suite.

That night, as usual while we were gone, Gene Veilleux, Yolande's father, had come in to lay a fire. Logs rested on a nest of kindling and crumpled newspaper awaiting the touch of a match. Soon the room was cozy and my cheeks flushed pink from the fire's heat. I moved back from the marble hearth and settled on the sofa with Winnie's new book— *Letters To Dear Abby*. Soon I was lost in another world reading Abby's pithy answers to people's problems.

Winnie and my sisters were busy. Grampy went back to his office to dictate to Yolande. On that February vacation my father had stayed in Dexter because he couldn't leave the office for a week. My mother had left for a few days alone in Boston or New York visiting museums. So, when it was bedtime, my sisters and I all slept on cots in Winnie's and Grampy's large bedroom.

If the boys were gone for Christmas vacation and both of our parents were with us, we slept in the boys' rooms on the third floor. It was exciting to be there and to snoop in their bureaus for shocking girlie calendars— but it was very quiet and less enjoyable with the boys home on vacation. I liked it better when the school was full of boys, even though I was too young and gangly to be noticed by them.

In the morning, we saw the boys at breakfast and during their break from class. We arrived at the spacious game room before they did, to roll the pool balls as hard as possible against the bumper so the balls would return to us. Sometimes we attempted to keep a ping pong volley going until the skittish white balls bounded, plunk, to the flagstone floor. We usually stopped to look for recent artistic additions to the life-size alabaster statue of a nude woman with a drape across her thighs, pouring water from an urn into the cupped hands of a little male cherub.

A rush of footsteps on the marble stairs signaled new excitement for us as the game room came alive with the bustle of boys on mid-morning break. The candy machine clunked repeatedly as the boys made their selections; sphu, sphu the caps snapped off green coke bottles, and cigarette smoke curled into the air. Pool balls clinked against each other, the boys' voices rose in excitement or annoyance as the balls rolled into or missed the pockets. My sisters and I sat on the couches near the television across the room watching and listening to the commotion and frivolity.

One of the boys worked the keys of the upright piano and the beat of *The Bumble Bee Boogie* filled the air. The toe-tapping rhythm rose above the other noises, drawing the boys into a semi-circle around the player. One boy stood to the left, leaning against the Rubenesque flank of the alabaster woman who sported blue nipples because some wag had found another use for the pool cue chalk. I walked closer to the piano away from my seat in front of the TV, and listened enraptured by the rock and roll and the moment of abandon. Then the buzzer pierced the air; it all stopped as quickly as it had begun. The boys hurried off to their classes, and the magic was gone.

During the seven years of our visits, while the adults were busy, we had free rein to wander about the house exploring. When we explored the school, we occasionally lost our way in the labyrinth of corridors and stairways that connected more than seventy rooms. Sometimes Randy and I climbed the winding back stairway and peeked into the boys' rooms. We often found what we were looking for—the newest 1957 or 1958 desk calendars with titillating pictures of scantily clad young women, posing seductively in lacy underwear or see-through negligees.

One day, as we emerged from one of the boys' rooms, in a corridor of doors, we almost bumped into Gene Veilleux. Yolande's father had moved his family from Dexter for his job as janitor at Hatch Prep. He walked along mopping the floor, his keys rattling. Flustered, we feigned confusion, saying we were lost. Gene had black hair with a shock of white in the front. With his pipe clenched in his stained teeth, he told us in French accented English how to find our way. Randy and I went down the back stairs to the kitchen where Winnie and Auntie were planning the meals.

On other days, I might wander off without my sisters, walking through the first floor, fascinated by the sound as my shoes clinked across the marble floors. That was a distinctly different sound from the sound of the hollow creak of the polished parquet floor. My footsteps on the marble echoed up to the twenty-foot ceilings even after I stopped to press the ivory keys of an old harpsichord. The taut wires vibrated in a melodic plink, plink. Huge old tapestries on the walls did little to absorb the clicking footsteps of my patent leather shoes, as I walked down some steps and turned to examine the lion's head marble fountain.

I sauntered on, caught up in the spell of looking at and touching objects from centuries ago, examining, thinking, imagining, storing up images and memories. When I read historical novels in the 1970s and 1980s, I could vividly picture rooms walled with mirrors, carved gold leaf moldings, ceilings painted with angels and cherubs, ornately carved fire-places so tall that a child could stand up in them, and huge ballrooms with leaded glass doors leading to verandahs and garden terraces—because I had been there in Newport.

We spent most of our holidays at the Hatch Prep School. One Christmas our cousins Nancy, Donnie, and David Rust and their parents drove down from West Newton to join us. That was the year my sisters and I each received a saucer sled. Our teenage cousin Donnie gave us spinning rides on the mosaic tile and polished flagstone floor in the Great Hall.

Under the piercing and watchful eye of the gargoyles, stuffed moose, elk, and bison trophies mounted high on the wall, we played unmindful of the room's dignity. The hall, with its sixty foot ceiling, dark oak balconies, walls adorned with tapestries, and an imposing life-size statue of Joan of Arc mounted on horse back hanging over the arched doorway to the library, hardly seemed like a place for children to play. But there we spun and spun in the center of the colorful Persian tile floor, giddy with the thrill of it, with no chance of bumping into antiques in a hall as large as a gymnasium.

On some rare mornings or afternoons when Grampy wasn't busy, and if the office door was open, we went in to visit him, Yolande, and the other secretary. I loved getting one of Grampy's pencils with red on one end, and blue on the other end. We stapled together pieces of bond typing paper to make books. By flipping the pencil over, I could add variety to my pictures, and still erase if I made a mistake. Before we left, Grampy gave us one of his Canada peppermints from his shirt pocket. He ordered them by the gross, and sometimes he gave us a whole box of mints. Other than that, we saw little of Grampy until evening time in the upstairs suite. We didn't think it odd, because we were caught up in a whirlwind of activity with Winnie.

During our school vacation in 1957, 1958, and 1959 we spent much of our time with Winnie in the suite reading *Eloise At The Plaza*, *The*

Collected New Yorker Cartoons or the Dear Abby book. We also watched *The Arthur Godfrey Show* with Winnie. She taught us how to knit, gave us ginger ale, S.S. Pierce canned pears, and imported Collard and Bowser butterscotch candy wrapped in foil. It was almost as good as the old-fashioned butterscotch candy Winnie made in the summer at the cottage back in Dexter.

Winnie planned outings for us every day. We all piled into the 1948 turquoise, three-seat, Chevy beach wagon with wood trim, and headed down Ruggles Avenue to Belleview Avenue, then downtown. First, we drove to the post office to pick up the mail. We usually stopped to chat with Tom, a blind man who sold newspapers. He made me think of Bobby Downing, the blind man who peddled his bike around Dexter selling greeting cards to Aunt Teddy and other townspeople. Tom's eye lids were also closed all the time and he didn't wear dark glasses. It seemed like magic that he could recognize Winnie by her voice.

Once on the way back to the school, Winnie told us that T H A M E S was pronounced Tems, not THames, after one of us misread the sign. She explained that the street on which we were driving was named after a river in London, England. As we drove up Belleview Avenue, past other imposing mansions, Winnie slowed down so we could look at the ramshackle former gate house that was causing such a controversy in the newspapers and the town.

The land was owned by an elderly, eccentric recluse called "Timothy The Wood Hooker" who collected discarded lumber and furniture and stored it in his yard. If we were lucky, we might see the stooped over old man, in his shabby clothes, shuffling about the yard. We were awed by his eccentricity and his disregard for what the town or visitors thought about his way of life. His yard and house looked like some places back in Dexter, while every other place on Belleview Avenue was an immaculately kept mansion.

Sometimes, when we went to get the mail at the post office, we saw hordes of young men in Navy blue coming ashore from their ship in the harbor. Winnie sang the song, "Bell bottom trousers, suits of Navy blue I've got a…" and we spontaneously joined her. On other days, we went to feed the ducks at the pond near the radio station, taking bags of left-over bread from the school. We went to the movies to see *South Pacific* and *Oklahoma*. Winnie had the records of all the Broadway shows, and we listened to them by the hour and sang along with her, "Oh, what a beautiful mornin'…" In 1959 we saw the unforgettable movie, *Some Like It Hot*. I couldn't take my eyes off Marilyn Monroe in the see through black dress. It was more revealing than the calendar pictures.

Although I was curious about catching a glimpse of developed bosoms, I found other equally interesting things to do. For years Winnie drove us to Bailey Beach to ride the carousel until the hurricane of 1954 smashed it to bits. My sisters and I each had a favorite horse and rode round and round. When I was seven, I even dared to show my bravery and nonchalance by riding without holding the reins or the brass pole. My sophistication didn't prevent me from enjoying the merry-go-round or other things of childhood, like dolls.

Our favorite place was the doll store, a small, dark, cave-like emporium filled with beautifully dressed dolls on glass shelves which also held cellophane-centered boxes of colorful clothes. Every year, we saved our money, and Winnie and Daddy gave us extra so we could buy outfits for our Vogue dolls—Ginny, Jill, Jeff, and Ginette from the incredibly beautiful and vast array on display. We looked longingly at the more expensive Madame Alexandre dolls. One year, I bought a little Dutch boy outfit with real carved wooden shoes for my Ginny doll. Another year, I bought my teenage Jill doll a green velvet coat with rabbit fur collar, muff, and a hat made to look like leopard. It was so hard to choose among the beautiful clothes. The doll store was magical, and so was all of Newport.

I was at that in-between stage, still old enough for dolls, but interested in boys. My sisters, Randy, Sally, Susie, and I each had a boy we admired from afar. Sometimes during dinner we sat at the table with the boys. At eleven or twelve, I was closest in age to the boys, since some of them were fourteen. One night I was placed at a table with Jerry Dedrickson, whom I secretly liked. Mr. Dilloway, one of the teachers, Yolande, and the other boys occasionally acknowledged my presence, but, as usual, I was too shy and quiet to participate in the conversation. In addition, on that night I felt too ill to do more than answer in monosyllables.

My extreme nervousness at being in such close proximity to the boys was only a partial contributor to my nausea. That night I was wearing nylons and my first garter belt. I sat through the entire meal enduring the constriction of the stretchy elastic tube with its spidery elastic snaps digging into my thighs. The belt's six-inch diameter was crushing my intestines, causing such a stomach ache that I could only wish for a chance to be excused so I could remove the long-coveted garment of womanhood. That night I didn't go to the library to help pour coffee. I felt so ill after dinner that I went right to bed. I hated being sick and missing out on all the fun at Newport.

In February 1959, Grampy had a gala celebration with a big basketball tournament, a lavish dinner, and a dance with an orchestra from New York City, and I missed the whole event because I was sick. During the entire ride from Maine to Rhode Island, I felt nauseated. Being carsick was a common occurrence after traveling in the back seat for five hours, looking at the scenery, and playing the alphabet game with road signs or the states game with license plates. I had a headache and a stomach ache as we drove along, and it didn't go away after we arrived at the school.

Consequently, I didn't get a chance to wear my beautiful black velvet skirt and the fancy white blouse that my Aunt Barbara had given me for Christmas. Instead, I put on my flannel nightie, had some ginger ale, and spent the evening in Winnie's bed listening to the big band sounds float up the grand staircase. I lay there imagining the scene of the elegant soiree in the mirrored ballroom, picturing the boys in their black tuxedos and their dates in gorgeous gowns. I was so disappointed to have missed the ball. All of my relatives were there for the festivities, even Aunt Teddy.

At least there is some comfort in the fact that the previous year, when I was in the fifth grade, I had the opportunity to go to Newport with a friend from Dexter accompanying me. My friend Carol's parents (much to her disappointment) wouldn't let her go. I chose Mary Batson, who was two years older, to be my companion. My cousin Patty, Mac's daughter, came from Walpole to join us. Patty was three years older than Mary, which meant they were both at a closer age to the boys.

During that February vacation, I passed my autograph book around. Grampy, Winnie, Auntie, and Yolande each signed their names and dates of birth. Patty wrote, "When you grow old and rewards are few, remember the mighty oak that was once a nut like you. Love 'n luck, Patty DeForest." Mary autographed the green page with these words, "May you never be the color of this page." The singers in the jazz ensemble, Retha Harris and Zootis, each signed their names with a flourish. Zootis's printed signature looked like the way Zoro signed his name with the sword at the beginning of each TV episode.

The music was grand and we sat on wooden folding chairs in the ballroom with mirrored walls and gold leaf trim. Oddly enough, with all that so vivid in my memories, I can't remember if the boys had dates that night, nor how Mary and I traveled to Rhode Island. (Perhaps by train.) It doesn't really matter though, because the main thing is—we were there. Patty had attracted the attention of a student named George. Mary and I mostly hung around the game room. Since she was attractive and was a teenager, the boys also talked to her while I stood off to the side. Patty and George saw each other during her vacations. Winnie took their pictures together, and over the months, the romance blossomed. The next year, Patty was George's date at the gala house-party with the formal dance. Grampy even let George drive the limousine for movie dates with Patty. Manny, the chauffeur, had the evening off.

It was exciting to watch my cousins with their Hatch Prep boyfriends. I knew my time would come when I was a teenager and developed from an awkward duckling into a swan. Or, at least I hoped so, and I could hardly wait. Since she was eight years older than I, my cousin Nancy Lea had been first. She was a bubbly, enthusiastic, starry-eyed, red head who spoke in superlatives. She loved ballet and modern dance. Sometimes she twirled and pirouetted around the library. Other times she did the Egyptian or turtle walk to entertain us. We tried to imitate her and make our necks and arms move the same way.

I was eager to be like my older cousin Nancy Lea, who had the good fortune to be a teenager while the Hatch Prep School existed. Of course, the adults were not pleased that Nancy Lea thought she was madly in love with a boy from Bogota, Columbia instead of Grosse Pointe, Michigan. Roberto was enchanting in his swarthy handsomeness, and he gave Nancy Lea perfume. She swooned, and I observed the romance of it all. Sometimes, we could follow them to the library and sit on the oak bench in the middle of the large oriental rug that was like a small island on a sea of parquet. Randy and I read magazines, played checkers, or lined up the chess pieces while Nancy and Roberto talked and laughed on the brown velvet sofa near the huge fireplace.

Soon the adults had something new to discuss and worry about; we children learned the details later. In 1959, the board of trustees eased my grandfather into retirement, out of his position as founder headmaster because they faced rising expenses and debts brought on by his acquisition of six nearby furnished mansions for faculty and students. Grampy wanted the boys to each have a private bathroom and the kind of living conditions to which they were accustomed. He also wanted the boys segregated by grade level in different mansions spread around the vicinity of Ruggles Avenue. To Grampy it seemed logical to buy six mansions for faculty and students.

In order to finance these purchases, he had offered a special deal of three years' tuition payable in advance for only ten thousand dollars (a goodly sum in 1957 when most families in Dexter lived on four or five thousand dollars income per year). Unfortunately, he spent the money the first year on mansion acquisition, for remodeling and maintenance of buildings, purchasing expensive athletic uniforms for all sports, creating tournaments, and for the lavish house party where the boys invited dates for the weekend dinner dance with the New York orchestra. Grampy was a pioneer in the field of education, but he was not a financial manager. Overburdened with the costs of maintaining and heating buildings that each emptied a fuel truck every week, and exasperated by Grampy's extravagant spending, J.J. Newberry, former student at the Wassookeag School, now Chairman of the Board of Trustees, called a halt to the situation. The Hatch Preparatory School was moved to Massachusetts and became a part of The Winchendon School.

Life changed for Grampy after 1959. He and Winnie went from the glamour of Hatch Prep and the seventy room mansion to the twenty room stucco house on High Street in Dexter—back where it all began in 1928.

The empire had crumbled, the magic of Newport was gone, captured only in glossy eight-by-ten photos and in our memories. My sisters and I had Winnie and Grampy living next door, back in Maine, and we saw them often, but we never forgot those seven years of visiting the Hatch Preparatory School.

For years, memories called me back in time to those vacations in the house on Ruggles Avenue. The vivid dreams came night after night in adolescence. I searched and searched, opened doors to new rooms familiar, yet different. Or, I drove over the crunchy pebble driveway through tangled brush and over-grown trees, seeking admittance. When I read the first page of Daphane Du Mauriers' *Rebecca*, I thought of my dreams of the house on Ruggles Avenue. The television Gothic soap opera in the 1960s, *Dark Shadows* began with the camera slowly closing in on what had been the Hatch Prep School and the girls' summer school, Burnam By the Sea. I couldn't bear to watch, although many of my high school classmates did.

When articles appeared in Associated Press releases about Claus von Bulow, a Danish born socialite who was accused of trying to murder his wife Sunny von Bulow, I read that his mistress Alexandra Isles, was a socialite and former star of *Dark Shadows*. That night the vivid dreams returned.

The house on Ruggles Avenue is different now. My cousin Donnie visited in the 1980s and went inside. The huge library was partitioned, and the building was in disrepair. I attempted to visit on Columbus Day in 1992, with a folder full of pictures from the past under my arm just like I did in the dream. The building, now a part of Salve Regina University, was in an even sadder state of neglect. I knew I would find only disappointment inside. I left, never gaining admittance, feeling grateful that I still have the eight-by-ten photographs and the memories of those days of my childhood.

Prudy, Randy and Sally at the Hatch Prep School—1953

The Hatch Preparatory School and Burnham By The Sea

Lloyd Hatch in the Great Hall—1957

The library (or part of it) where coffee was served

Randy, Patty DeForest, Prudy, Sally, Susie

Grampy and Yolande in the office at Hatch Prep School

Susie, Prudy, Grampy, Randy, Sally, and Winnie in their suite at Hatch Prep—1957

THE HEADNASTER EMERITUS

In his retirement years, with the recognition and glory behind him, my grandfather became obsessed with his past accomplishments. He inserted a bookmark in the thick red volume of his *Who's Who in America* 1956 edition, no doubt reread the entry with his name countless times, and referred to it for newspaper articles in which he called himself "headmaster emeritus."

Grampy was also obsessed with his alma mater. It was as if Bowdoin had been his whole life, and certainly more dear to him than his children. The cottage on Lake Wassookeag contained a collection of college memorabilia—Bowdoin chairs, Bowdoin glasses, the Bowdoin beer stein, the set of Bowdoin dishes, a Bowdoin black wool felt banner, and a black felt pillow with white lettering and the sun shaped college emblem. *Bowdoin Alumnus* magazines, Chi Psi fraternity magazines, and articles enumerating Grampy's activities for Bowdoin fundraising and reunions were piled on his desk at the office cottage next door. Grampy filled the void of his retirement with work for the college commencement and gathering of alumni.

In 1961, Grampy offered evening study hall as a way to further fill his time and earn some money. Characteristically, that endeavor produced little net income, because Grampy spent money in advance on a small pool table and having a ping pong table built. He bought copies of the text books the boys used at Dexter High, and once again the third floor of the house on High Street sheltered students.

Billy LaBarge, Skipper Champeon, and Donnie Brooks arrived five nights a week to study and be tutored. Grampy sat at his desk with a glass of amber liquid at his side. When my grades hovered in the D's because of my letter writing and time spent skating and playing football at the rink instead of studying, I joined them with my own card table desk in another room. At break time we went to the finished basement to shoot pool or play ping pong. The basement game room was a pathetic imitation of the big one at Hatch Prep in Newport.

When he was retired, Grampy seemed to identify more with his college moniker. He signed his nickname and Winnie's ("Pop and Peg Hatch") in his bold, squarish script written with a flourish on white, greeting card size, green tasseled calendars, engraved in black with the twelve months in small blocks.

During the 1960s the printed calendar heading said, "The Hatches" instead of the former "Hatch Preparatory School" or "The Wassookeag School." Grampy insisting on keeping up the Christmas tradition of sending the cards to hundreds of people even when he and Winnie were in diminished financial circumstances and were thousands of dollars in arrears to R.C. Whitney and Sons (my friend Carol's family) for oil to heat their twenty-room house on High Street.

My sister Randy told me a story about Grampy that I had never heard before. Randy had to memorize and recite a poem for school. She was nervous and afraid she wouldn't do her poem well enough to earn her usual A. She mentioned it to Grampy on Thanksgiving Day when the family gathered for the holiday. He told Randy about the time he had to deliver a poem and how his dramatic presentation moved his Bowdoin professor to tears.

Grampy stood in the old fashioned kitchen in the house on High Street, with the slate sink behind him and his ever present glass of amber liquid set on the rectangular work table in the center of the room. To Randy's amazement Grampy performed an emotional rendition of Walt Whitman's "O Captain! My Captain!" with the same histrionics and theatrics that had won him an A+ at Bowdoin. Grampy stood on the balls of his feet, just as he had decades before, leaning slightly forward, explaining how that threw him off balance and added to the drama by making him tremble as he spoke. With his arms thrust out, lurching ever so slightly, tension mounting, Grampy's plaintive delivery evoked all that he had summoned five decades before. Randy remembers vividly the verses of "O Captain! My Captain!."

In 1966, Grampy sent my father a letter with an itemized list of the expenses Grampy had incurred raising and educating him, asking for money in payment. Grampy was desperate, his debts were high, and Daddy was incensed.

"L.H. is off his rocker now," raved Daddy. "Can you believe it? Telling me I owe him for my upbringing and schooling...Papa Hill took care of us for years. There's no mention of that."

There is something else about Grampy, something shameful and embarrassing to the family. In 1966, when Winnie was very sick after a stroke, and the unpaid bills were mounting, and his alcoholism was at its worst, Grampy did some unspeakable things. Grampy did something— exposed himself or touched a young girl, after she came inside from skating at the rink beside the house. I was married with a baby when I found out and couldn't bear to hear the details.

My father and Aunt Barbara discussed it long distance over the phone. They were appalled and knew they had to get Winnie and Grampy out of the house on High Street where there would be fewer opportunities and fewer problems to prompt the drinking. That summer, the house was sold to Mr. May and Winnie and Grampy moved to Dennis Cleaves' trailer park.

The following summer, they still had the cottage. Grampy hired a young woman to type and take dictation. Unfortunately, she had to field his advances as well. She told me and my friend about it, and I was incensed but couldn't do anything, except let her know that the family in no way wanted her to have to deal with it. She was poor and needed the money and I guess she managed somehow to keep him at bay. At least I hope she did. That's one memory that I let fade.

Decades later, I told my sister that I have no memory of Grampy doing anything like that to me. She didn't either. I said, "I don't think it is one of those blocked memory things like we so often read about." She voiced what I felt, that Grampy was far too preoccupied with problems and plans to spend much time with us, to say nothing of inappropriate touching. That's the way it was. Winnie was the light of our lives when we were children. We spent hours and days with her with nary a sight of Grampy, even after they returned to Dexter. Ironically, since Grampy outlived Winnie by ten years, it's he whose life seems so large. Winnie is the one who is most loved by those who still live and those who have passed on. Grampy is remembered for his genius and brilliance…and his excesses.

In those waning years, when Grampy's deeds and accomplishments had faded into the past, he was just another alum in charge of fundraising and reunions for the class of '21. He made such elaborate and expensive plans, doing everything in such a grand style that he needed a wealthy classmate to bail him and the class out of debt for costs incurred for the reunion of '71.

Grampy had reserved the entire Harriet Beecher Stowe House, arranged a catered lobster dinner, run up terrific bills for Thomas taxi for chauffeuring him from Dexter to Bowdoin's Brunswick campus and back and around town on missions he deemed vital for reunion planning.

After one night of reunion partying with old classmates, Grampy's excessive drinking became a story in the Brunswick newspaper. The incident was treated as if it were just some elderly Bowdoin boys, fraternity brothers out for a night of fun. My father laughed in his usual rueful way when he told me about Grampy's indiscretion and the headline that appeared after he drove his friend's car on the train tracks. It was a bit embarrassing to read: "Hatch rides the rails."

After Winnie died, Grampy moved to an apartment across from the Crosby Funeral Home. A few years later, he moved to an apartment up over a Main Street store. When he became less able to take care of himself,

he moved to Dover-Foxcroft to a boarding home, and put all of his possessions in storage in Hopkin's barn.

Four decades before, it had been The Wassookeag Farm. In 1971, all of
Grampy's possessions—beds, tables, chairs, paintings, pictures, dishes,
vases, with other household items were stored in that barn on the farm
that had once been his.

Grampy's books and the green bookcases were in Aunt Teddy's dining
room, not at Hopkin's. One day I visited her when Hector Hebert was
there at Grampy's request, choosing history books that he might like for
his library. The colorful book from PBS of *The Wives Of Henry VIII* was in
his hand at the time, and I wished that it could be mine so I could learn to
keep the wives straight.

In 1973, Grampy decided to send all of his possessions to me in
Skowhegan since the storage fees were getting expensive. My husband and
I had just purchased a large Victorian house and had little furniture.

My sister Randy and I went through the boxes and found the remnants
of Grampy's life: the three tuxedoes he bought to wear at house parties and
reunions at the Waldorf, the purple and gold Chi Psi felt banner and the
black and white felt banner, the Bowdoin memorabilia, the Phi Beta Kappa
pin, hundreds of pictures of the rooms of the house on High Street and the
mansions in Newport, pictures of men, long ago young in photographs of
the Bowdoin debate or track team or honor society or graduation in 1921,
childhood pictures of Barbara, Harvey, and Mac taken by Bert Call that
once hung in Winnie's and Grampy's bedroom at the house on High Street,
large framed photographs of Wassookeag Summer and Winter Schools
hand colored by Bert Call, boxes of Wassookeag bulletins and brochures,
dozens of duplicate pictures of the stages of construction of terraced bankings when the hockey rink was built with the money—$40,000—from the
sale of Wassookeag Summer School Camp in 1947.

That was the year the Winter School reopened after being closed in
1945 and 1946 because of the war. In 1951 Grampy and Winnie were off

to Newport, Rhode Island for a more prestigious setting and his eventual downfall eight years later, when he was asked to retire.

One day when my husband and I visited Grampy at the boarding home in Dover-Foxcroft, we asked him about the old days at The Wassookeag School and at Hatch Prep. Grampy talked of the 1920s, 1930s, and 1940s when the school and camp were in their heyday.

He spoke of the years after he moved the school to Rhode Island and changed the name. He listed the names of all of the mansions he had purchased to house the students and faculty in Newport, just down the street from the Vanderbuilt's Breakers estate. He told us about the day a mansion on Ruggles Avenue across the street from Hatch Prep was to be auctioned. Everyone else stood in the rain waiting for the auction to begin. Grampy joked and bragged that he had Manning, his chauffeur, drive up to the rear entrance, and that Grampy "went in and bought the building and entire contents for $50,000, while the other saps stood waiting with their umbrellas in the rain."

No one really knows for sure how Grampy finagled the finances, but it involved multiple mortgages with banks and with parents, prepaid tuition, bartering and a lot of juggling and chutzpah.

He told us the story about the summer when he stayed in Newport to work while Winnie went ahead to Dexter. Two hapless burglars broke into Vernon Court with the intent of robbing Grampy.

"Give us your money, they demanded."

They tied him up in the large marble bathtub with his feet on the faucet. They took his cigarettes, keys, peppermints, and his Phi Beta Kappa pin, and gagged him with his linen handkerchief. Grampy, the lecturer, had tried to use his speaking skills to make the robbers leave and give up their folly. One of the robbers said, "Don't get smart or we'll make it tough on you."

After they left, Grampy struggled for hours to get free or at least remove the gag. Finally, after his mouth was uncovered, he "bellowed like a bull" for help. He needed a cigarette and his 'pepmints. Someone heard him bellowing from the mansion bathroom and called the police. Later they found Grampy's gold Phi Beta Kappa pin on the lawn, glinting in the sun, but his cigarettes, keys, and Canada peppermints were gone with the robbers.

The tale of Grampy's escape made me think of O. Henry's *The Ransom of Red Chief* that I read in ninth grade. It made me wonder if Grampy's robbers had second thoughts, too, after they were scolded and castigated by the headmaster of Hatch Prep. Maybe the robbers thought he had lots of money after they saw the picture of Grampy in the paper in 1954, the summer of hurricane Carol, when Newport was devastated by the storm's high winds. The eight-foot high stone wall that graced the Ruggles Avenue entrance to the mansion's driveway lay in a pile of rubble, demolished by the wind's force and fallen trees. The beautiful big willow tree that I once sat under with my Ginny doll, was uprooted. The power was out for days, and Grampy needed a shave. He had a generator delivered and his picture was taken perched upon it, electric razor in hand. That was Grampy, nothing but the best would do.

One day when we visited at the boarding home, he sat in his worn, but still classic, clothes from Louis of Boston—the red gaberdine, loose flowing pants rolled up at the cuff as they were for lobster parties in the 1950s. With them he wore the pale yellow rayon shirt with over-stitching on the pocket and collar and his Moroccan leather opened-toe sandals. His long yellowed toenails, as hard as tortoise shells, protruded through the once expensive footwear. At his side he had a green box of his Canada "peppermints," his cigarettes, and paper clipped lists of items he wanted to discuss with us, one by one.

In the long hours of his days which no longer had purpose, Grampy had drawn plans to remodel the boarding home. He contacted carpenters, had conference calls on the telephone. The owners finally put a stop to Grampy's, plans which were as elaborate and unrealistic as the design he once told me about for a ketchup bottle. He would use plungers, vacuums, and devices to push the remaining condiment out of the bottle. Even as a child, I thought maybe making the jar-opening wider and using a spoon would make more sense though I never mentioned it. I can't look at a bottle of ketchup without remembering Grampy's characteristically unrealistic, expensive, imaginary contraption to get the remaining table-spoons of ketchup out of the bottle.

Grampy changed even more after he left the boarding home for the nursing home. He had always been a very social person, the giver of elab-orate parties, the pontificating headmaster. In the late 1970s after Winnie was gone and when he was no longer the celebrated educator, Grampy preferred sleep and dreams of the past. He stayed in his dreary room at the nursing home, avoiding contact with others. He felt above everyone at the nursing home, demeaned by being there. He had nothing in common with the other patients, except that he was old and waiting to die. Sleep and dreams of the past blocked out the reality of his day to day existence.

Perhaps Grampy dreamed of the house party days at Bowdoin when Winnie arrived with new evening gowns purchased by her parents. Winnie was accompanied by some of her friends from Dexter, and Grampy's mother to serve as "patroness and chaperon" for a gala weekend of dinners and dancing. Maybe Grampy dreamed of the evenings at Camp Wassookeag when he stood like a king before his court, lecturing into the wee hours of the morning while his teaching staff tried to stay awake as Headmaster Hatch went over each student's academic program. Perhaps Grampy dreamed of the grand days at Hatch Prep School in the mansion on Ruggles Avenue in Newport, Rhode Island.

Nothing in Grampy's experience prepared him for the defeat of old age and his final years, unless it was the earlier humiliation and loss of his rightful role as the Valedictory speaker at his graduation sixty-four years before his death in 1980.

So many words that begin with "P" characterize Grampy—particular, precise, persnickety, pompous, pedantic, proclivity to pontificate, pro-claiming his philosophy, program, proposals, penchant for parties and puns, pictures and pamphlets, photographs, punctilious, perspicacious, pertinacious, posturing, prodigious purchases, in a pickle, preparatory, preoccupied, pensive, pedagogue, pinnacle, plummet, past…The list goes on and on.

After Grampy died in 1980, my father handled the funeral arrangements. When he saw the obituary Grampy had composed, Daddy decided that he could not give it to Mr. Crosby at the funeral home to send to the newspapers unless he did some condensing and editing.

"Father wrote EVERY detail of his life. It would cost a fortune to print it," Daddy told Aunt Barbara over the phone. Years later, he told me again that it was too embarrassing and self-promoting to put all of the old accomplishments in the obituary, especially in light of the depths to which Grampy had sunk with unpaid bills and inappropriate touching of young girls. Daddy abbreviated Grampy's obituary, but it was still much longer than is common.

When I look through my collection of clippings, pictures, pamphlets, brochures, furnishings around our home, and sift through the memories they all evoke, I wonder if Grampy ever hoped that some day someone would write about his life. When I listen to the audio and video taped interviews with my father, Hector and Renee Hebert, and Aunt Teddy, I sometimes wonder if Grampy's spirit prods me on to tell his story and his rise to fame, if not his slide to infamy.

I have learned a great deal as I have looked back on the lives of my grandparents, father, aunts, uncles, and cousins. I have learned that time telescopes, that life is brief, that fame is transitory, and change is inevitable. I found a quote once that sums it all up. I wonder if Grampy, the student and teacher of history, ever read these words by Heraclitus, "Nothing endures but change."

Lloyd Hatch shaving using a generator after Hurricane Carol—1954

THE HOCKEY RINK

When I drew a map of Main Street with the special places of my childhood, I gave the hockey rink prominence, because it had such a magnetic attraction for all the kids in the neighborhood and beyond. The rink was the hub, the paths from our houses were the spokes, and the seasons rolled on through childhood and adolescence, moving us on to our futures.

Our futures led us in different directions. We haven't been together as a group for decades. We have little in common now, yet, in a way we have so much in common—we have a history and the memories of our times together at the rink. We were classmates from 1951 until 1965 and we met at the hockey rink in the fall, winter and spring until the middle teenage years. After that, dating outside the circle of friends seemed more alluring.

We had our youth, our discoveries, our conversations, as we were on our way to becoming the people we are now. We had the experience of growing up in a small Maine town where everyone knew us and our families, and where we could feel a link to the past. Being with my friends at the hockey rink was vital for me; it shaped my youth in ways I am only beginning to understand.

The hockey rink, which surrounded the flat, grassy area at the top of the terraced hills, might have been one more monument to my grandfather's folly and ego when he had it built in 1947 for his students. But, it was a wonderful place to play in the 1950s and 1960s. The rink was the gathering spot for ten childhood years until my friends, Carol, Gene, Larry, Phillip, and I had outgrown such things.

We five spent afternoons, evenings and occasionally entire days of vacation at the rink. Often we were joined by five to fifteen other neighborhood friends. In our early years the children in the area gathered to play Hide and Seek, Kick the Can, Giant Step, or Red Light-Green Light in the fall or spring. In the winter, we slid down the bankings on our saucer sleds.

We played cowboys and cowgirls or soldiers, copying scenes from TV westerns and 1940s war movies. We crawled on our stomachs, peeking around the rink corners, waiting for the right moment to pelt each other with the hard, orange berries from the Rowan tree that grew near the fence.

My sisters, other neighborhood girls, and I tried to walk around the top of the rink boards, cautiously placing one foot in front of the other on the inch and a half wide edge, with one of us on each side holding right and left hands to help with balance. Larry and Gene worked on mastering the entire perimeter of the rink, once, striving for a second trip around the boards, one foot step after the other.

The barn-red boards formed a corral-like balance beam around the interior of mowed grass. Perched bravely, four feet above the ground, we girls unsuccessfully attempted to inch our way around the entire rectangle of the regulation size rink. Sometimes we made it across the short end of the rink, about eighty-five feet from one corner resting spot to the other, but the side that was two hundred feet long was too difficult to master.

On the short end, closest to Main Street hill, there was a flat, five feet wide border of grass outside the rink before the tiered bankings dropped off. It gave us the illusion of being on a mountain as we looked down at Main Street. We found it safer to look in the other direction, inside the board fence where we could only see the four feet below. When inching along heel to toe on the board edge, it was best to look down only at the narrow path to be conquered.

I failed to do that once, or perhaps the friend holding my hand moved too fast. I fell straight down, landing with a painful jolt, straddling the edge of the fence. By the time I reached the bathroom of our house next door, blood was gushing out between my legs. I was scared and in pain. No great damage was done, fortunately. However, I lost interest in the challenge of balancing and walking on the fence edge after that. Then, in about the fourth grade, the boys began arriving for ball games, and I began to join them.

Larry Richards lived up on the hill beside the road to the cemetery. He walked down through the woods behind my grandparents' house, carrying his football or bats and glove, sending his younger brothers back home.

Larry had a dark, wrinkled burn mark on his neck, so he always wore a shirt to cover it. I had a neck scar from the removal of a birthmark, and sometimes I felt like a kindred soul to him, although I wasn't embarrassed about my scar. Larry had a dark complexion with high, prominent cheek bones and looked as if he had some Native American ancestry, although we never heard that he did, nor even thought about it. He had dark circles under his eyes, as if he were chronically tired. That combined with his perpetual scowl, gave him a serious look, unless he was laughing.

Larry laughed like a horse, with his mouth wide open. The noise came rippling up from his toes in a huge guffaw and turned into a sound similar to that of a hyena. His laugh was at its maniacal worst when someone else was the butt of his ridicule, but that was when he was a teenager. When he was younger, he threw burdocks rather than barbs.

Larry was my friend and my enemy for most of my growing up years in Dexter. He hated me and liked me simultaneously and intermittently, depending on the season or the year. In the sixth grade, we secretly liked each other. My diary for 1958 has a reference to him on every page. One day I liked him, the next day I didn't. We had a strange affinity for each other, which intensified and then disappeared as it was consumed by resentment, jealousy, and anger only to reappear later as respect. The power of those emotions affected my self-esteem and his, both positively and negatively as the years went by.

Gene Kortecamp and I lived the closest to the rink, each about a hundred yards away. His parents called him Butch, and he had a blond crew cut waxed stiff in the front. In the fifth grade Mrs. Dearborn called him Eugene, and we secretly snickered because it seemed so poetic and formal.

Gene's ruddy coloring was a characteristic he inherited from his father, who was known around town as "Red." Gene had a penetrating stare, with bright blue eyes that challenged. His face became a deeper shade of crimson when he was embarrassed or angry, and his nostrils flared like those of a wild stallion. My father used to tease and call him "Butch Cotta Pin" or "Caught a Cramp," and Gene's face got red, but he didn't really mind the nicknames.

When it was time for Gene to go home from the rink, his mother stepped out on the back porch, thrust her fingers between her lips, curled her tongue and sent out a shrill, piercing whistle with an unmistakable message. Gene might grumble, but he vaulted over the fence and headed down over the bankings to his house.

When he was younger, Philip Ramsey was allowed to come to the rink, because he could walk safely through several back yards to the rink. He was an only child of a doting, older mother who whistled him home on her trusty metal whistle much earlier than any of us had to leave. He had to go home and read the encyclopedia so he would be smarter. Gene remembers Mrs. Ramsay bragging about Phillip's reading of the encyclopedia. He was accepting of the fact that he must read the volumes, sometimes ambivalent, but never proud. Philip was shorter, younger, and less athletic than Gene, Larry, or the other six boys who joined us. Phillip was part of the group, but neither Carol nor I ever had a crush on him.

Phillip was my first neighborhood playmate, because my parents and grandparents were friends of his parents. When we were preschoolers my grandmother invited Phillip to the birthday parties for me and my sister Randy. Phillip's father went to Bowdoin College, and that made all the difference in the world, since my father and both my grandfathers were

Bowdoin men. Philip would carry on the tradition for his father, or so his parents hoped.

Once we started school, Phillip and I spent many Saturdays at his house. When warm weather arrived, our cowboy and cowgirl games would leave his basement and be held outside at the rink. Gene, Larry and other kids joined us when they heard our voices.

When Carol Whitney was at my house, we gravitated to the rink. I didn't want my younger sisters hanging around us, so I spent as much time as possible at Carol's house or the rink. When Carol was seven, her mother gave birth to twins. This gave Carol a little more freedom, because then she wasn't the only focus of her mother's attention. Mrs. Whitney worried about Carol's heart murmur and excessive playing. Carol lived a little farther away. She had to cross Maple Street, turn on to Forest Street, then cross Main Street to get to the rink, a distance of perhaps a thousand yards.

Carol and I were both slim and tall for our ages. Her long, brown hair was curled on the ends and more sophisticated looking than my medium length brown hair with bangs that were sometimes trimmed too short.

Gene liked Carol, and once when we were about eight years old, we three stood under an apple tree while Gene twisted Carol's arm behind her back until she let him kiss her. I didn't help much, but I held staunch to my beliefs and shouted, "Leave her alone, leave her alone." To Carol, I shouted words of encouragement, "Don't let him. Don't let him kiss you." I hoped she could out maneuver Gene and remain pure and unkissed. I was disappointed that she gave in, but he was hurting her arm and she wanted to be free. We never let Gene forget his cruel way of getting a kiss. When we became friends again, especially during the early teen years, we talked about the old days and the squabbles or disagreements about which was better—Cub Scouts or Brownies— and the cruelty of a stolen kiss.

As the years went by, we met regularly at the hockey rink after school, in the evenings, on weekends, and during school vacations. For the third and fourth grades, my sisters, and I were sent to Spring Street School, while Carol, Gene, and other friends from the north side of town stayed at Pleasant Street School. Larry stayed there until fourth grade, because his parents had not yet built their home on Bryant Hill. Phillip's mother intervened and insisted he stay at the same school. Her wishes were granted, and I begged my mother to ask if an exception could be made for me too. I was devastated to be leaving Carol and my other friends, but the large size class and our location on the south side of Main Street dictated the move.

In the fifth grade, we were finally reunited at the N.H. Fay School, which had room for two fifth grades and two sixth grades. The years of separation in school and our approaching teenage years meant we had forged stronger bonds of friendship. Carol and I began to hang around more with the boys at the rink. Since kindergarten, the rivalry and friendships had developed, and the interest grew.

We seldom planned a meeting at the rink. I telephoned Carol, but we never called the boys, because we knew girls were not supposed to call boys on the phone. We were allowed one exception to that. In the sixth grade, Polly Thomas's dance school came to town from Bangor. Carol and I called Gene, Larry, Philip, and others to see if their mothers would let them join. We convinced the boys that it might be fun. So, on Wednesday evenings they put on sport coats, dress pants, shirts, ties, and stiff leather shoes, forsaking dungarees, sneakers, and tee shirts. They joined us girls who wore our church or party dresses. We learned the Box Waltz, the Lindy, the Jitterbug, and the Charleston at the Dexter Club, in the rooms up over the Rexall Pharmacy on Main Street.

Since we never called the boys about going to the rink, we either made plans at school or we listened for the boys' voices, looked out the window, and sauntered over. As we became older, the sauntering became more forced, a bit casual appearing as we began to think of the boys in new ways, and to develop self-conscious feelings.

Once we had our own footballs, it was easier for us to walk purposefully over to the rink. At the age of ten, Carol got a football, so I had my father buy me one at the Dexter Hardware store. We carried the footballs over to the rink to practice kicking. We wanted to be good enough to punt and play touch football with the boys, although we only watched when they played tackle roughly with a gang of boys.

The football was my trophy of acceptance. When we played, I enjoyed the feeling of delivering a good kick, even if it did make the instep of my foot smart as canvas sneaker top connected with pigskin. My football had a bumpy texture like the crust of Vienna bread, and I liked to toss and catch it, or to practice my grip and try to throw a spiral.

We played football in the evening when I was in seventh grade, because my grandparents had moved back from Rhode Island to the big stucco house and Grampy turned on the six flood lights that towered on poles above us. After the game, we lingered to talk until my grandfather flicked the lights a few times to remind us it was time for young people to go home.

Sometimes we stayed for a few minutes more, talking in the dark under the starlit sky and the full moon. If we finished the game early or took a break to rest, the boys sat enthroned on the corner seat created by the fence. The boxed in sheet metal-covered corners were perfect for the boys' swinging, banging, awkward feet. Carol and I leaned on the fence, tearing apart autumn leaves or grass, or picking at a rotted spot on the old fence. Sometimes the acrid odor from the fall leaf burning ritual wafted its way up over the bankings and hung in the air. The nights were still, the sounds of occasional cars didn't intrude. The rink was our place, a world with no adults, until we were called home. We made up the games, the rules, and we learned to negotiate or compromise. We discussed, criticized, argued, and defended. We joked and laughed, flirted, and came to understand each other a little better.

From the fifth grade to the ninth, we played football in the fall and baseball or badminton in the spring. Carol and I learned a lot about the ways of boys, and it almost made up for not having older brothers. We weren't full-fledged tomboys, but we liked being at the rink with our friends and perfecting our skills so the boys would accept us in the games. We considered it unique and adventuresome that we played football and baseball with the boys, since most of the girls in the families we knew wouldn't do anything like that.

That fall of 1959, when my grandparents returned to Dexter, was the first time that the hockey rink lights had been turned on in a decade. When winter arrived, the rink was used again for its intended purpose— skating. The boys could play hockey on Saturday mornings and at other times when children weren't skating. On week-end afternoons, hundreds of children skated on the ice created after my Uncle Mac, or Louis Chabot, had worked through the frigid nights using a garden hose to flood the rink.

The rink hadn't been flooded for the previous seven years, because my grandfather's prep school was moved to Newport, Rhode Island, and the house and land in Dexter were vacant, waiting for Winnie's and Grampy's return. Louis Chabot and his sons kept the extensive grounds mowed regularly, and quite naturally, the rink became a gathering spot for neighborhood kids in the fall and spring. In the winters before 1960, the rink filled up with snow, and we only used the bankings for sliding.

After his retirement, my grandfather needed a project to keep himself occupied, so he and other interested people formed the Dexter Winter Sports Association. Families and businesses donated or raised money to pay for the electricity for the lights and wages for Mac and Louis Chabot and others to flood the rink or shovel it after a storm. The back porch of the stucco house was lined with benches and became a place to put on our skates or to get warm, and to socialize.

Since my friends and I became teenagers that winter, my thoughts turned to boy-girl parties. I'd watched *The Mickey Mouse Club* on television with the serialized story of a teenage party, called The Missing Necklace. I was one of the top magazine sales people in the sixth and seventh grades, and the *Teen* and *Seventeen* magazines I ordered gave me even more ideas about parties. Our ballroom dancing lessons were progressing well.

Gene, Larry, Philip, Carol, and I, and about seven other friends felt a little less awkward about holding each other in the proper dancing position. I convinced my parents and grandparents to have a few parties during the winter. During February vacation, several families contributed money so dozens of friends, who skated regularly at the rink, could have a supper and hot chocolate after skating. We gathered our 45 RPM records and waltzed to *Teen Angel, Hang Down Your Head Tom Dooley, Running Bear,* and *The Lion Sleeps Tonight.*

Then came mud season, and a brief hiatus during which we all missed the rink and its activities.

We began to gather for baseball during April vacation if the weather was good. The grass was still brown and the air smelled of the earth awakening after a long winter. We'd worn permanent dirt bases (first and third were by the light poles) and the area rubbed free of grass the previous year had a stronger scent of spring ground thawing. As the days warmed and lengthened, we gathered at the rink after school and in the evenings.

Playing baseball with the boys had a positive effect on my self-esteem and on Carol's. We learned how to have a good batting stance with the bat held poised in the air, elbows up, ready to swing. We could hit fairly well, for girls, especially when Larry or Gene threw "a good pitch" across the plate, not too fast. They gave Carol and me extra pitches, four to their three. Sometimes we played 500 or we just had batting and fielding practice and didn't run the bases. The boys pitched "steamers" and "threw smoke" for each other to show their prowess or to strike out male opponents. Carol and I didn't want them to just lob the ball in to us, but we still wanted to hit.

I loved the feeling of power when the bat connected with the ball. I relished the look of admiration on the boys' faces after I hit the ball my hardest sending a line drive to the left of second base. The whistle of acknowledgment and "Good hit" echoed in my head each time I stepped up to the plate, hoping to belt the ball over the fence.

Hitting the ball over the hockey rink fence meant an automatic home run. How I longed for such a hit, but I never achieved it. If we sent a foul ball over the fence behind us, it meant Larry or Gene had to leap over the fence and scramble down over the terraced bankings to catch the ball before it rolled down Main Street hill past Kortecamp's house, toward downtown. I preferred batting to catching and wanted to stand at home plate hitting the ball rather than being in the field holding a glove.

I never really became very good at catching. If the boys hit a line drive, I was afraid of getting hit in the chest or face or stomach. I stepped aside rather than try to be a heroine and it made the boys mad that I wouldn't at least try. I didn't mind when Gene or Larry hit a pop-up for field practice, but I avoided getting hurt by the ball.

Carol could catch though. She had the confidence and skill that I lacked and which I didn't try to develop. She loved to impress the boys and draw compliments for her catching just as I craved praise for my batting. Carol also knew the names of the professional ball players and their teams, almost as well as the boys did.

I listened, but I didn't care enough about baseball to worship the players in the Major Leagues or to collect baseball cards the way the boys did. I just liked the feeling when the bat connected with the ball. I had given up vying for attention with professional baseball. (My father was a Yankee fan.) So I made my own fun with my friends out of the house, away from the sound of Curt Gowdy, the organ music, and my parents' quarreling. The hockey rink was my escape.

When we were at the rink, Carol and I were participants with the boys, not just observers. No parents organized our activities. Little League had arrived in Dexter, but its influence was minor compared to today. Our families had owned televisions since 1954, but we still knew how to entertain ourselves. The boys orchestrated the games. Carol and I helped them create the rules, make the calls, and judge the strikes or foul balls. We helped make the decisions and arbitrate the differences. We didn't need an adult coach or a crowd of parents. If Gene and Larry got in a dispute, Carol and I tried to appease and cajole them into a truce before things escalated and they went home with the equipment. There was a rivalry and a competition between Larry and Gene, and they liked each other even less as the high school years wore on.

In September 1959, after a summer of seldom seeing Gene, Larry, Phillip, or the other guys in the neighborhood, we had a reunion at the rink. We were shy and feeling a bit awkward at first, and we noticed the changes in each other since our adolescent bodies were maturing. Gene's and Larry's feelings were tinged with resentment because of Carol's and my summer flirtation with the wealthy, out-of-state boys at the Wassookeag School Camp, which was located six cottages down from ours at the lake. During the summer, Carol and I made every possible effort to meet the dream boats from the camp.

I hardly gave Gene and Larry a thought until we saw their scowling faces at the Little League games. Carol and I went to all the games. However, we stood behind the fence where the cute boys from away sat on the bench while their team was up at bat, and the Dexter boys were in the field. We made fools of ourselves that summer, and for a few more after that, flirting with the Wassookeag boys, treating them like Greek gods. We worshipped everything about them—their classy clothes, their accents, the allure of their being from Massachusetts, Connecticut, New York, New Jersey, or beyond.

That fall at the rink, Gene and Larry called the interlopers "the Wassookeag fairies" because they wore chinos or madras Bermuda shorts, Weejuns loafers, and blue cotton oxford cloth shirts, rumpled and hanging untucked. Wassookeag boys were cool because they wore Izod shirts like those Brooks Brothers advertised in *The New Yorker* magazine that I skimmed through at home. Carol and I were entranced by such sophisticated attire.

In comparison, Dexter boys wore dusty dungarees, striped jerseys, and black lace-up, high-top Red Ball Jets when they played at the rink or their baggy, gray flannel Little League uniforms for the games at Crosby Park. Gene, Steve Bassett and Ralph Smart proudly played for the team sponsored by Fay & Scott. Larry played for Dexter Shoe, feeling like a pro in his new uniform.

That September of 1959, I persuaded Walter Abbott, a Dexter boy who attended Wassookeag Camp, to sell me his two foot long group photo of the boys at camp. I added it to my collection of pictures of the Hatch Prep boys. I didn't collect baseball cards, or have Fabian or Ricky Nelson or Elvis as my idols; I had the Wassookeag boys.

That fact was a source of great annoyance to Gene and Larry. They didn't like to have their roles usurped by a bunch of rich kids from the city. Carol's and my admiration of the Wassookeag boys amounted to disloyalty in the minds of the Dexter boys. We had more arguments that fall with Carol and me defending the wearing of Bermuda shorts by boys. Gradually, we renewed our friendship during the football games at the rink, but Carol and I never forgot the Wassookeag boys for long, and we were ready for another batch of them the following summer. Larry and Gene never forgot that being from away and wearing blue oxford cloth, button-down collar shirts conferred status and turned girls heads. Perhaps those memories influenced their life choices far more than they ever realized, since they each now live away from Maine in affluent suburbs, working and dressing for the corporate world. I, however, am still here in Maine, married to a man who wore madras in his teen years and went to prep school, but was also once a boy much like Larry and Gene, playing neighborhood baseball in a nearby town.

The cycle of the seasons brought Gene, Larry, Carol and me together for sports and conversation at the rink. We played football that seventh grade fall of 1959. We had skating parties, and I had my first teen-age party when I turned the magical age of thirteen. In the spring, we played baseball again. Carol and I honed our skills to make us more acceptable as teammates. We picked up information from Larry about Satchel Page and the Pittsburgh Pirates. Larry was going to play on that team when he turned professional, and I really thought he would.

In September of 1960 or 1961, when we met at the rink, Carol and I found out what Gene, Steve Bassett, Larry, and his cousin, Garry Gilbert, had been doing for fun. While Carol and I fantasized and chased the Wassookeag boys and were away at Girl Scout camp, the boys played telephone games. They called people getting them to answer questions for a phony radio quiz show, telling the winners to pick up their free bag of groceries at Lagasse's IGA.

Larry was hysterical with laughter, practically rolling on the ground, his mouth yawning open, teeth bared in his characteristic howling laugh. He could hardly control himself as he retold the story of the questions, the answers, and the people they had fooled.

I never liked kidding or teasing and thought the phone game was cruel. The boys thought I just didn't have a sense of humor. They liked the challenge of seeing how long they could keep gullible people on the phone talking. When *The Gazette* featured an article on the prank calls, with a quote from Chief Harold Knox that he expected to apprehend the culprits within the week, the boys were scared to death, fear rising in their throats rather than laughter or glib talk.

Talking was something Gene, Larry, Phillip, Carol, and I enjoyed. We listened to each other, and we complained about problems with parents and teachers. We offered advice and divulged secrets. As we matured, we discussed philosophies of life and controversial topics. We might disagree, but we could express our opinions, and we were all voracious readers. We loved to debate. Gene and Larry were the instigators at school, asking teachers if we could skip the planned class and "have a debate." The interest in discussion helped occupy many hours at the rink. We talked about every imaginable topic, comparing ideas, stretching ourselves. Sometimes their boy-talk shocked Carol and me, although we pretended not to hear their snickering comments to each other about what hormone driven boys do.

The boys enjoyed telling tales of their adventures. One day after school, Larry and Gary discovered an old tire on the side of the road, just below the skating rink. They decided to "test the laws of physics by rolling the tire down Main Street Hill." The boys watched with glee as their experiment far exceeded their expectations. The tire gathered momentum and rolled along the center line with unerring accuracy down the hill toward the traffic light intersection, about four hundred yards. Larry and Gary ran to Gene Kortecamp's side of the road, just in time to see the tire stop on the side of Chief Harold Knox's cruiser, parked in front of Fossa's store. The tire gracefully flew through the air and landed on the cruiser's hood.

Fixed in horror, they watched as Harold Knox, barrel chested, proud in his uniform, a chief of police personified, rushed out of the store, put the tire in his back seat, and sped up Main Street Hill, with the siren screaming. Larry and Gary took refuge in the rink, ducking down behind the boards, quivering as they knelt on the grass. Chief Knox went speeding by, having failed to spot them. They spent days of anxiety. Gary's brother Mark told their parents and punishment was swift for Gary and Larry. They meted out their own kind of retribution to Mark, tying him to a tree in the woods with his pants down in hopes that a girl would find him. No girl found Mark and Chief Knox never found the owner of the tire, but Gary's story of the mishap still triggers Larry's laughter.

*　　*　　*　　*　　*　　*

As the seasons of our life rolled on, the events of childhood evolved into the events of adolescence and we became interested in more exciting things than meeting at the rink. We felt so mature, looking back on our childhood and childishness. Carol and I thought of Gene, Larry, Philip, and all the others as "our boys" in a sisterly, patronizing way. We were interested in seniors, rather than sophomores, as potential boyfriends which meant our days at the rink began to dwindle.

Slowly, the group drifted apart, and reformed with other friends who had sometimes been at the rink. In 1965 when Gene, Larry, Phillip, Tommy, Ralph, and Steve signed my yearbook, they each referred to the fun and talks we had over the years at the rink. The sentiment and synthesis of childhood memories were in our minds, and we spoke of the rink as the place that bound us together.

Most of us were together in the senior play, which was intended to include as many classmates as possible. Gene had a leading role in a comedy. He looked as suave as a Wassookeag boy, wearing a blue, button-down collar shirt, beige Levi jeans, a madras blazer, madras belt, and brown Dexter Shoe loafers, all of which Carol and I encouraged him to buy when we accompanied him on a shopping trip in Bangor. Larry, Ralph, Tommy, and I had parts also. Carol and Steve were on the play committee.

Our amateur performances evoked laughter from the audience, both for the scripted dialogue and the mistakes. Afterward, the cast gathered at the fire hall.

I left the cast party early that night in November, since being there seemed anti-climactic and somehow disloyal to my new boyfriend who was away at college. Later, I regretted that I cut myself off from my old friends because of a misguided sense of fidelity. I still had in-depth conversations with Larry and Gene a few more times in my senior year, but my letter writing to my boyfriend, Brian, at Villanova took precedence.

My last time at the rink was with Brian, when he was home for Christmas break. After skating, Brian, Carol, her boyfriend, and I went inside to play cribbage, pool, and Ping Pong at my grandparents' house, just as Gene, Larry, Carol, and I had done so many times in previous years.

The winter of '65 was the death knell for the rink with so many neighborhood kids in high school. A year later, my grandmother had a stroke, and my grandfather's condition worsened. It was a time for letting go, and moving on.

Our worn paths to the rink filled in with new grass. Gene, Larry, Carol, and our classmates were off meeting new people and having new experiences, creating different paths to follow.

In the summer of 1966, my grandparents moved to a trailer on the other side of town. The rink and house were sold to Mr. May who, years ago had bought the summer camp from Grampy. The last of my grandfather's link to the past was gone. Years later, when I was in my twenties, I used to wonder how my grandfather coped after everything changed, and his empire had crumbled.

Once, in 1971, when he rode with me to the hospital to see Aunt Teddy, I noticed that he didn't look as we drove down Main Street and up High Street past the hockey rink and the big stucco house where his dreams began.

I looked at the building where he and my grandmother had lived, comparing it to his tiny apartment filled with pictures from the past, and I wondered how he endured it all. Now I think I know. Time passes. Events unfold. People change. Places change, and it is a relentless process. Now, when I drive up Main Street hill, where the barn-red boards of the hockey rink once topped the terraced bankings, I don't want to look either.

My grandfather had to let go, to accept change and loss. I have had to also. I have been learning to do it over the years, as I watched him let go of it all—the Wassookeag School Camp, the Hatch Prep School mansions in Newport, the big stucco house on High Street, the cottages on Lake Wassookeag, then my grandmother in 1970. His world diminished even more as he lost independence and moved to an apartment, then to a boarding home, and then to a nursing home until his death in 1980. Everything faded away in pathetic denouement over the years, and all that is left are the pictures and the memories. Sometimes that is enough. It has to be.

When I drive up Main Street, my glance is drawn to the right to see if the rink is back in its place after all. It isn't.

Instead, a tastefully decorated dentist's office with fading, natural cedar siding and contemporary windows perches on top of the terraced hill. The building is an intrusion, ill-suited for the site. I feel a jolt of disbelief every time I see it. The hockey rink, our place of childhood games and adolescent conversations belongs there, not a dentist's office.

Now, I am struck by the fact that my sons are more than twice as old as I was when I stopped going to the rink and began having dates. I think of how the years can telescope, and I am in awe that the memories can be so real.

I see Carol and me with our footballs, heading to the rink. I remember the surge of pride when I walloped the baseball with the bat. I remember the excitement of conversations with friends as we were coming of age in Dexter. I hear Philip's mother tweet on her metal whistle and call, "Phil-LIP." I hear Gene's mother's whistle pierce the night before she calls out, "Butch, Butchie." My sister leans out the door and calls through the trees those words I hated to hear, "Prudy, time to come home." Carol gathers up her things; Larry gathers up his bats, ball, and glove and heads up over the hill to his house beside the road to the cemetery. My map of Main Street looks much different than the street does now. My map shows the hockey rink crowning the terraced hill. Like my grandfather, I prefer the terraced hill of my memory.

Clockwise, far left: Gene Kortecamp, Larry Richards and Gary Gilbert (outer circle) Prudy, Candy Wiley, Carol Whitney, Teresa Ronco, Cathy LaBarge, Randy Hatch, Judy Nedeau and Mike Ouellette playing Wink'em

SEVENTH GRADE—THE AWAKENING

1959—1960

I'm in Mrs. Mealey's seventh grade homeroom. At home, I have an old photograph of Mrs. Mealey and seven other mothers, standing behind the Hepplewhite style chairs ready to wipe any frosting spilled upon the brocade covered seats at the party for my sister Randy's fourth birthday. Randy sat at one end of the long mahogany table, wearing her paper crown. I was at the other end with Robbie and his mother, Mrs. Mealey, to my left. That was six years ago, half my life time. Now she's my favorite teacher.

Mrs. Mealey is a short, pleasantly plump woman. She has a simple, girlish hair style, with straight bangs and the straight sides cut in a short pageboy just below her ears. She has three children; Robby, who is in Randy's class, a daughter named Barbara, who is in my sister Sally's class, and her youngest, Mikey, who "is like a little butter ball," Mrs. Mealey says affectionately.

Mrs. Mealey likes the color red and wears it often. One day she appears in our classroom wearing two different red shoes. She hasn't noticed until one of the boys, the class clown, points it out to her. She laughs at herself and tells us the story of her rushed morning and why she hadn't noticed the mismatched shoes. She is easy going, and doesn't mind if we laugh too.

Another day, she chuckles as she tells us the story of how she was sprayed by a skunk the previous night. She had to stay in the barn attached to her house and take off her smelly clothes. She says she had to use fourteen cans of tomato juice to remove the scent from her skin and hair. I try not to picture Mrs. Mealey naked in the barn waiting for her husband to bring her fresh clothes and tomato juice to sponge on her body.

Mrs. Mealey teaches English, reading, and social studies—subjects I enjoy the most because they are easier for me. I like diagramming sentences, even though I make some mistakes. The process appeals to my sense of order, having a place for everything and everything in its place. It helps me understand the different parts of speech. I haven't done as well memorizing all of the prepositions. I keep getting stuck when I reach *down, during, except* and then *be, being, been* pops into my head.

Mrs. Mealey teaches us about objective and subjective case pronouns. We must never use one of the subject pronouns after a preposition. If there are two pronouns in a sentence— "from him and me" or "from him and I,"—we cover one with our finger or say one in our mind to see if it makes sense. I like the exercises and I can understand that we shouldn't say "He gave it to Bob and I." Some people think they are always supposed to use "I," but I understand that it isn't correct.

Mrs. Mealey says, "You must all remember the importance of good diction and pronunciation. The word is pro NUN ciation—not pro NOUN ciation. You say SPOONSFUL and HANDSFUL, not SPOONFULS and HANDFULS. We say PER spiration—not PRESS piration. And we certainly don't use the word sweat. Animals sweat; people perspire."

I like her attention to such words. I have learned, from my parents and from Grampy and Winnie Hatch, that it's important to speak correctly.

We learn about syllabification and marking words with long and short vowel sounds. I sit silently puzzling and pronouncing words in my head to see if I can determine if a vowel is long or short. I can't figure it out. I try to listen to hear if the vowel is said for a long time or a short time. It doesn't make sense. Everyone else seems to get it. It takes a while before I connect it with our recitation of the chant a,e,i,o,u done in two ways.

Mrs. Mealey does a unit on poetry. That's how we learn about rhythm and rhyme. She teaches us about Henry Wadsworth Longfellow. He was born in Maine and went to Bowdoin just like my two grandfathers, only he went there in 1839. Mrs. Mealey believes in the importance of memorization. We will have beautiful verses always in our minds and jewels from our lips just like she does. She recites from memory, Longfellow's "The Children's Hour," "Hiawatha," "Paul Revere's Ride," "The Village Blacksmith" and "The Highwayman." I'm learning to recognize the first few lines of each poem.

She recites, and we do along with her, "The Landing of the Pilgrim Fathers" and every morning we say "The American's Creed"—I believe in the United States of America as a government of the people, by the people, for the people...."

When we have to memorize a poem. I choose a sad poem from a book of my mother's that is one of her favorites—*Little Boy Blue* by Eugene Field. I memorize the first three stanzas then flounder in front of the class. My oratory and memory aren't as good as Grampy's either.

I bring in *The Golden Treasury of Poetry* that my sisters and I received for Christmas. From it Mrs. Mealey reads the tragic story of a Medieval huntsman, Llewellyn, who stabs his faithful dog with a sword when he sees blood on the dog's fangs. Lewellyn thinks the dog has killed his baby. As the dog, Beth Gelert, lays dying, a betrayed, plaintive look in his eyes, the baby cries from under bloody blankets, and the father finds a dead wolf. I am moved to tears by the story. I see how tragedy can happen when people jump to conclusions.

We write limericks for Mrs. Mealey. I share some of the ones in my *Golden Treasury*. Some of the boys—Tommy, Brent, Larry, and Gene—write nasty lyrics and snicker in the back of the room. Someone writes one about an old lady from Millinocket who puts her finger in a light socket.

My class is the last seventh grade to be taught at the high school. Because we are such a big group, we are told we will also be the last eighth grade. Next year the students following us will stay at N. H. Fay School. We are the first wave of the postwar baby boom and we will be the largest class ever at Dexter High School when we become freshman and are joined by the kids from nearby Ripley and Garland. There are sixty-six of us in the seventh grade photograph for the yearbook.

Seventh grade is a good year for me in many ways, but my report card is peppered with Cs and Ds. For the first time, I am faced with mid-term exams and semester averages. I'm lucky to be with my friends in the top group for a few more years, even if I am on the fringe. I learn from observing and listening to the brainy kids who answer all the questions. Unfortunately, I'm not very diligent about homework. (It's my grandparents' first winter back from Newport, Rhode Island and I choose ice skating at the lighted rink beside our house in the evening instead of studying.)

I'm finding out that math and science are difficult for me. The good news is that with a large clock in the classroom, I have finally learned how to tell time when the big hand is pointing on a number other than the twelve. This year we have electronic bell signals for different periods of the day when classes are over. Now, the term "quarter past" or "quarter of" or "ten forty-five" makes sense to me. I am wearing my glasses more, and noticing the hands on the clock as they move, ticking away seconds and minutes of class time.

Brent Slater sits in the back of the room, his chair tipped against the wall, until Mrs. Mealey notices. His dark hair is oiled back with more than a little dab of Brylcream. He keeps a small black comb ever ready in his pocket. He is the only boy who needs to shave. He wears form-fitting black chinos with little tabs connected to a metal buckle in the back over his bottom. In his wallet, he has a little package sealed in cellophane that he keeps to show the other boys. I overhear them call it a "safe." We don't know if he actually uses them or not. Brent is a class leader and more worldly than most of us. He's smart and has a large vocabulary. He'll probably be a lawyer some day because he likes to present his case and have debates.

The seventh grade is located at the far end of the school, but we walk the same hall as the sophisticated upperclassmen. Carol and I know some of them because they live in our neighborhood. Marcia Hebert, a perky blonde cheerleader, is a senior. She and her friend Barbara Landry went to Philadelphia to be on American Bandstand in the summer, and are the envy of us all. On the way home from school one day, we see the pictures Marcia and Barbara took, and we ask them about the regulars on the show. Marcia is five years older and it makes us a bit tongue tied.

Marsha's father used to work at Grampy's school in the 1930s and 1940s. Now, Mr. Hebert teaches at Dexter High School, and for Mr. May at Wassookeag School Camp in the summer. The Heberts live near us in a yellow house with green trim and a vine covered front porch. The yard around the Heberts' house on Maple Street is always roped off with string and wooden stakes, because Mr. Hebert is meticulous about his lawn. He rakes and cuts and weeds and doesn't like dogs or kids on it. He sweeps and hoses off the dusty road in the late spring and listens to his jazz records on his Victrola in the evening.

One of the other seniors is Donna Thomas, whose father runs the taxi service in Dexter. Donna baby-sits for Carol's brother and sister while we're at Girl Scouts since Carol's mother is our leader. Donna asks if Carol and I want to join the Rainbow Girls, and gives us important looking papers. We decide to join, although my mother isn't wild about the idea. She makes it clear that she doesn't want to go to any meetings. I'm not sure why, but I guess she doesn't care for groups with rituals. Since my Aunt Teddy is in Eastern Star, she can sign a recommendation for me to join Rainbow Girls. (The evening meetings are another reason I don't get my homework done.)

I have Rainbow Girls on Monday evening and Girl Scouts on Wednesday afternoon. I go to ballroom dancing lessons on Thursday evening and I go to the hockey rink other evenings. After school, I usually go to Carol's to watch *Bandstand* and *Who Do You Trust*, because Johnny Carson is so funny. I read the teen letters in *The Methodist Magazine* and much of *The Saturday Evening Post* and *Look* magazines, which we don't get at our house. (We get *Time* and *Life* and *Ladies Home Journal*. Every month I read "Can This Marriage Be Saved?" I like to read about people's problems. Maybe it will help me when I'm older and married. I don't like hearing people argue. It gives me a knot in my stomach.)

When I think about the undone homework and my grades, I feel a little guilty and hopeless and my mother is worried. She hires Louis Chabot to build a study area in the closet of our former play room where my sisters and I once kept our toys. She buys a set of *World Book Encyclopedias* and *The Lincoln Library*. We have a globe and a small set of plastic drawers to hold the collection of shells our Uncle Mac brought back from Florida. Frankly, I'd rather be in my room on my bed reading a book or writing a letter to my pen pal in England.

In Rainbow, Carol is chosen to be installed as IMMORTALITY, but when the degree program is published, the *Eastern Gazette* prints it incorrectly as IMMO**RALITY**. We are mortified, but convulse with laughter. A month later another typo lists Carol's mother as Mrs. Robert L. Shitney, instead of Whitney. We find this even funnier.

I am chosen to be Outer Observer in Rainbow, which means I sit outside the inner sanctum until I am called inside. I feel like a guard, and I wonder what they are doing in there while I sit outside and wait for Inner Observer to knock on the door and invite me in. As a new, young member, I have to start out with a lower position and work my way through the stations.

Meanwhile, sitting and waiting in the ante room gives me time to think about my undone homework. When I'm finally inside, we go through all the formal ritual, the marching with squared corners and Worthy Adviser telling Worthy Associate Advisor to tell Hope to tell Charity to tell someone else to begin the meeting, which amounts to little business and then we have the closing ritual in reverse order. By the time I get home it's too late for homework and time for bed.

When we have the Mothers' Degree, I'm moved to tears as one of the girls sings "I walk through the garden alone while the dew is still on the roses, and He walks with me and he talks with me and He tells me I am his own." It's a beautiful hymn and I am impressed by the high ideals for living that Rainbow Girls teaches. I know I must never reveal what is in the pot of gold.

In October, the Rainbow Girls go on a Friday night hay ride to Sangerville. Most of the older girls invite boys. Carol and I go together. As the ride progresses, being in hay makes my breathing difficult, like the way I feel after being in the barn at Great-Grammy Ellms' farm. I feel wheezy and congested.

I notice my heavy breathing and in the silence, others are breathing heavily too. It is embarrassingly quiet. Carol and I feel uneasy and whisper about what we suspect is going on in the back of the big old truck. We feel disgusted, disappointed, and self-righteous.

I had expected the hay ride to be like it was on TV, on the Walt Disney, *Mickey Mouse Club* episode of *Spin and Marty*, with everyone singing and laughing. I think the couples are kissing and necking and maybe even petting (I've read about it in Dear Abby).

I am disillusioned and sputter to Carol about the evening when we get back to my house. The older girls seem so virtuous when they read their parts at Rainbow and sing the beautiful songs.

In the fall, I earn the status of high sales person in the magazine drive and win a trip to the Ice Capades in Bangor. I'm also chosen to be a cheerleader for the boys' basketball team when my classmates vote from a list on the board. At first when we cheer at the games, I feel embarrassed about jumping around and clapping chants in front of people. If the boys are losing and start to catch up, I forget to be embarrassed and yell and cheer until I'm hoarse like the others. We ride the bus to Dover-Foxcroft, Milo, and Brownville Junction to old-fashioned town halls and gymnasiums. On the bus ride home, we sing and giggle and talk. I think the bus driver gets tired of hearing "99 Bottles of Beer On The Wall." I know I get tired of singing it after twenty or thirty choruses.

I look awful in the cheering photo when we sit like attached train cars on the front bleacher, each with our left leg crossed over our right and our left feet all pointing in the same direction. Carol and I are the only ones who have forgotten our newly polished white canvas sneakers. She wears the black suede look-alike shoes that we both bought at Reed's Shoe Store. I wear my loafers and a sideways grimace. My bangs are curled too short, exposing my too high forehead, and my glasses finish me off. Carol's posture in the red corduroy jumper is more erect than mine, although I'm not slouching as much as Jackie. My red and white yarn pompom is a little droopy. We all have yarn pom poms we made to tie around our necks. I'm getting lots of exercise with cheering and dancing class.

One night I stay for supper at Carol's and we go to ballroom dancing lessons afterward. Carol lets me wear her jangly charm bracelet. Miss Connie disapproves of such a noisy, tasteless ornament, and I have to remove it because she says "It's an annoyance." I feel embarrassed and angry with her. When the boys, Larry, Billy, or Gene come hurrying and sliding across the room to ask me to dance, she makes them ask some of the other girls so everyone has a turn with a boy partner. At least when Bobbie Darrin's record *Mack the Knife* comes on, I have a boy to do the Lindy or Jitterbug with, instead of a girl. In the six grade, I was stuck steering a heavy, retarded girl around the room because the boys didn't choose her and there weren't enough boys to match with girls. In the seventh grade, she goes to special school and I don't have to feel embarrassed by or ashamed for my less than kind feelings about dancing with her instead of a boy.

After school Carol and I stop by Daddy's office to hang around and get some money for date bars at the bakery or an ice cream cone—chocolate on top and vanilla on the bottom—at the Rexall Pharmacy's soda fountain. Sometimes we go bowling at the small alley behind the Eastern Gazette newspaper. Often boys from our class bowl in one of the three lanes.

When something goes wrong, Mr. Dube goes in the back of the alleys to set the pins and fix the machine. His legs hang suspended like those of a marionette and Carol and I giggle at the sight. Before we pick up a ball, we roll our hands on the little moist metal spinning thing beside the alley. Then we wipe our fingers on the dirty cotton towel that hangs near by, and grab a ball hoping desperately to get a strike. We use small balls, not those big kind like Ralph Kramden and Ed Norton use on *The Honeymooners.*

Other days after school, Carol and I go to Winnie's and Grampy's house. We now know how to bluff our way through poker and we understand the electoral system in the 1930 Parker Brothers' game of Politics. When we play cribbage, it means we have no points if Grampy says one of us has a nineteen hand. I go to Winnie or Mac for help and Carol asks Grampy, and then we swap advisors. One day Carol gets a twenty-nine hand because she has the right jack. Sometimes I put down just the cards Carol needs to peg out on the cribbage board, because I don't remember her previous cards, and anticipate the cards she has left in her hand. Carol usually beats me in cribbage, just like she used to beat me when we played Monopoly.

I go to the public library with Carol after school sometimes. We are getting braver about venturing around in back of the wrought iron, jail-like bars that stretch across librarian, Miss Champion's, long oak counter. Carol finds a book called *A Lantern In Her Hand*, by Beth Streeter Aldrich. When Carol returns the book, I borrow it. Once I start reading the story, I can't put it down. I follow a young girl who lives in a prairie sod hut through her life until she is an old, old woman. I cry when I get to the end and she dies. I am amazed how quickly her life goes by. I think about Winnie, Auntie, and Aunt Teddy and wonder if it seems to them that their lives are going by fast. I try to imagine them as young girls. It's even harder to imagine myself as an old woman.

Life is different for my grandparents now than it was a few years ago. It's nice to have Auntie, Winnie, and Grampy back in Dexter year round, but I miss the excitement and beauty of Newport, Rhode Island. I wonder if they do, too. At first my sisters and I say, "Why did you leave the ping pong tables and the pool tables in Rhode Island? Why didn't you bring that big oak table and bench from the library?"

I have figured out that money is a problem for Winnie and Grampy now. They can't afford to live the way they used to. Winnie apologizes that she can't give us as many gifts now. I love the red, White Stag, nylon wind breaker with Scandinavian trim that I buy at Cortell Seigal's in Bangor with money from Winnie, Grampy, and my parents. It's perfect to wear at the skating rink and matches the red canvas, skate-shaped bag that my cousin Nancy bought for me at Best and Co. in Boston. Now I feel like a real teenager when I skate. I'm getting really good at backwards skating. Sometimes we make a whip of ten or fifteen skaters, but I don't want to be on the end and go crashing into the wooden fence.

My cousin David Rust comes from Massachusetts to visit in February. David takes lessons in Cohasset and is really good at skating. He and Gene become friends. Carol and I play cribbage with them after skating. David brings *Mad Magazine* with him for us to read. Carol and I love the humor and satire, especially the ads Mad Magazine makes fun of. We buy *Mad* every month after David leaves.

David and I write regularly. When he was visiting I helped fix him up with Loanne Hughes who is a friend of my sister Sally. David makes me a silver ring out of a fifty cent piece. He starts a rage for rings at his school in Cohasset and makes money telling other kids how to do it by pounding and reshaping the coin.

At Winnie's and Grampy's, we notice that the room where the long oak table once stood at Grampy's first school, is quite empty, because the table was left in Newport. It would be a great place for a party. Carol and I have always wanted to have a teenage party. For my thirteenth birthday, we invite all of the boys and girls who are in our ballroom dance class and friends from school who don't take the lessons. I ask my friend Cathie LaBarge's boyfriend, Dennis Frost, to come, too. He is two years older. The boys wear sport coats and ties.

We play Wink'em with us girls sitting in a circle on chairs with one empty chair. The boys stand behind us and the boy with the empty chair winks at a girl and she has to try and get out of her seat to the vacant seat before the boy behind her grabs her shoulders with his sweaty hands. We play our collection of 45s and dance to *Mr. Blue, Teen Angel* and Ricky Nelson's *Lonely Town.*

My friends give me some great presents. Someone gives me a necklace with a mustard seed in a little glass bead and a written message about it. I get a Strictly Private photo album and lots of little ceramic figurine animals in sets of three or individual—deer, bunnies, cats, dogs—that people buy at Ben Franklin, because they know I collect them.

I have a pajama party at Winnie's and Grampy's house. All of my friends like it there. We take pictures of each other in our bristle curlers and short baby doll pajamas. We hope no one shows the revealing pictures at school. If they do we will squeal and grab the pictures away.

The next morning we are downstairs in the kitchen in our nighties and pajamas. Winnie says we should cover up more or get dressed because the boys' who play Saturday morning ice hockey are on the closed-in porch warming up, and they can see us through the kitchen windows. I see Gene looking in with his face flushed brighter red by the cold.

On snowy mornings, I listen hopefully for the whistle blasts from the fire station—four blasts means no school. A certain number of frantic blasts with a pause and more blasts means there is a fire on a specific street and Daddy will be upset about his loss ratio, because he insures many of the houses in Dexter. It will mean a new black and white Gazette photo of an insured loss tacked on the bulletin board of Dexter disasters at his office. We check the Lloyd Harvey Hatch, Jr. Insurance fire alarm card for the code of whistle blasts if we are not sure what the number of blasts means. Daddy has big fire alarm cards and pocket size cards to give to people. I have one in my red leather wallet.

My wallet is personalized with PRUDY in black letters, and it's three inches thick because it's filled with pictures of my friends. I have a photo of Carol and me standing by the wall at R. C. Whitney and Sons Garage where her father works. We are about seven and our smiles reveal missing front teeth and too-short, blunt cuts. We're wearing white T shirts and dungarees and holding kittens. I cut out a telephone number and tape it to the front of Carol's shirt so it looks like a convict's number. It's a riot.

In my wallet, I have a lot of funny childhood pictures that I got from my mother's albums. Some of them are of me alone or with my sisters. I have pictures from the Dexter Gazette of the Rainbow Girls in antique women's dresses. My favorite photograph is of my sisters, Barry and me in dress-ups at Aunt Teddy's a long time ago when we were eight or nine.

There's a picture of my Uncle Mac's daughter Patty at Hatch Prep school. I have pictures of my cousins Nancy Lea and David. Another picture is of Nick Guitheim, a Wassookeag boy I met this summer. Larry still says the Wassookeag boys are fairies because they wear Bermuda shorts. Carol and I think the Wassookeag boys are SOOOOOOO CUTE, and SOOOOOO COOL! Nick lives in Newton, where my cousins used to live and he goes to The Fessendon School. He sends me letters on pine scented stationary. I feel kind of creepy when he writes. "Baby, you're the ginchest!!" and another letter that sounds like song lyrics "…Baby your the most. I really like it when you are close. You send a shiver down my spine that makes me feel so fine." We hardly know each other.

Someone gave Daddy a box of pictures from Bert Call's studio after Mr. Call died. Everyone knows that Daddy likes old pictures and things about the history of Dexter. I found some pictures of people I know. There is one of Phillip Ramsay when he was about three with slicked back short hair. He's holding a book titled *Animals and Little Ones*. I cut out and paste words on Phillip's picture that say, "Cute, but what's its price tag?" "Sells for $35,000." and "Brainy." I think it's really cool how I found so many perfect words to stick on the pictures in my wallet.

I have a lot of identification cards now with my name written on them—the Episcopal Church parish membership, Girl Scout and Rainbow Girls membership cards, and my $3.00 Athletic Ticket to get me into all the boys' football and basketball games at D.H.S. I have Father Gardiner's card with his Milo phone number and address and a plastic card for emergency rescue breathing. Daddy gives them out free with the fire alarm cards as a community service. I even have some joke cards that say "Charge It", "I Work Too Hard", and "Why Suffer? Don't walk around half dead when for $49.00 we can bury you on our LAY-AWAY PLAN. Its later than you think. Crokum & Plantum, Morticians." Daddy has lots of joke cards that people give him. I like to have funny stuff in my wallet.

I just LOVE my thick red wallet that has so many places for pictures and cards. I like to talk with lots of expression, like the book character, Eloise. Last year for Christmas, Winnie gave me the book *Eloise at the Plaza*. Sometimes I try to sound sophisticated like Eloise. I also try to sound like my cousin Nancy Lea. Now I say "Oh, Mother!" like Nancy does in a certain disdainful way. Saying Mommy is too babyish, but I still say Daddy. It seems like I'm always saying, "Daddy, kin I have some money." (We used to play Mother-May-I and I know we're supposed to say may I, but it's almost like one word DaddykinIhavesomemoney?) If he's in a good mood or if some other people are around, Daddy says "Sure." or "What for?" reaches into his pocket for the thick roll of bills and peels off one or two or more.

Back in September when we start seventh grade, Carol and I earn the money we get from Daddy. We stop by the office after school and do errands or clean the back room. We help his secretary, Phyllis, by empty-ing all the envelopes of school insurance money that most of the parents bought in case their kids get hurt on the school grounds. We open hun-dreds of envelopes and count the money—two dollars or three dollars for extra coverage. We have to make sure parents put three dollars in the enve-lope checked for extra.

Seventh grade is the year when I notice so much more about the world and the people around me. This is such a momentous time in my life. In January of seventh grade, we start a new year and a new decade. It's the year when everyone in our class turns thirteen. It seems as if 1960 is such an important time. So much is happening and we see it every night on the Huntley Brinkley news report.

This is the year I hear about the Olympics, and go to Winnie's and Grampy's to watch figure skaters and slalom skiers on TV. Everyone is so interested in the Olympics. I guess it's because not many people had televisions when they held the last Olympics.

I watch old movies— *Johnny Belinda, Gunga Dinn, A Tale of Two Cities, The Good Earth, Rebecca of Sunnybrook Farm* and all of the Shirley Temple movies. We see Fred Astaire and Ginger Rogers swirl and dance, listen to Rosemary Clooney sing, and watch the girls in the Ziegfield Follies perform. We watch Esther Williams and her co-stars in the scenes of synchronized swimming. (They look much better than we Girl Scouts do when we choreograph swim movements for our Swimmers' Badge.) My sisters and I like watching movies that my mother saw when she was young. On Sunday, I am glued to the TV movies until one or two in the afternoon and then go over to the skating rink to see my friends. I seldom get to my homework.

My lack of diligence and fear of asking for help earn me a D in math on the third report card. My mother arranges for me to be privately tutored after school. I walk through the snow or Daddy gives me a ride to Mrs. Hutchinson' s house on Pleasant Street, across from the house where my second grade teacher, Miss Call lives. Five years ago she tried to teach me to tell time. Now I finally get it. But I'm faced with fractions and numerators and denominators and other mathematical mysteries. Obviously, I didn't inherit Grampy's math brilliance.

When I am at Mrs. Hutchinson's and she methodically explains the steps to me, I feel as if a warm gossamer veil envelops me. Her voice sounds soothing and distant and my brain and eyes glaze over. (That's what happens when people try to help me, I kind of zone out and go into a trance.) While her baby sleeps in a cradle in the next room, we go over the mistakes on my school papers, and I understand some of it, but when

I leave I'm often as befuddled as when I arrived. I'm too shy to admit that I still don't really understand most of it.

The only books in our classroom other than the text books in our desks are on a short shelf near the pencil sharpener. There's a wonderful blue book with many biographies telling about the lives of famous women. (In the second and third grade I read biographies and I recognize some of the women's names from the old orange books Carol found on the shelves at the Abbott Memorial Library. The stories in the new blue book have more details and nice drawings, not black silhouettes like those books from the 1930s.) I read about Abigail Adams and how she saved some paintings and furnishings in the White House before the British burned it. I read about Jane Addams and Hull House, Dorothia Dix, Louisa May Alcott, Marie Curie, Florence Nightingale, Amelia Earhart, Clara Barton, and other women who were important in history and I feel proud of them. I hope I can be like them someday and help people. I've moved beyond Dale Evans and Nancy Drew as heroines.

We have Barter Day so we will better understand how the early settlers managed to get what they needed without money. We all have brought things from home to barter with classmates. I have an ID bracelet of silvery metal with a stretchy band and a flat rectangular piece that flips up to reveal a place for a tiny photo. I got it for fifty cents and a lot of Bazooka bubble gum wrappers, but I don't tell them that. The other kids think it is great and I get a really good deal in the swap because they think it's neat.

I sit in the third seat back from the door and one day in the middle of class, Mrs. Rowe, her face ashen, appears in the doorway from her room across the hall. It's not time for her to come teach us science or math, so I wonder why she's here. My ears perk up. I can tell by Mrs. Rowe's voice that she is upset and something is wrong. Everyone is working quietly and I overhear when Mrs. Rowe whispers to Mrs. Mealey, "Ohhh Fran, I've just shut myself in the drawer!"

Mrs. Rowe is old, very old. She has gray hair cut short and shaved severely up the nape of her neck. She has posture that leans back as she leads with her lower torso, her hips and stomach protruding with a duck-like walk. She wears full length slips with straps that slide off her shoulders and show through her blouses. Her straight wool skirts, smudged by chalk, hang like sacks on her, the seams and stitched front placket are usually twisted so they are not centered in the front or on the sides. (We girls have discussed it and we don't think Mrs. Rowe wears a bra, though thankfully we all need them now.) She wears a slip and undershirt or other old-fashioned garment. Her breasts seem to hang, saggy, deflated, and low like the African natives in *National Geographic*.

We learned later, out at recess, that a few minutes before she came to our door, Mrs. Rowe was at her desk intently searching for something in the middle drawer, when some students' murmuring became audible in the back of her classroom. In exasperation she snapped, "All right, what's going on....?" slamming the desk drawer to emphasize her annoyance and quell the disturbance. Unfortunately, Mrs. Rowe was leaning over her desk at the time, her breasts at risk. A stricken look came to her face and she hurried out of the room. She was in agony, and the students sat stunned as she left the room. I will never forget those words Mrs. Rowe said to Mrs. Mealey, "Oh, Fran, I just shut myself in the drawer!"

Mrs. Mealey takes over both classes while Mrs. Rowe goes to the teacher's room to recover for a few minutes. Before long others realize or guess what has happened, and the whispers ripple through the room. Some students don't do a very good job of smothering their snickers, and Mrs. Mealey has to step back into the class to shush them. At recess the boys mimic what happened after talking with the kids across the hall.

We treat Mrs. Rowe with respect, but sometimes the boys can't help laughing when she stands in front of the class with her leaning-back-stomach-protruding posture, lecturing about math or science. She gestures with her chalk-covered hand to make a point, her middle finger poised in the air. I don't know exactly what pointing with a middle finger means, but I know from observing the boys that it is bad. When the laughter from

Larry Richards or his cousin Gary Gilbert becomes too loud to ignore, Mrs. Rowe asks, "...And what may I ask is so funny?"

Mrs. Rowe seems to have something against Gary Gilbert, maybe because his cousin Larry sets him up for trouble so often. When Gary makes a mistake or is caught answering Larry's whispered question, Mrs. Rowe says, "GAY-REE, GAY-REE, GAY-REE," shaking her head at the hopelessness of his behavior and pronouncing his name in such a way that Larry can barely smother his loud hyena laugh. Gary is a thin boy with glasses, dark hair with cowlicks, slumped posture, a protruding Adams apple, dark peach fuzz on his upper lip, and nervous insecurities brought on by Larry's teasing. Larry says that Gary likes me.

Carol and I tell Gary and Larry we'll meet them downtown Saturday afternoon. As we walk down the sidewalk, I feel embarrassed and shy and don't know what to say. So Carol and I walk by and say nothing. Later Larry tells me I am a snob, that I don't like Gary because his father is a meat cutter at the A & P. I protest that it's not true, but he won't believe me. I think Larry is still mad because Carol and I like the boys from Wassookeag Summer Camp. Carol thinks Larry secretly likes me, but just says that he doesn't. Out of the corner of my eye, sometimes I notice him looking at me when Mrs. Mealey is teaching.

Mrs. Mealey makes learning about American history and WW I and WW II interesting. She brings in ration cards that people used for sugar and gas during WW II. We learn about what it was like for our grand-parents and parents. (Carol's mother was a secretary in Washington D.C. during the war and that's where she met Carol's father. We think maybe when we are nineteen or twenty we can go to Washington and be secretaries too and meet our future husbands.) We learn about how weak President Wilson was during WW I and the treaty he signed and how his wife assumed his responsibilities when he was sick. I realize that he was president when Grampy was in college. We learn the songs from the war and practice them for an evening performance. I love the feeling of unity and solemnity when we sing as a group.

I am full of nervous excitement that evening when we all appear at school on the night of our program. The girls have to wear a black or navy skirt with a white blouse and the boys wear dark pants with white shirts and ties. Since I don't have a plain dark skirt, I wear a navy wool pleated skirt of my mother's that's too big, but is cinched up with a wide belt. My white cotton blouse with the Pandora collar sets it off nicely, but I feel like Second Hand Rose. My mother says, "It's only for an hour."

When we all gather on the stage in the Dexter High School gym, it is a magical moment with Mrs. Mealey poised at the piano. We come together as a group and sing those stirring songs that had been popular when my grandparents and great-aunts were young, and WW I was at its height. We sing the jaunty tune "Over there, over there, the Yanks are coming, the Yanks are coming, the Yanks are coming over there, Say a prayer..." and my favorite:

"It's A Grand Old Flag.
It's a high flying flag,
and forever in peace may she wave.
She's the emblem of, the land I love,
the home of the free and the brave.
Every heart beats true to the red, white, and blue
and there's never a boast or a brag..."

Our voices are as one, swelling with pride for our country that had saved the day in Europe.

One Sunday I see the old black and white movie, *Sergeant York* with Gary Cooper. It is a true story about a pacifist who is forced to go to war and becomes a hero. I'm struck by the tragedy of war. It makes what we have studied seem so much more real. I learn that my Uncle Harold and both of my grandfathers served in WW I, but they didn't have to go to battle.

On the night of the medley of patriotic songs, we end with *God Bless America*. My heart stirs at the beauty of our voices and a feeling of pride in my country. I am so glad that "the war to end all wars" is over and that

America is such a good country—tops in everything, according to the bar graphs in our social studies book.

In December, Mrs. Mealey invites us to tell about our memories of Christmas and when we first found out there was no Santa Claus. Skipper Champion mentions that he knew when he found limp carrots in the trash, carrots that he had left for the reindeer. I mention that I knew when I overheard my father telling a visitor where he bought some wooden hutches for doll dishes that my sisters had received from Santa. Another Christmas Eve I woke up after hearing Daddy complaining and swearing in a voice too loud about the complicated assembly of metal cribs for my sisters' dolls. We all speak of our disillusionment and sadness to have discovered the magic of Christmas was gone.

One of the girls in Mrs. Rowe's seventh grade room is pregnant in the winter and, before long, the word is out. During gym class, wearing her regulation burgundy gym bloomers, she jumps and jumps on the trampoline, as if she hopes to loosen the baby growing inside her. She drops out of school and has to marry the baby's father who is a senior, much too old for her.

In the late winter, we begin to study Maine history. We each have to make a Maine history notebook with a varnished plywood cover. My Uncle Mac makes the cover for me, drilling holes for three rings and sanding and varnishing the wood until it gleams. He delivers it to me. Like many of the kids, I have nothing to do with the process. I glue a sprig of pine needles on the cover, glue booklets on pieces of oaktag, and write a report about Maine. I do little more work on the contents. The tradition is to see who can make the thickest Maine history notebook. Seven or eight inches high is the goal.

We all send to Augusta for every possible pamphlet, brochure, map, and advertisement that the Maine Publicity Bureau and State House have to offer. Dexter postmen have extra heavy, leather bags to tote up and down the hills of town, delivering Maine information to sixty-six homes. We don't really read most of the booklets. We just glue them in the notebook to make it look thick and show that we used our letter writing skills to gather facts about Maine.

In the spring, the whole school has dress-down day when we girls are allowed to wear slacks for one day instead of our usual skirts or dresses. We and the boys move all of the desks out of rooms into the hall just before we go home so the janitors can clean and wax the floors during vacation. Two weeks later, we have dress-up day when the girls wear church or party dresses, constricting garter belts, seamed nylons, and our inch and a half American Girl Jet Heel Pumps. The boys all wear sport coats and dress pants with shirts and ties.

One day, Steve Bassett arrives at school wearing very neat red chinos and a bold colored shirt. He has been shopping in Waterville at Levine's with his mother. Steve's new colorful clothes create such a stir in the school that he is sent home to change. It doesn't seem fair to us, and we think the principal is over-reacting.

A lot of the girls are wearing Ben Casey or Dr. Kildare shirts since the TV shows about the doctors are big now. Carol and I are disdainful about those trendy imitative blouses with buttons on the shoulder and down the side. I don't want to look like my dentist. I go to Burdell's with my mother to buy some new spring clothes. I am growing so rapidly that I need many things. I choose a cute outfit—a black, white, and red plaid cotton skirt with a black boat-neck blouse and red cotton, white lace-trimmed, knee-length pantaloons that go under the skirt. The outfit gets me lots of attention. My friends pay me a quarter to walk from the girls bathroom down the hall past the upper classmen with the pantaloons showing below my skirt with the waist band rolled up. I wear the outfit to ballroom dancing lessons and Mrs. Brown thinks the old-fashioned pantaloons are cute and tells me to show Louise Gudroe, our pianist, and the instructors.

In May there is a benefit fashion show. Most of the kids in our ball-room dancing class participate. I have to model a dress from Avis Davis' dress shop, and some white Jet Heels from Reed's Shoe Store. I walk across the stage in shoes with masking tape on the soles so they can be returned to the store. I turn to face the audience, then slowly do a complete circle to show the back of the dress. I'm nervous. This is different from our summer fashion shows on Aunt Teddy's lawn when we were little. There's a big crowd sitting on folding chairs in the high school gym. I try to be calm and poised and to stand straight and tall.

As I start to proceed across the stage and off the other side, I realize that the one and a half inch Jet Heel of my shoe is wedged tightly between the sections of the wooden stage. The stage is made up of large, rectangular, gray wooden boxes and my shoe is stuck at the spot where four of them meet. I step forward. My right foot suspends and paws the air like one of the Three Stooges about to do a pratfall. My left foot won't lift up. I try to tug the heel out by scrunching my toes and pulling my foot. It seems as if I have been on the lighted stage for half an hour. I feel hot and flushed. I think I hear chuckles from the vast, unseen audience. For a second I think about just stepping out of the shoe and leaving it there as I walk off, but I don't want to look like Gunsmoke's limping Chester with my one shoeless foot shorter than the other.

Finally, in desperation to get off the stage, I scooch down and pull the tiny heel loose. As I walk off the stage with a crimson face and ears, I hear the commentator say,...and that dress from TITCOMB-DAVIS was so gracefully modeled by Prudy Hatch." I know she is just saying it to make me feel better, but the round of sympathetic applause rings in my ears.

I write to my cousin David and ask him if he would come to Dexter to take me to the Cabaret. It is a formal dance for Dexter High School students and local towns' people. Carol goes with Gene Kortecamp and we sit at a table together. Cathie goes with Dennis. I buy a pale yellow chiffon dress and realize later when I see the pictures that it washes me out. The red taffeta I wore to Rainbow is a more flattering color.

We have a good time at The Cabaret, but I realize that it was silly of me to ask my cousin to take me to a dance, especially since David likes Loanne. We dance or sit at our table and watch Mr. and Mrs. Wilbur dance gracefully to all the songs. The Wilburs know how to do the jitter-bug and the waltz perfectly. They make it look effortless, not boxy and stiff. I watch Maxine Wilbur, a big woman, in silver shoes with straps, glide and twirl around the gym that is decorated with crepe paper, lattice work, and fake flowers.

We each have a decorated card table which makes the gym look like a bistro or cabaret. That's how they get the name for the dance. We don't mind sharing the evening with dancing adults from Dexter. I'm just glad to be at the Cabaret.

One day Mrs. Mealey tells the class that even Dexter once had a branch of the K.K.K. I mispronounce it as Clue Klux Klan when I tell my mother. Everyone of us is shocked to learn that years ago men in our town wore those hoods and burned a cross on a hill. We have studied the Dred Scott decision and the Underground Railroad and slavery. We learn that in Maine, it is not because of Negroes that the Klan is organized. We learn that it has something to do with French people, Catholics who came from Canada to work in the woolen mills. Dexter has a telephone book full of Clukeys, Gilberts, Chabots, and Goullettes. Most of them work at Amos Abbot Mill, or the Dumbarton Mill, or Fay and Scott Machine shop, or the new shoe shop, or are carpenters or they own small stores.

Carol's father tells her that when he was a boy he saw the Klan parade through town. A dog grabbed at one man's hooded robe exposing my Uncle Harold Hatch, Grampy's brother. We also learn that one of Dexter's most prominent citizens (who became governor and a U.S. senator) was once a member of the Klan, like other Protestant men in the community. My father tells me that when he first went to work for Mutt Small's insurance agency he was shocked to see white hoods and robes in a closet. We can hardly believe that people we know would do such a thing.

I read in *Time* that for the Centennial of the Civil War, the movie *Gone With the Wind* is being rereleased. The article makes the movie sound really good. Carol and I go to see it in Bangor and a second time when it comes to the Park Theater in Dexter. We cry rivers of tears when Melanie dies and when Rhett leaves Scarlett. I am struck when Scarlett says, "I won't think about that now. I'll think about that tomorrow." I realize that's the way I think when I hear arguments at our house or Winnie's and Grampy's. It's how I deal with my homework when I decide to go skating or to Carol's instead of doing my assignments. Thinking that way is becoming a habit for me. I'm a cross between Scarlett O'Hara and Alfre E. (what me worry?) Newman.

I'm hearing a lot about the 1960 census and the election with Nixon and Kennedy. Some people are saying the Pope will have more power if Kennedy wins, because the Kennedys are Catholic. We have debates with students taking turns telling their opinions. Gene is an altar boy and he defends John Kennedy. Gene's face gets beet red when he makes a point. We keep up the debate at the rink.

I feel as if I have just awakened from the sleep of childhood. I notice things about the world around me. I have a new awareness of how drinking changes Daddy, Grampy, and Mac that slipped by before.

Every Sunday night, my parents watch *You Are There* with Walter Cronkite. Daddy likes to see the old film clips of the war. At first we used to complain because we wanted to watch *Bachelor Father*. Now I watch and recognize some of the names—Normandy, Pearl Harbor, Berlin, Iwo Jima. Afterward, when Walt Disney comes on Daddy says he's going to the post office to see if the new mail is in his box (having a postal box means he gets mail more frequently) or he has some work to do at the office. "Who wants me to get some gum at Fossa's?" he asks.

We all chime in with requests for our favorite brand and flavors—Beeman's Pepsin or Clark's Teeberry, Blackjack, or Clove. My mother has a certain look on her face. An hour or two later Daddy comes back.

"Here's the gum girls," he says slowly. We all scramble greedily for the packs, and unwrap the gum as frantically as we do Christmas packages from Aunt Barbara. I notice that Daddy keeps asking the same question over and over. "How rya doin' girls?" or he says, "How's my Salsie

Palsie?" to my sister Sally. Susie is playing with her Chatty Cathie doll and doesn't notice.

I think I'm the only one who watches as Daddy goes out to the kitchen. He walks on the balls of his feet in a way I've come to recognize. He keeps patting his chest and licking his lips as he repeats things when he returns. While we sit with gum wrappers on the floor beside us, chawing on wads of gum and watching *The Ed Sullivan Show*, Daddy decides to go to bed. I notice that when he goes up the stairs, he seems a little unsteady. He holds the banister with his left hand and slides his right hand up the wall. "gnight girls...I think I'll go to bed now," he repeats.

I never see Daddy with a drink. He just comes back from the office and his voice and walk are different. I notice that Grampy has a glass of whiskey by his side often. Sometimes his face is flushed, and his voice is different, but I hope it's not too noticeable to my friends at the skating rink. Mac has his beer and sometimes when he has too much he argues a lot with Grampy. I notice that Grampy is bossy and scolds Mac as if he were still a boy.

Now that I am finally a teenager, I'm beginning to see that life is more complicated than I ever realized. I'm noticing so much more and understanding things better like telling time with quarter past and quarter of and how men in my family change when they take a drink. I wonder if I am the only one of my sisters who knows this. I don't mention it to anyone. I look for signs in the faces of my friends' fathers when I visit. I'm feeling quite grown up and sometimes weighed down by the burden of having so much knowledge that my younger sisters don't have, but then, I'm a teenager now and they are not.

Prudy and Carol at R.C. Whitney and Sons Garage—1956

AUNT TEDDY—WORKING WOMAN

Aunt Teddy was a working woman. From the date of her high school graduation in 1909 until her retirement in 1967, she held jobs as a bookkeeper and secretary. An independent woman who felt a sense of responsibility to her family, Aunt Teddy never married. "I had boy friends and an offer or two for marriage, but I felt I was needed at home," she told me when she was ninety.

Born Estelle Margaret Hill in 1890, she was called Stell by many people and Aunt Teddy by more than those who were related to her. I never found out how she got the nick name Teddy, but her middle name was chosen to honor her grandmother, Margaret Fairgrieves Tait who was born in Galishields, Scotland in 1828, and who emigrated to America in 1852.

Aunt Teddy's mother Jennie Tait was a member of the first graduating class of Dexter High School in 1882. Twenty-seven years later, in 1909, Aunt Teddy was valedictorian of Dexter High. Within days of graduation, her high school principal, Mr. Bucknam, telephoned and said, "Ernest Blaisdell's coming down to see you about work."

"What kind of work?" Aunt Teddy asked.

Mr. Bucknam responded tersely, but with encouragement, "You can do it."

"That's all he said to me," Aunt Teddy told me years later. "Mr. Blaisdell came down to our house on lower Main Street and I went to work as his bookkeeper. I didn't take bookkeeping at all in high school; I took the Latin course, Aunt Teddy said, emphasizing the T in the last syllable. "Everything worked out all right though. Ernest's wife Inez was pregnant at the time and she taught me all the bookkeeping procedures."

For about seven years, Aunt Teddy worked in the office of Blaisdell's electrical shop. Then she decided to further her education and enrolled at the Gilman Commercial School in nearby Bangor, where she lived for a year. Using money she had saved from her small salary at the Blaisdell's, Aunt Teddy paid for her own tuition.

"When I came home from school," Aunt Teddy explained, "Fay and Scott machine shop was starting in with the war business. Myrtie Leighton, who was a bookkeeper there, asked me why I didn't come down and work. I went down to see Mr. Fay and he said I could come to work any time."

Aunt Teddy stayed at Fay and Scott until work slacked off. Her next place of employment was at the Eastern Trust and Banking where she worked until a fire in an adjacent building destroyed the bank, and she was out of a job. Aunt Teddy next found a position at Eldridge Brothers' sawmill as a bookkeeper. They made clothes drying racks, one of which was still in Aunt Teddy's pantry decades later. It had folding arms like rigid octopus tentacles climbing the circumference of the five feet high pedestal. Aunt Teddy bought it with her pay. She also took dictation from one of the men who was the overseer and needed someone to write letters to suppliers. "He'd say 'you write to so and so; we haven't received that thing.' That was how he dictated."

Aunt Teddy continued to live at home and to pay room and board. Her two younger sisters were married by then, and between 1916 and 1920 Winnefred gave birth to one girl and two boys. Elsie gave birth to two girls and one boy. The six children, their mothers, grandparents and Aunt Teddy lived a frugal, but comfortable life with a big garden, a cow, and chickens to provide food for the growing family. Winnefred cleaned houses when she could and Elsie earned money as a cook. Papa Hill earned $21.00 dollars a month. Aunt Teddy contributed part of her salary.

At some point during this time, Aunt Teddy worked part time for noted Maine photographer Bert Call. Using skills she learned from him and the necessary chemicals, she turned the pantry off the kitchen into a dark room to develop pictures of her three nieces and three nephews.

During her vacation in the summer, Aunt Teddy hiked the Katahdin wilderness area with friends, including Jere Abbott, son of the owner of Dexter's Abbott Woolen Mill. Years later he was a co-founder of the Museum of Modern Art in New York City and a benefactor of the Colby College art museum. But, in the 1920s and 1930s he was just a Dexter boy, albeit a privileged one. Jere, photographer Bert Call, Aunt Teddy, and her friend Alice camped and hiked in the Katahdin wilderness before it became Baxter Park. They stayed at York's camps at Daicey Pond and Aunt Teddy filled a photo album with snapshots of the wilderness around them. She was inspired to write a poem in white chalk on the black pages, expressing awe at the beauty of the wilderness, "with apologies to Tennyson."

One summer Aunt Teddy joined the group later and hiked part way in with a guide, gamely helping him carry part of the load in her leather pack, with her eyes on the lookout for bears.

In 1926 Bert Call photographed her kneeling by a stream, cup in hand for drinking water, wearing full hiking gear including wool knickers. "When the photographs appeared in Maine Central Railroad's magazine, *In the Maine Woods*, it created quite a stir from men who wrote saying they didn't like seeing a picture of a woman in pants on the cover," said Aunt Teddy, still surprised and indignant by the response.

From about 1928 until 1951, Aunt Teddy worked as the bursar for my grandfather at The Wassookeag School Camp for boys and at the winter school. Aunt Teddy kept track of the $2,000 tuition, the bills, and tried to keep things straight with the bartering deals Grampy arranged. Then that job ended, when my grandfather with the grandiose dreams moved his preparatory school to Newport, Rhode Island in 1951.

Aunt Teddy began looking for work again. She found it at Perley Pines' Dexter Bottling Works where she continued to work part time as a bookkeeper until she retired at the age of seventy-six. In the summer Aunt

Teddy would bring home a wooden case filled with an assortment of seven and a half ounce bottles of Moxie, birch creme soda, and gingerale that she bought at a discount price or that Mr. Pines gave her as a bonus.

In addition to her job at the bottling plant, Aunt Teddy worked part time for Avis Davis at the Titcomb Davis dress shop during the years of my childhood. This gave her the opportunity to earn money for a new dress for meetings of the Dexter Literary Club, the Sunshine Club, or to wear to work or church. The Sunshine Club offered help to people in the community by making sandwiches and serving food after funerals or preparing Thanksgiving and Christmas baskets. Aunt Teddy was a reader and a social person. The afternoon meetings of the Literary Club provided an opportunity for the group to hear lectures on books and authors. She didn't mind taking a few hours away from her work to be a part of the literary discussion.

The most important job Aunt Teddy ever did was to nurture children. For her first nieces and nephews—my father, uncle, aunt, and their cousins—and the next two generations, Aunt Teddy was a memory maker and she welcomed our visits to her house.

My sisters and I arrived on a Friday night, bag and baggage for the week-end. In exchange for the child care, my father paid her real estate taxes and helped in other ways. I never heard a hint that Aunt Teddy was tired from a week of work and a life time of activity. She returned to her job on Monday morning after a week-end of taking care of my sisters and me, as well as our cousin Barry and our friends who visited. When I thought of it as an adult, I wondered how, as a woman in her mid sixties, she had the stamina and energy to do it all.

In November and December, she stayed up past midnight at her sewing machine fashioning elegant clothes—ball gowns, fur wraps, nylon net tutus, and dozen of other outfits for our Vogue dolls—Ginny, Ginette, Jill, and Jeff. Then she made complete layettes for the baby dolls anticipating our delight on Christmas morning. One year Aunt Teddy made each of us personalized muslin laundry bags. Another year, she sewed each of us a different colored denim over night bag with our names Prudy, Randy, Sally and Susie sewn cursively with red ricrac.

Aunt Teddy seemed to have endless energy, probably the result of vigorous daily exercise. In addition to all her wilderness hiking, Aunt Teddy, who never learned to drive, walked to work every morning and then walked home for lunch. She walked back to work for the afternoon and then left for home at five o'clock. When she was seventy-six, she fell and broke her leg while walking to work in a blizzard. After that she retired.

Although she no longer worked, Aunt Teddy kept busy with activities at the Universalist Church, the Sunshine Club, and taking care of her adult nephew Mac who still lived at her house. She washed his clothes in the wringer washer and hung them on the clothes line, cooked meals for him, and overlooked his drunken rages.

Aunt Teddy's character has taken on almost mythical proportions. Members of a writing group once told me, "You need to make your aunt more real by having balance and showing the negative side of her personality."

I have no memory of such characteristics. Aunt Teddy was even tempered, self-sufficient, and adaptable. I saw her as patient, generous, and thoughtful with all those she knew and worked for.

Aunt Teddy's first boss, Ernest Blaisdell, was an entrepreneur of the times. He was the first person to introduce the automobile to Dexter. Mr. Blaisdell took his entire staff to Boston to get a fleet of cars to drive back to Dexter and sell. While he was gone he needed someone to take over his duty of "town switch puller." In those days Dexter citizens didn't have the luxury of electricity twenty-four hours a day.

At midnight the power was turned off. Every day, early in the morning, Ernest Blaisdell drove to the town hall, pulled the switch and illuminated the homes as people readied for work. Since he was going to be in Boston with his staff, he asked Aunt Teddy to take over his job. She got up earlier that morning, when it was still dark and walked a mile to the town hall near the Abbott Memorial Library. Mr. Blaisdell had shown her the location of the switch in the town hall. "I was short, but I knew there was a box there. He told me to stand on the box and to throw the switch, and he told me not to fall."

Aunt Teddy, who had climbed across the Knife Edge on Mount Katahdin, assured him she'd be fine.

And so Aunt Teddy took over Mr. Blaisdell's responsibility of town switch puller. Not only did she bring light into people's lives for 97 years, quite literally she once brought it to the whole town of Dexter.

VISITS WITH AUNT TEDDY

I figured out that there are eight hundred and thirty two Saturdays and Sundays in the prime years of childhood—ages five to thirteen. Added to that are school vacations, other holidays, and the long lazy days of summer. Looking back on my childhood, that means I had over 1,500 non-school days to explore the world around me, to go to my friends' houses, to the hockey rink, to visit relatives, and to have new experiences.

My sisters and I traveled to see our grandparents in Newport, R.I. during school vacations and we stayed at Aunt Teddy's on many weekends. Because of the vast disparity of the experiences, I learned about two very different worlds that shaped my values and expectations.

Aunt Teddy lived on lower Main Street for over eighty years in the house her father hired built. She helped take care of her three nieces and three nephews when they were little. She took care of her parents when they were old, her nephew Mac when he was defeated by life, and my sisters and me (her grand nieces) when our parents were away or when we just wanted to visit.

Aunt Teddy was our link to the past, since she was born in 1890 and lived in a house filled with old things—a tin candle mold, antique dolls, a large mahogany-framed picture of Abraham Lincoln, his wife and little Tad before he died, another of George Washington and his crew crossing the Delaware, the little instrument Aunt Teddy used as a child on her high button boots, a thick warm striped flannel night shirt we took turns wearing, a stereopticon viewer with sepia-toned post card size photos, a two feet high dancing girl statue, drawings done by an ancestor in the Civil War, hundreds of antique china dogs from her mother's collection, a framed copy of Burns Grace by the Scottish poet, and an alphabet sampler stitched by a six year old girl in 1848. The closets and entry way cubby hole near the back stairs revealed even more old things when we asked to look on rainy spring days.

We arrived to visit on Friday in the late afternoon toting the canvas over night bags that Aunt Teddy had made for us. Everything about Aunt Teddy's was in sharp contrast to our routine and surroundings at home. Some of our happiest moments were spent in Aunt Teddy's old-fashioned kitchen, which looked nothing like our new Youngstown kitchen with turquoise and yellow metal cabinets.

The kitchen at Aunt Teddy's house hadn't changed much since she was a girl there or since the days of my father's childhood. A new electric stove stood near the old gray cook stove which had been converted to kerosene. That old stove was the very one in which tiny, sickly baby Harvey, our father, was placed to warm that December morning of his birth. I thought of that on Saturdays as I watched Aunt Teddy check the pot of beans and molasses she cooked all day.

Her house was cozy on winter days with warm air blowing up through the wrought iron floor registers from the coal furnace. I went down to the cellar with Aunt Teddy and watched her feed gleaming, midnight-blue chunks of coal into the cavernous furnace. The furious flames reminded me of the Bible story of Shadrach, Meshach, and Abednego and their walk through fire to safety. My fourth grade teacher, Mrs. Cleaveland, read us a Bible story each morning during opening exercises and the vivid details stayed with me. As I watched the flames roar in Aunt Teddy's furnace, I shuddered to think of being surrounded by fire with flames licking at my legs.

When we played beauty shop with old metal wave clips, slim brown rubber curlers, combs, towels, and glasses of water, we had a perfect place to sit Indian style—over the hot air registers while our coiffures dried. To pass the time while we waited, Randy and I played Cat's

Cradle, an old-fashioned game Aunt Teddy taught us using cotton string from a ball in the pantry drawer.

Earlier in the fall while visiting, we kids had helped Aunt Teddy put evergreen branches and the heavy wooden banking boards around the foundation. Aunt Teddy wielded the hammer, and my cousin Barry, my sisters, and I carried the boards and positioned them. We felt so needed and important to be helping Aunt Teddy.

At home we didn't work together as a family. My father wasn't handy, so he paid Louis Chabot and his sons to do all the yard work or repairs. Helping Aunt Teddy made me see the value of people pitching in. After the work was done, we went inside to have hot chocolate and play cards.

The game of Old Maid was our favorite. The cards were so worn, we could recognize Baker Ben or Cowboy Carl or other cards just by the creases. The Old Maid card had been crumpled rather severely on more than one occasion when one of us was left holding it, so we had to keep it hidden in our hand. I think we made the connection about Aunt Teddy's not being married, but she was such a good sport she played right along with us, not minding when we chortled to the loser, "You're the oh-uld maaaiid; you're the oh-uld maaaiid."

Even in the winter months, I used the rope swing in the center of the screened-in porch. I swung back and forth, back and forth, pumping higher and higher, until, with my feet out straight I left tread mark prints of my PF Flyers on the white ceiling. I kept, swinging and pumping, trying to reach my goal and match my prints to the first set, until Aunt Teddy tapped on the window, shook her head back and forth, and I could read her lips saying, "No more." I went back inside feeling chagrined.

"What do you say we all go sliding after lunch," Aunt Teddy asked?

After lunch, Randy, Sally, Barry, two neighborhood kids, and I, bundled up and took the old sleds to the hill behind her house in Hanson's field, led by Aunt Teddy in her old-fashioned boots and wool winter clothes. The thick crust made by rain a few days before held the heavy sleds even with our weight. We all posed around a little pond and Aunt

Teddy snapped a photo of the six of us. Then we trekked back to her house an hour later and stored the sleds in the shed. My feet were frozen, because instead of wearing several pairs of socks in packs like most boys did, my sisters and I wore shoes with one pair of socks under and another over our shoes inside the rubber boots. I had on my new saddle shoes with a pair of wool socks over the shoes, but that wasn't very effective.

Back in the house, we each huddled in different rooms over the black register grates, warming our bodies and red feet, our toes tracing the curlicue design, while Aunt Teddy started making biscuits in the pantry.

"Could we make molasses pull candy after supper," I asked?

"I think that would be a good idea," Aunt Teddy said. "We haven't made any for quite a while."

When it was time to clean up after supper, we took turns washing the dishes. I liked swishing the small, long-handled wire basket, that held a bar of brown soap, to make soapsuds in the metal dish pan. After everything was washed, Aunt Teddy showed us how to wipe the slate sink clean so the wetness evaporated more quickly. Then we were ready to begin preparations for making candy.

"Land sakes. This takes me back," said Aunt Teddy. "Sixty years ago my sisters and I made candy in this kitchen with our mother."

We each took turns measuring the ingredients—water, sugar, vinegar, molasses—and pouring them into the heavy sauce pan on the new electric stove. As the molasses mixture bubbled and boiled, it gave off a sweet, tantalizing odor. For a while we hovered around the stove waiting impatiently for the taffy to reach the right temperature and thickness.

Randy placed two stainless steel trays on the oil cloth-covered oak table where Aunt Teddy and our grandmother sat as girls. Sally greased the trays readying them for the candy. Barry measured three tablespoons of butter to add at the end of the cooking cycle. Nearly drooling in anticipation of the first taste, I filled a Pyrex custard cup with cold water to test if the syrupy mix had reached the hard ball stage.

While the mixture bubbled, we adjourned to the front room and Aunt Teddy played the piano. Her eyes twinkled behind the black, cat's eye pointed frames of her glasses and in a steady voice she sang, "Little Sir Echo, how do you do?" and we echoed her refrain, "Hello, hello." and then began "Daisy, Daisy, Give Me Your Answer Do…" our favorites of Aunt Teddy's piano repertoire. Gathered around her, we sang until the timer dinged. Then we hurried back to the kitchen to check the bubbling taffy.

Eager to taste and test, I held the spoon above the dish of cold water. A gooey strand of molasses plopped to the bottom as evidence that the mixture was not quite done. My fingers in the water made a soft ball of the molasses. It was obvious that we needed to wait. A few more times of testing gave each of us a chance to savor the taste. Stray drops of sugary molasses left the linoleum so tacky underfoot, that my saddle shoes made a sticking, snapping sound as I walked with the custard cup to the slate sink for more cold water. Aunt Teddy used a knife and an old rag to clean my shoe and the floor. It seemed like hours until the candy was finally ready.

"Now stand back so you don't get burned," Aunt Teddy warned as she carried the hot pan to the pantry to set on a cutting board near the slate sink.

Aunt Teddy turned the thick, sticky candy onto one of the buttered trays to cool and using a wooden spoon, pushed the mixture around the pan until some of the heat escaped and the taffy thickened more. Gingerly, she took the first glob of hot, sticky molasses and began to work it with her buttery fingers until it was cool enough to pass on to one of us. Then she worked another glob of taffy to give one of us until we each had some. Shirt sleeves pushed back, our hands glistening with butter, we tugged, twisted, and folded the hot taffy into long golden ropes, trying to lighten the candy's color just as Aunt Teddy said her mother used to do.

I had to use my teeth to pull my sleeves back when they crept down to my wrists, because everyone had buttery fingers. The palms of our hands were bright red from the heat of the taffy. We pulled and pulled until our arms ached. Then we placed the long molasses snake-like lengths of candy onto the other greased tray to harden in the cold entryway outside the kitchen. The scent of cooked molasses floated through the house.

Our anticipation mounted until the candy was finally ready, and Aunt Teddy brought in the tray covered with glossy, mahogany colored strips. We broke the taffy into pieces by whacking it with the handle of a table knife. Tiny pieces of taffy went flying. With bulging cheeks, we returned to the front room just as the theme song for *Gunsmoke* began and sat down to watch Matt Dillon save the day. Randy, Sally, Susie, Barry, and I spent the rest of the evening gorging ourselves on the taffy until the insides of our mouths puckered from the sweetness, and Aunt Teddy had to say, "I think you've had enough. It's time to brush your teeth and get ready for bed."

I slept in the little bedroom with rosebud wallpaper and a single bed. I read a Nurse Cherry Ames book under the sheets with my flash light, eager to see what was going to happen. It wasn't as good as my Nancy Drew books, but the story kept my attention, until Aunt Teddy came to bed and saw the faint light from under the door.

Randy and Sally slept in the big room which had the large maple bed with a high, pointed head board and matching marble topped commode, bureau, and vanity. The linoleum floors were cold on our stockinged feet, because the heat from the furnace was lower for the night and so we snuggled under layers of blankets.

Susie slept with Aunt Teddy, and we all gathered there in the morning and played, "I'm thinking of something…" while we gave clues and hoped the guesses stayed "Cold or Colder" not "Hot or Hotter."

When I looked around the room for objects, my gaze stopped at Aunt Teddy's bureau. On top of it she had the miniature china cabinet that once held her set of doll dishes. After she was an adult, the shelves behind the little glass doors held Aunt Teddy's large collection of costume jewelry. When it was my turn to think of something, I chose the translucent beads on the shelf of the little cabinet. When she wore them, they glistened like soap bubbles in the sunlight. We played the game for half an hour, then got up to start the day.

After breakfast we lingered at the table and listened as Aunt Teddy entertained us with stories about our aunts, uncles, and our father, telling anecdotes of their growing years. We could picture the December day, in 1917 when Dr. Foss arrived by horse and sleigh to deliver our father, and had difficulty coming up the icy driveway.

She told us, that the new baby, Harvey, (Later rechristened Lloyd Harvey Hatch, Jr. when he was three) was sickly and suffering from a severe rash. Nanny Hill covered him with black salve and surrounded him with cotton in a box on the open oven door. My sister, Randy, told me with a laugh, that for her whole childhood she had a mental image of Daddy as a tiny baby in a cotton-lined shoe box in the oven. I had pictured him looking like a mini member of a minstrel show with black salve covering the rash all over his little body.

"Tell us a story about Mac," Randy asked as we lingered at the table after a breakfast of pancakes and Maine maple syrup.

Aunt Teddy said, "Mac's antics and mischief got him quite a few scoldings from your grandfather. One day Lloyd had just boarded the train to return to Cornell where he was teaching and studying. Mac was about three. After the train was out of sight, Mac stamped his little foot on the piazza, folded his arms, and said, 'There, I'm glad he's gone. Now we can do what we want to do.'

I understood about Grampy's strictness because I had seen him scold the adult Mac as if he were still a misbehaving boy.

"Tell us the story about Mac and Mr. Call," I asked, wanting to hear the tale again. Familiarity with the story didn't dull our anticipation of the punch line.

"Well, one summer when Mac was about eight, Mr. Call came to take some photographs for your grandfather's glossy brochures. Afterwards, Mr. Call had to speak to Grampy about Mac's most recent hijinx. Mr. Call lined the students and faculty in long rows with Mac and your father on the left in the back. Using his camera that scanned the long rows from left to right, Mr. Call photographed the whole group. He discovered that Mac was in the picture twice, because he had run around behind and positioned himself on the other end before the camera moved to the right side. Mr. Call had to do several retakes. Lloyd wasn't amused. That Mac was such a little imp," she said with a chuckle.

I learned many valuable lessons from Aunt Teddy, but one in particular still evokes powerful memories. My part in the event must have caused Aunt Teddy some embarrassment when she heard about it, as well as making me ashamed of what I had said to Carrie Palmer's granddaughter.

Mrs. Palmer lived behind us and was a friend and contemporary of Aunt Teddy's. Mrs. Palmer's granddaughter sometimes visited at her Grandmother's, and I joined her to play a few times. Janet, who had long dark braids, and held her head stiffly to one side, was different acting, not like the rest of us, and somehow I heard that her mother had the measles before Janet was born. As she became older the differences became more pronounced. After the six grade, she still lived in Dexter, but was no longer in our classroom.

Before that time, Mrs. Palmer always drove to school to give Janet a ride home. As I walked home from school with Carol or occasionally by myself, I'm ashamed to say, I was calculating enough to wave as they went by so I could get a ride home rather than walk in the cold and snowy weather. I felt like Eloise, the character in a book, who feigned illness, only I put on an act of being weak and needy of a ride, using people for my own benefit.

I knew it was not kind the way I ignored Janet except for the ride. Later, in sixth grade, I did have to dance with her sometimes at ballroom classes when there was a shortage of boys. The worst thing I ever did was tell Janet things about her grandmother that I overheard my father say. Unfortunately, when my father pointed to the hill behind our house and complained about "the cheapness of that old woman" when my parents bought our house on Main Street from her, he was not speaking of Carrie Palmer, but of Mrs. Carsley, who also lived on Bryant Hill.

Mrs. Carsley had removed all the light bulbs from the sockets and had done other things that still made Daddy's blood boil when he spoke of them. My thoughtless comments and misinformation eventually taught me a few lessons.

Shortly afterward, while I was at Aunt Teddy's, by her side at the sewing machine, she told me about a girl who had hurt Janet Parson's feelings and told her things that were all wrong. The girl had confused Mrs. Carsley with Mrs. Palmer. As Aunt Teddy told me what the girl had said and how it had upset Janet and Mrs. Palmer, I became more and more ill at ease and guilt-ridden.

I prayed that Aunt Teddy would never find out that I was the awful girl who had done such a thing. Aunt Teddy handled the episode in such a way that saved me the embarrassment of a scolding and defensiveness, but made me ashamed and sorry. Years later, I realized that she had known that I was the girl, but it was her way of letting me save face, while teaching me a valuable lesson. Over the years, I have thought of that story frequently, and it affected how I reacted to my sons and to my students.

Years after that day by Aunt Teddy's side, I went to a used book sale at the Universalist Church. It was in 1985, two months after I had studied Dante's *The Inferno* with Professor Dan Gunn at UMF. I found two used books at the book sale that I had to have.

One is a large book of the *Divine Comedy* with haunting black and white pictures of the Inferno, Purgatorio, and Paradiso. The other is a book titled *The Tomb of Tutankhamen* by Howard Carter and A.C. Mace. I had been fascinated with the topic previously and borrowed some books from the Skowhegan and the Maine State libraries when the treasures of King Tut toured the U.S. As I browsed through the books that day of the sale, I opened *The Tomb of Tutankhamen* and knew I would pay the four dollar price. Inside, the fountain pen inscription says, "Carrie Palmer." Some how it seemed that the book was there waiting for me. One more synchronicity of many in my life. Owning the book didn't expiate my sin or unkindness, but having it on my shelves is a reminder.

Aunt Teddy's Shed

Whenever I see the pictures that my aunt took with her Brownie box camera, I am transported back to summers of the 1950s—to Aunt Teddy's shed, where my sisters, cousins, friends, and I dressed up for our make-believe fashion shows and plays.

Vines of sweet peas climbed the trellis beside the wide doorway to the shed. Their scent mingled with that of pansies and snap dragons and wafted around us on breezy summer afternoons as we rehearsed. Wearing vintage clothes from the dome-topped trunks in Aunt Teddy's shed, we pirouetted on the grass. As the afternoon wore on, we returned to the large shed for costume changes and a final rehearsal.

The shed was built when Aunt Teddy was a little girl. In those days, it contained the outhouse where she and her two younger sisters emptied white china chamber pots on winter mornings. Years later, after a first floor room in the house was converted to a bathroom, the family no longer needed to perform that dreaded chore. In those later days, when my father was a little boy, the shed sheltered the family cow and assorted chickens from the harsh Maine winters.

Aunt Teddy's father, had bought the cow to provide milk for his six grandchildren. Yankee frugality, with its roots in Scottish ancestry, enabled Papa and Nanny Hill to maintain a comfortable home for themselves, their three daughters, and their six grandchildren. Having a big garden and a cow provided for the extended family. The shed was a perfect place for Bossey and the chickens.

As Bossey grew, she produced more milk than the family could use, so Grampa Hill offered the extra milk to a needy family who lived on nearby

Railroad Avenue. He gave them milk regularly until the day they arrived in an automobile to get the glass jars filled. Walter Hill, who couldn't afford a car and walked everywhere, decided it was the last time he would give milk to that family.

"If they can afford to buy an automobile and gasoline," he reasoned, " I guess they can afford to buy milk."

The shed, during my childhood, held a treasure trove of elegant dresses stored in old trunks which flanked one side of the second section of the shed. On the opposite wall, a workbench stretched along the three windows. We placed all the tiny brass sample tubes of Avon lipstick and cast off compacts of rouge and powder at one end of the bench. On the other end, we arranged outfits for costume changes between scenes. That dressing room section was two steps up from the stage area of the first shed, with a door separating the areas.

Most of the clothes we wore were those my Aunt Barbara and grandmother received as part of the tuition barter deal Grampy arranged with the owner of the exclusive dress shop in New York City.

What a collection we had—old hats, evening gloves, feather boas, capes, shawls, velvet, crepe, and chiffon dresses from the 1920s and 1930s, and pins with clusters of silk violets or daisies. The clothes fit as if made for me, because I was tall, even as a ten-year-old, while my grandmother and aunt had been petite. I felt like Greta Garbo in the celery green brocade taffeta dress with a rhinestone studded bodice and thin straps. The slinky crepe de chine floral print dress flowed about me, and the scent of the old trunks was my perfume.

When Randy, Sally, Susie, Barry, and my friends helped me prepare the shed for plays, we created quite a mess before the place finally came together. We tugged and shoved the old wardrobe chest, an old church pew, and wooden crates to the back of the shed's first room. Then we draped blankets over the shelves of gardening implements and assorted junk. To do a more thorough job, we took turns beating the old threadbare carpets with the fan-shaped wire rug beater, whapping out the dust.

Next we swept the layers of dirt from the wide, creaking boards. Sweeping with exuberance and determination, we pushed open the large sliding door, letting fresh air in and expelling the billowing clouds of dust.

Once those preparations were complete, we worked on our ideas for performances, which were usually based on Nancy Drew mysteries. I had read all of them, plus The Dana Girls and Judy Bolton mysteries so we had a wealth of material to consider. My sisters were beginning to read the books too and helped decide which scenes to include. We arranged the props on the make-shift stage—the shed floor—creating a kitchen with an old-fashioned box oven, discarded furniture, and dishes.

I, being the eldest, orchestrated the plays, prompted the dialogue, announced costume or scene changes, and gave the fashion show commentary, using the names of companies mentioned on the television show *Queen For A Day*—shoes by Grace Walker, jewelry by Sarah Coventry, hats by Adolfo, and dresses by Classic Designs. Barry and my sisters stepped out of the shed, walked down the grassy runway, and whirled around before striking a pose while I did the commentary. Then I modeled my outfit.

Later in the afternoon, Barry's mother invited us all in to taste the new batch of her home made root beer since it had reached the proper point of effervescence. The event was magnified by our anticipation and the knowledge that we could only partially quench our thirst. At home my sisters and I would have quaffed big glasses of soda. Instead, I politely savored each swallow from the little jelly glass and told Margaret it tasted better than the Frosty Root Beer made at the Dexter Bottling Works.

Refreshed, we returned to the shed and rehearsed the basics of the scenes and dialogue most of which was impromptu and ad-libbed once the play began.

We took another break in late afternoon for croquet using the old set my father, aunt, and uncle had used with their cousins. After a picnic supper, Barry, Carol, my sisters, and I readied ourselves for our presentation while Auntie and Aunt Teddy did the dishes with their visiting friends. When they finished, they were our audience.

Every summer Aunt Teddy's former girlhood chums came to stay for a few weeks. Aunt Teddy would take some time off in July from the office at Perly Pines' Dexter Bottling Works, even though things were busy. If her guests stayed beyond Aunt Teddy's vacation, they visited Auntie next door while Aunt Teddy was at work. Aunt Teddy walked home for her lunch break every day and had a brief visit before she returned to work. It was probably helpful that she was away from the house during the day since after a while the house guests began to annoy each other.

When we were in the shed Barry mimicked their conversations, complaining that Alma and Aunt May "scrapped like cats and dogs." Alma Graham was sour, complaining, and disagreeable—quite a contrast to Aunt Teddy's sunny disposition. We weren't overjoyed when we heard that Alma was coming up from West Buxton.

Aunt May, Aunt Teddy's childhood chum, was jovial and friendly with a toothy false-teeth smile, a thick chin, and pointed frame eyeglasses. She spoke in glowing terms of her nieces who also lived in Maryland. They seemed like perfect princesses. We felt inferior, but Aunt Teddy spoke up about us.

When curtain time arrived, Auntie, Aunt Teddy, Alma, and Aunt May, came to the shed eager to watch our production. After paying the five cent price of admission, they sat on an old church pew awaiting our entrance— all full of smiles and applause. Aunt Teddy especially had a way of making our efforts seem professional with her compliments to each of us.

After the performance, Aunt Teddy, the sparkle in her eyes enlarged her glasses, smiled and said, "You look so lovely in hats, Prudy. I wish I could look as good in them as you do."

"This is my favorite hat," I responded, fingering the wide brim of the old-fashioned beaver hat with the long, fluffy ostrich plume swept jauntily to one side.

We stood side by side the same height because I was in a growth spurt. Aunt Teddy seemed younger and more lithe and spry than her friends and she was glad to have us playing in her shed.

*   *   *   *

In the summer of 1976, Aunt Teddy began the process of sorting through a lifetime accumulation of memories and possessions, as she prepared to sell her house and move into a senior citizen apartment complex. My sisters, Barry's mother Margaret, and I were there to help, but Aunt Teddy did much of it herself, alone in the night.

"I went to an auction at the old Springer homestead, fifty years ago," she said. "It made my heart ache to see framed photographs and once treasured family items spread out for the highest bidder. That won't happen to folks in these pictures," she said, showing me a box of ripped photographs.

She saved the old tintypes of family members and the youthful photos of herself, her brother, Tim, her sisters, Elsie, and Winnifred. She kept the pictures of her parents and the photographs of her stern looking aunts in their turn of the century clothes, some of which she still had stored in trunks. She also saved the photographs of my father, his sister Barbara, and brother Mac, along with those of their cousins, Jimmy, Bunny, and Margaret.

She saved all of the pictures of us four little Hatch girls and those of our cousins. She saved snapshots of our children, who were the next generation, but she slowly and methodically ripped up and burned all the others.

When she told me that they were old Civil War pictures, and early photographs of people her parents or aunts must have known, I winced, feeling certain that some valuable historical information was now lost. She gave my cousin John, Barry's older brother, the rolled parchment of Civil War drawings that an uncle had done when he was at the battles. They were like treasured scrolls, a connection to the past that Aunt Teddy kept in a drawer of the oak buffet in the dining room.

Aunt Teddy told me about the pictures on the summer day when I arrived to help her sort through things stored in the shed. As we were about to begin the work, I asked about the old trunks that held the collection of clothes.

"Oh, the trunks are all gone now," she said with an obvious note of relief in her voice. "I just didn't know what I was going to do with all those things now that I'm selling the house and moving into an apartment. A nice antique dealer gave me fifty dollars for all of the trunks."

I stood stunned. Fifty dollars for the trunks. Fifty dollars for all those trunks filled with clothes, a veritable treasure trove of fashion—gone! After I heard those words, I couldn't bare to look into the rambling shed at the empty spot where the trunks had rested for eighty years.

Heartsick, I tried to share, and voice, Aunt Teddy's gladness to have found someone to cart off the trunks, but the memories and images crept into my mind. I could almost smell the musty scent of age that escaped when the trunk lids were lifted. I remembered the feel of brocade and chiffon.

The vivid memories of the dresses and the feel of the fabrics were so real, yet as evanescent as a wispy cloud of fog. I wanted to reach out and pull the clothes back to the present with the memories. I thought of one of Aunt Teddy's photos of the four of us in dress-ups gathered near the shed with a back-drop of sweet peas climbing on the trellis, their scent mingling with that of her favorite purple pansies and pink snap dragons.

I, a skinny ten year old, stood striking the pose of the sophisticated vamp holding a feather poised in the air, wearing the favorite 1930s midnight blue velvet dress with its matching bolero. My sister Randy sat beside me in a black lace gown with long evening gloves and the wide-brimmed black hat with fluffy fronds. Beside her sat Susie, our youngest sister, a precocious four year old in too large, black suede, open-toed pumps, with one foot jutting out as she tried to keep her balance on the metal picnic bench.

On the other end stood nine-year-old Barry. He posed clutching a white purse and was enveloped in the gold brocade evening gown with the spaghetti straps slipping from his shoulders and a lacy flounce swirled about his ankles. The bright print silk kimono, a blond doll's wig, and a veiled, bejeweled pill box hat completed his ensemble.

I wondered what would become of the flowered, gossamer silk kimono and the blue velvet sheath. What about the paisley shawl that came over on the boat with our Scottish ancestors, and the wide brim, black beaver picture hat with the fluffy feathery fronds? Or the celery-green silk gown with the rhinestone-studded straps and brocade bodice? Where is the white cotton eyelet lace dress with the magenta velvet bows at the neck and waist?

What about the clothes that were seventy-five or a hundred years old, the ones people came to borrow as costumes for plays or events that celebrated the past? What about the grass hula skirt with woven grass brassiere that Barry wore to his third grade Halloween party? Where is the fringed Indian dress, Aunt Teddy's Camp Fire Girls outfit, made from imitation deer skin that I wore in a Girl Scout skit when I sang the song *Pretty Red Wing*.

"You girls had such fun dressing up in those clothes," Aunt Teddy said wistfully, interrupting my reverie. "I remember when you girls arrived, you'd set your overnight bags in a row on the piazza and rush off to the sheds. You hardly said good-bye to your parents. You'd play in the shed all day long."

After her move from Lower Main Street, we had twelve more years of visiting Aunt Teddy at the apartment and then the nursing home.

Aunt Teddy's shed is gone now. The people who bought her house tore it down and built a two-car garage where it used to stand.

Over the years, I've had dreams that I am in Aunt Teddy's shed again. I discover another long room, around the corner near the stage area, that is filled with wondrous articles and antiques I hadn't noticed before. I go through the items one by one like Howard Carter cataloguing Tutankhamen treasures. I awake tingling with a feeling of heightened awareness almost as excited as when I stepped into Aunt Teddy's shed on a summer afternoon.

Barbara Hatch with the baby chicks—1920

Barbara Hatch with Bossie—1920

Susie, Prudy, Mac and Randy—1954

Dress ups at Aunt Teddy's—Prudy and Randy Hatch and David Rust—1956

Outside Aunt Teddy's shed—1954

CELEBRATING AUNT TEDDY

Aunt Teddy's birthday was in July, when family members who lived out of state returned to Dexter for vacation. Auntie and Winnie helped us plan a surprise party for their sister. As the plans developed, my sisters and I were sure Aunt Teddy never suspected, and she never let us down, always acting surprised.

We spent the afternoon frosting the cake, mixing the Zarex fruit punch, and helping Auntie make sandwiches, which she covered with a damp dish towel to keep them fresh. We changed into our party dresses, patent leather shoes, and anklets, Then we helped carry plates, cups, the plate of sandwiches and the covered birthday cake to the picnic table behind Auntie's house.

My sisters, visiting cousins, and I stood poised on the piazza, shushing giggles and anticipation. Barry was stationed behind a tree at the end of the driveway. We waited until he spotted Aunt Teddy striding toward home. After Barry whispered loudly, "Here she comes," the minutes ticked and tingled slowly by, until Aunt Teddy finally reached the driveway hilltop. We rushed at her, shouting, "Surprise, Surprise! Happy Birthday, Happy Birthday!"

"Land sakes; what a surprise! What a surprise," Aunt Teddy exclaimed.

When she had recovered from her astonishment, we guided her over to Auntie's backyard for the picnic supper, and birthday cake. Aunt Teddy pretended she hadn't guessed the plans, protested and fussed about all the attention. "You shouldn't have done all this. I'm getting too old for birthday parties." But, she put on a paper party hat and tweeted the paper party whistle.

After sandwiches and fruit punch, my sisters and I pressed close with the presents, hoping she would like the new necklace and earrings we bought at Cotes jewelry store. Auntie served the cake and there we all stood, around Aunt Teddy, her sisters, her friend May, her nieces and nephews singing happy birthday.

Our childhood visits with Aunt Teddy were out of the pages of Tasha Tudor's beautifully illustrated, *A Time To Keep* with seasonal activities drawn from another era. In the early spring, we walked up the railroad tracks to the area where pussy willows grew. We cut branches for a bouquet and for an art project. When we arrived back at Aunt Teddy's, my sisters and I glued the gray furry buds on pieces of black paper. I made a soft cat sitting on its haunches with its back to the viewer. It looked a bit like Aunt Teddy's beloved gray cat, Bootsie.

In the fall and spring, neighborhood kids came over to Aunt Teddy's to join us in games of Giant Step, Red Light, Kick the Can and Hide and Seek. If we stayed outside beyond dusk that made it easier to sneak back to the steps to touch the Goo. Shouts of "I got my Goo." and "olli-olli in free" rang through the neighborhood.

We made May baskets with colored tissue paper, old satin ribbons, pipe cleaners, paper cups, and berry boxes. After the baskets were all decorated and filled with nuts, chocolate babies, gum drops and mints, we scampered across the lawn to Auntie's house, rang the bell, and chanted, "May basket for Barry." Then we ran off so he'd have to catch us. I wondered if Aunt Teddy had given a May basket to a neighborhood boy when she was a young girl.

In the morning, after breakfast, we rang the buzzer, which signaled to Barry in the house next door, that we were ready to play. Sometimes Barry came over with his new wooden wagon, but we weren't allowed to play with it. We had many toys at home, but we didn't always take the best care of our possessions or appreciate the work that went into paying for things. Barry's wagon was special, and his mother, Margaret, my father's cousin, didn't want Barry's toys to get scratched or broken.

Sometimes we got into squabbles about sharing, but Aunt Teddy knew how to settle our disputes wisely. She'd separate us for time-out, or send Barry home for a while if need be. Although she never had any children of her own, she surely understood kids.

We gathered around the sewing machine while Aunt Teddy showed us how to stitch doll clothes and warned of the time the needle went into her finger. Aunt Teddy was cool-headed in the event of calamity. She had plenty of Mercurochrome for cuts and abrasions and Mentholatum for congestion, aches, and pains. Once while we visited, Randy ran to the window behind the sewing machine to see the passing train, and she poked the corner of her eye on the glass shelf that held cactus plants. The scariest time was when Randy caught her arm in the wringer washer, and Mac helped pull her free.

When Susie was a toddler, standing at the window, she slapped the pane in excitement, shattering it. Aunt Teddy handled these incidents calmly. Her years of experience with her nieces and nephews and her easy going nature helped her be ready for anything. Although, sometimes, when I was a pre-teen, I felt as if Aunt Teddy hovered over us or worried too much about possible injury.

One Saturday, Barry and my friend Carol joined my sisters and me for an afternoon of play. We found the lovely old baby doll and began playing hospital in Aunt Teddy's bedroom. Some of the other dolls, swathed in bandages, lay in their beds. We made a delivery table out of the flat top green trunk, that came over on the ship with the Scottish ancestors. Carol and I, garbed in old sheets with white bands on our heads, and white handkerchief masks on our faces, assisted my cousin Barry, the doctor.

My younger sister Randy was the mother, writhing on the trunk, screaming out in agony during the arduous, painful labor, inspired by our cinema recollections. We must have made a fearful noise, because Aunt Teddy came rushing up the stairs breathlessly to see what was the matter, no doubt imagining the worst, remembering other accidents or injuries.

"It's okay," we assured her. "Randy's having a baby." At that moment, the old baby doll, guided by the expert hands of the attending staff, was emerging from under the sheets that covered Randy's wriggling body.

Aunt Teddy, sixty-five and unflappable, exclaimed, "Well land sakes... I thought someone was hurt. Tell me, is it a boy or a girl?" Then she went back down stairs to finish making biscuits for supper.

While the new mother, Randy, was in the delivery room, Carol's father arrived to take her home. We heard voices at the bottom of the stairs. "They've had quite an afternoon," Aunt Teddy said to him. "I don't know if she's ready to go yet or not. She's been delivering a baby this afternoon."

*   *   *   *   *   *   *   *

Aunt Teddy had three more decades of birthdays after those surprise parties of our childhood. The most celebrated was in 1980 on her 90th when she still lived in her apartment. All the relatives came from afar. We rented the church hall, filled it with dozens of bouquets of wild flowers and perennials and over one hundred of her friends and relatives. Aunt Teddy, the eldest in her family, had outlived her younger siblings, but she had three generations of nieces and nephews who remembered her kindness and sacrifice.

In 1986, on Aunt Teddy's 96th and last birthday, most of her nieces and nephews gathered at our lake-front cottage. My father went to the nursing home to get her and bring her to the party. When she arrived, my sister and I stood to assist Aunt Teddy as she clutched the aluminum walker with her slim age-spotted hands, and maneuvered her way over the protruding roots. As she inched along, I noticed that Aunt Teddy still made an effort to be festive. She wore a black and white print dress with a pink corsage. A grayish-looking rhinestone bracelet, won at the nursing home Bingo game, encircled her frail wrist, appearing to cut into a purple bruise on the translucent, parchment-like flesh of her arm.

Feeling as if I towered above her shrunken, stooped-over form, I helped ease her into a rocking chair and my sisters' daughters, Dierdre, age two, and Anne, age five, came rushing to Aunt Teddy's side with gifts to be opened.

"Oh, my goodness," Aunt Teddy exclaimed, "You shouldn't have done all this. I'm getting too old for parties."

I gave her a bouquet of pink, purple, and orange flowers from my perennial garden, as I had for twelve years, and a box containing a pair of gray and pink New Balance running shoes.

"Why, I never thought I'd have a new pair of shoes," she exclaimed over and over, chuckling along with all of us as Anne and Dierdre excitedly tried to force the partially tied shoe onto her foot, lifting it into the air. I knelt to help. We took pictures of Aunt Teddy standing with her walker, showing a spark of her fun-loving self, holding out her foot in a high kick, to show off her new shoes. Then we had the ice cream and cake.

The following summer, the pink spirea, purple monkshood, and orange day lilies that grew in my garden bloomed three weeks early. For twelve years they had been at their prime for Aunt Teddy's July 19th birthday. In 1987, the flowers were in full radiant bloom on June twenty-fourth, the day my father called to say that Aunt Teddy had died.

I walked out to my garden and stood fingering a purple pansy, its petals as soft as a velvet dress. Then I cut stems of pink spirea, purple monkshood and orange day lilies and arranged them in memorium.

Barry and Aunt Teddy—1952

At Aunt Teddy's house before birthday party—1954

Aunt Teddy blowing her party whistle—1957

Aunt Teddy's birthday party—Susie, Prudy and Randy Hatch and Bobby Milone—1956

Auntie and Aunt Teddy—1962

Aunt Teddy age 89

DIFFERENT PEOPLE

Dexter had its share of unusual and reclusive characters when I was growing up. Two of them lived right down the street at the corner of Forest and Maple Streets, across from Mrs. Card's house where the front parlor served as a chapel for Messiah Mission—the Episcopal church we attended.

One of these characters was Reynold Pierce. When I had to walk home from Carol's house on cold, dark autumn afternoons, I picked up speed as I rounded the corner by his house. Reynold often stood silent and forlorn, on the lawn in front of his parents' house, with a trace of a smile on his lips and a distant look in his eyes. The smile seemed sinister, and I was always afraid he would get me. When I read *To Kill A Mockingbird* in high school, I knew firsthand how Scout and Jem felt about Boo Radley. Some said Reynold Pierce had a metal plate in his head from the war. He never said anything; he just stood in the yard staring and smiling, his torso rocking back and forth ever so slightly.

Across the street, another odd person, Knight Otto, lived with his mother and father just beside the Heberts' home. Reynold and Knight were in their late thirties, about my parents' age. I visited the Otto's when their grand-daughter Debbie and her family came to visit from Fort Fairfield. Knight's father had potato houses in Corinna, Newport, and Dexter. Sometimes we rode with Mr. Otto when he went to check wooden barrels of potatoes.

One Saturday I arrived in my brown oxford shoes, newly polished with Scuff-Coat, and Debbie's mother commented that I must have new shoes. When I responded that I had just polished them, I glowed with pride at the comments about my industriousness and responsibility.

Ivan Bath, an older neighbor whose father was the Universalist minister, came up the street to Otto's, and we made May baskets with colorful tissue paper. Later we went in the cluttered house where Mrs. Otto had paths around piles of papers and accumulated clutter. We went upstairs to see Knight's electric train set in the quarters where he lived.

Knight was bald, and always grinning like the Cheshire cat in *Alice in Wonderland*. He liked to tease, but he acted a bit skittish at times. When he had too much to drink at the Sterling Hotel on evenings in the years that followed, he'd call up my mother or Carol's. His voice slurred and melancholy, he talked of their beauty, professed love to them, and played juke box songs into the phone. My mother remembers his favorite was *To Each His Own*, and his lament was that everyone had somebody, but he was all alone.

If my mother hung up, he was very persistent, and called back. If my sister, Randy, or I answered, he'd talk to us a while, wanting us to hear one more song. Randy and I didn't want to hang up on him, even though our mother warned us not to encourage him. We felt sorry for him, so we listened and strung him along a bit. It was funny, yet disconcerting to listen to a drunken man who transferred his feelings for our mother to us. The phone calls continued for years until the fall of 1962.

The last night that he called, he rambled on and on, making us extremely uncomfortable. The next day we found out he took the garden hose, methodically attached it to the exhaust of his car with tape, and ran it through the car window. In the morning they found him slumped over in the seat. I overheard some details when my father came home for lunch.

For years after, when I walked down Maple Street I thought of Knight's soul. I looked nervously to see if Reynold was out, and hustled around the corner toward home. It was so eerie to know someone who had committed suicide and to have spoken to him the night he did it.

Sometimes it seemed that wherever I went there were strange old men. I wasn't comfortable at my great-grandmother's house. Nanny Hatch took in boarders. They all seemed like such timid pathetic souls shuffling around in carpet slippers, old cardigans, and round tortoise shell eye glasses. An empty, old-fashioned, woven cane wheel chair dominated the living room after Nanny's cousin Susie died. It seemed like the ghost of Nanny's star boarder was still there.

The house smelled uninviting with the cooking odors of cabbage and greasy food. Nanny Hatch's eyesight was failing and she wasn't much of a housekeeper. She did have Yankee thrift, and my father bought all the nearly spoiled cantaloupe, bananas, or vegetables from the A & P or the First National so she could cut away the bad spots and salvage something for meals. Daddy didn't like to see anything wasted.

One day in 1954, I sat in our car in her driveway playing with the Muskie for Governor pins and bumper stickers Daddy had on the front seat. He had brought Nanny the lobster bodies with the tiny claws left over from a shore party. Every week he also took her the leftovers that Walter Yeo had cooked at the Dexter Club. What she couldn't use went to her pigs. Even then, I saw the disparity, if not the irony, of Nanny Hatch's taking in boarders and salvaging food, while her son, my grandfather, was in Newport living beyond his means in the Newport mansion. (Grampy certainly preferred the company of people who where in high society.)

Winnie's and Grampy's friend and former classmate, Jere Abbott lived on Free Street in a beautiful Georgian style house with large windows overlooking Dexter.

Usually, two or three times in the summer the owner of the Spring Street Green House, arrived at my grandparents' cottage in her denim coveralls with two dozen yellow roses from Jere. Other times he arrived with a basket full of peonies from his garden and a container of his homemade vegetable soup.

It was an event when the roses arrived. Winnie chuckled and I overheard joking comments about how much Jere must have recently imbibed because the flowers always arrived after such an episode when he was feeling sentimental. I wondered if he had been her beau before she married Grampy. Winnie put the roses in a green glass vase, and each night she put the roses in the refrigerated bar unit and kept the bouquet fresh for over a week. I thought Jere carried a secret unrequited love for Winnie from the old days when she and Grampy were his classmates.

Jere was also friendly with my grandmother's sister. Aunt Teddy's black photo album is filled with pictures taken by her and photographer, Bert Call, on expeditions to the Katahdin wilderness in the 1920s. In many photos of the group of hikers, Aunt Teddy, Jere and others posed on the precipices and boulders of Katahdin's trails.

These Katahdin photographs were taken after the summer when Jere toured Europe's art museums with his mother. He had just finished his graduate studies at Harvard. Aunt Teddy, a bookkeeper, but lover of literature and poetry, was comfortable hiking and conversing with Jere.

As a child, I knew Jere Abbott was different, just as I knew my cousin Nancy's friend Leo, the waiter at the Lakewood Theatre Inn was different. Jere's life was discreet and sedate. As the director of Smith College art museum, he came to Dexter only in the summer during the break. When he came to visit, I was all eyes and ears, as I sat on the colorful Navaho rug playing Chutes and Ladders with my sister. Jere had a friend named Lawrence who helped him tend the flower gardens and was a caretaker and companion. When Jere Abbott died in 1982, he left the house to Lawrence who sold it and continued living at his own house.

That was the sad irony. In the 1960s and 1970s, Jere Abbott bought two houses on Free Street that he considered eye sores and had them torn down. He tried to buy another to tear down, but the owners wouldn't sell. The word was that Jere Abbott had decreed in his will that his house was to be torn down rather than face the disgrace of being on a street with houses that were shabby.

The Abbott house was elegant, an interesting piece of architecture built for his parents. As a teenager, Grampy went to the Abbott's to study after school. I think visiting there must have opened a new world to my grandfather, fueling his desire for the finer things in life. There was a great deal of competition between my grandfather and Jere for grades. Aunt Teddy once told me that when Grampy lost the honor of being valedictory speaker, Mr. Abbott spoke to principal Bucknam in hopes Jere would be chosen in Grampy's place.

The genius of both boys and their classmate, Edward Ellms, my other grandfather, was obvious. The wealth that the Abbotts took for granted looked very appealing to my grandfather, whose mother was a widow with little money. Jere's house was grand by comparison to Helen Hatch's place with pigs in the barn.

After he died, Jere Abbott's house was sold to someone from away. After that, the Abbott house on Free Street fell into a state of disrepair. The once manicured lawn was not mowed for years and turned to hay. The expansive front steps and verandah slowly rotted. The paint faded and chipped. Across the street, where the old houses once stood, grass and a few trees grew. The eyesore buildings had been removed, but Jere couldn't save his own house from neglect. Every time we went by, my father would say, "Jere Abbott would roll over in his grave if he could see this. It's such a shame."

In the early 1990s a local couple bought the house and did some work to improve the looks of the exterior, although, that included vinyl siding. A couple from away are the most recent caretakers and owners and they are lovingly restoring the home on the interior and exterior. They feel a committment to the history and the architecture of the house.

Jere Abbott's name was a familiar one to me. Daddy would go to LaGasse's I.G.A. and have Buck LaGasse or Gubby Cleaves fix him a "Jere Abbott roast"—a six pound sirloin tip, boned and rolled roast. Daddy came home bearing the beef wrapped in butcher paper, exclaiming over the beauty and tenderness of the cut of meat, fondling it like a baby, anticipating our Sunday dinner. I thought later how those cuts of beef probably contributed to my father's stroke when he was seventy. They probably didn't help Jere's arteries either, although he did live to be eighty-five.

In the collection of books at Winnie's and Grampy's cottage, was one called *Fairy Tales from France*. The fountain pen inscription read: "This is Harvey's book. Jere gave it to him. Jere Abbott, Dexter, September 21, 1925." My Grandfather inscribed it to my sons in 1970. I had loved the stories as a child at the cottage. My favorite was the one about the couple who abused their chance for a magic wish. The foolish wife inadvertently wished for a sausage, her upset husband wished it attached to her nose, then had to wish it off, which used up all three wishes. Winnie read these stories to us over and over.

In 1986, I noticed an article in the arts and books section of the Maine Sunday Telegram about the Colby College museum and Jere Abbot. I knew that when Jere Abbott died, his money went to Colby College. My father always wondered why Jere did nothing for Bowdoin or Smith Colleges and why he chose Colby. The article helped explain his philanthropy to Colby.

As a child, I had not realized that in 1929 Jere Abbott and his former Harvard roommate, Alfred Bart, had co-founded the Museum of Modern Art in New York City. The Telegram article, featuring a conversation with Hugh Gourley, curator at Colby College's art museum, explained that before Jere Abbott died, he left a bequest to Colby of $1.8 million for unrestricted new acquisitions. At the time, it was one of the biggest gifts ever made to an American academic institution. It was Jere Abbott's friendship with Hugh Gourley and their mutual love of art that prompted the gift to Colby.

When I go to the Colby Art Museum, I think of Jere Abbott's philanthropy and I think of the Dexter mill workers, like Louis Chabot, who with sweat on his brow and the sinewy muscles in his arms, ran the looms during years of long shifts at the Amos Abbott Woolen Mill, helping the Abbott family amass a small fortune that paid for Dexter's library and ended up purchasing art for Colby College.

At my other great-grandmother's farm in Ripley, I encountered another eccentric. Grammy's brother Harold Weymouth always seemed shy and fearful. The moment we arrived he'd slip off toward the cavernous barn. It was as if he couldn't stand to be around the ebullient chatter of little girls. If we went out to the barn to explore, he was usually nowhere to be seen. Sometimes, we saw him silently attending to barn chores in his denim barn jacket. I wondered what made him so strange and timid.

My sisters and I played in the hay loft and watched the cows and pigs until my hay fever acted up. Then we went outside for fresh air and stood on the wooden platform, taking turns working the hand pump to fill the tin cup with water. We were intrigued by the three-holer privy in the connecting shed. Grammy kept a wooden barrel with a small tin can for the lime to sprinkle down the hole after using it.

Another odd man was Aunt Teddy's brother Tim. It occurred to me years later that there was some similarity to Winnie's brother Tim in Dexter and Timothy the Wood Hooker in Newport, Rhode Island, who kept the yard full of junk on Belleview Avenue. I wondered if Winnie ever thought of it.

Tim Hill died in the early 1950s, so my memories of him are hazy. He was a reclusive alcoholic. I can remember going to the basement when Aunt Teddy shoveled coal into the furnace. That was where Tim lived in the winter—in the cellar. The wooden walls of his corner were covered with beer signs and memorabilia that would be worth a small fortune today. I'm not really sure why he lived there instead of upstairs. In the summer, he lived in a little shack in back of Aunt Teddy's and Auntie's houses. I heard that when he was a young man, his wife left him. He was never the same after that.

Although most of the town's eccentrics were men, there was one woman who occupied a great deal of my thoughts. Her name was Gracie and she was the town recluse. She lived on Lincoln Street and we went by her house when we drove from the cottage to Aunt Teddy's in the summer, or with Mac on the way to Snyder Provost's market.

Gracie lived across from the railroad trestle beside Bernard Mountain's house. Mr. Mountain and his sons knew her well. Her dilapidated house, overgrown with a tangle of vegetation and sprouting trees, held an eerie attraction for me. She lived alone in squalor, filth, and poverty, with her German Shepherd Queenie, assorted cats, and tamed garbage-eating rats, one of which was named Weenie.

Gracie was a curious sight in the summer, wearing a wool hat, leaning on her cane, stooped over, dressed all in black, wearing clothes that she never changed as the seasons and years went by. She always had her battered, black purse clutched to her side.

We knew she was crazy. We knew because she lived in that tumbled down house, with floors, ceilings, and roof rotted out. She told us that when the Sunshine Club at the Universalist Church brought its yearly Thanksgiving basket, she fed it to the rats, because she thought people were trying to poison her. I never figured out how that could be. If she loved the rats as pets, why did she feed them food she thought was poisoned?

Riding by Gracie's was an event. We never thought of it as a freak show, but that is what it was. We begged Mac to go by and he'd stop if she was out or toot and call to her so she'd come out. Mac tried to get her talking. He could humor her if she became contentious and string her along in conversation with a wink at us. Sometimes she came over to the side of the car wreaking of foul odor and filth. Her skin was leathery and wrinkled like that of a dried apple doll.

We were very curious about Gracie. One summer I was playing at Doug Whitney's, my friend Carol's cousin. Doug and I went for a bike ride down Lincoln Street, and when the sky clouded over and the thunder and lightening started as we passed Gracie's house, I was scared. Dressed all in black, she seemed witch-like. I thought she might get us and take us inside. When we stopped to stare and whisper, she spoke sharply to us.

We got on our bikes and peddled home as fast as we could in the rain. I was drenched and had to change into Doug's clothes. When Dot Whitney drove Doug and me downtown, I was mortified, and certain everyone on the Main Street and in Ben Franklin knew I was wearing boys clothes with a zipper in the front instead of in the side pocket, and a flannel shirt with buttons on the wrong side. Besides, I was still shaken by the encounter with Gracie.

We heard that she slept on the back seat that was removed from a 1922 Nash. My father told the story of Gracie's roof. She once put in a claim with one of his insurance companies for her roof that collapsed in the winter. They replaced the roof, but she tried to send the money back, because she said God came down and told her it was the wrong color roof. Gracie had many visions from God. She also had a strange past.

Once she had worked as a nurse. She came to Dexter from Massachusetts. Her husband had a wheelbarrow for picking up garbage. Aunt Teddy remembered his pulling it backwards up the driveway to her house. Gracie and her husband poked through the garbage, keeping the good stuff for themselves and giving the rest to the pigs that shared the house with them. As a young woman Gracie was big and dirty. There was no water in the house. After her husband died, she deteriorated even more.

The Mountain family looked after her as much as she would let them. She was suspicious and had a temper that could flair up at the least thing. The Thanksgiving of my seventh-grade year, when Winnie and Grampy were back in the big house on High Street, all of the relatives gathered there. Mac suggested we take some left-overs to Gracie to see if she would want them. My sisters and I went along wanting to share the abundance. Gracie finally came out and talked for quite a long time that afternoon. That was when she told us about the food from the Sunshine Club that she thought was poisoned.

That was probably the last time I saw Gracie. Later in the winter, on one Monday night when my father and the other selectmen had just left the Dexter Club after their weekly dinner and card games, they got a call from Chief Harold Knox or the Mountains. Gracie was deathly ill and they needed help getting her to the hospital.

Clair Wiley (my friend Candy's father), told me years later, "Your father came in the door and said, "Get your hip boots on, Clair, we're going with

Harold Knox to Gracie Richards' house to take her to the hospital. What a night that was!" Mr. Wiley said shaking his head at the memory of the filth and piles of animal and human waste. "We all got sick, and threw up our roast beef dinners," he added.

As my father, Clair and Ray Whitney (Doug's father) made their way through the dark house, the sights and smells were so horrible. The ground floor, what there was of it, was knee deep in pig manure. Newspapers layered with animal and human excrement were stacked chest high. Mr. Mountain opened one door on the second floor and his grip on the handle was all that kept him from falling through the floor. They opened one drawer in the kitchen and found egg shells—hundreds of them.

To make matters worse, Chief Knox, confident and proud in his duty to save the town, pulled his gun from his holster and shot all the animals on the spot as Gracie stood near by. Even in her delusional state of mind, Gracie knew that her pets had been killed. She became enraged and resisted her rescuers. The old black hearse from Crosby's funeral home took Gracie to the hospital since Dexter didn't have an ambulance in those days. That night, I was ice skating at the rink and I remember distinctly being in the cold and wondering what it had been like for Gracie to live like that. I pondered the details I had heard, that the nurses and Dr. Taylor or Dr. Shurman had to cut the clothes off her body. She had worn them so many years that they adhered to her skin. It was such a shock to her system that she succumbed to pneumonia the next day.

Two years later when I read *Great Expectations*, I thought of Gracie when I read about Mrs. Haversham, even though Gracie's house had much more than dust and cobwebs and mice on uneaten wedding cake. I always wondered what happened in Gracie's life and how she went from being a public health nurse to living in such squalor. The town destroyed her house that summer.

I didn't give Gracie much thought in the years following. It was quite an accident, literally, that I found out more about her. In 1989, I was in

Dexter on Labor Day weekend. I had been cooking baked beans at our family cottage on one side of the lake, and drove from my friend Cathie's cottage to ours to get the pot of beans. As I returned to Cathie's, I drove past Doug Whitney's parents' house and approached the place where Zions Hill is bisected by Lincoln Street. A car drove through the stop sign. I saw it coming too late from the corner of my eye. I slammed on the brakes, veered to the right, but couldn't avoid the collision. Baked beans went everywhere, including up under the dash board. (The station wagon never smelled right after that. When the heat was turned on, there was a most distinctive odor.)

Soon the neighbors called the police and before long my father, who was our insurance man, my husband, and our friend Dennis Frost arrived. Curiosity seekers stopped to see what had happened. Among them were the Mountain brothers, Billie and Ronnie. Their father Bernard, known as Nig because of his dark coloring, was no longer living. I struck up a conversation with the brothers who had been young men when I saw them riding in an antique car in a Fourth of July parade a decade or two ago.

Once they realized I was Harvey Hatch's daughter they were more friendly. I had been at a writing course that summer and had thought of Gracie. When I asked them for details about her, they poured out their memories about the filth and almost falling through the rotted floor. The Mountain brothers now own the land where Gracie's house once stood. The area is seeded over with grass. A large butternut tree flourishes in the soil rich with humus—all that remains of Gracie's life save the memories of those who knew her.

There is one more memory tied to all of this. It has to do with the men who ran Mountain Motors where my father took my sisters and me to visit sometimes on Saturdays. The men all sat around swapping tales, jokes, and sports stories.

Even as a child I was bothered by the way my father and the other men joked with Colby Gerry, an obese, mentally retarded young man who spent his days at the used car place. I was astute enough to see that it really wasn't funny the way they treated Colby. My father bought a cardboard box of all the old cupcakes, angel food cake, and doughnuts from the A & P grocery store and took them down to feed Colby. That was what they did, watch Colby eat and laugh until the tears came as he stuffed entire cupcakes into his mouth and swallowed in one gulp. The men egged him on and Colby obliged because he loved food and he wanted to please them.

Colby consumed prodigious amounts. My father made pickled eggs and took the gallon jars down for the men and Colby. He would pop one in his mouth, his face beet red and his eyes and cheeks bulging. I always felt embarrassed and a little sad to watch the grown men make sport of Colby. I must have said something, but Daddy dismissed it with the excuse that Colby liked the food. I still felt uncomfortable, but Daddy couldn't see the harm. I don't remember what happened to Colby Gerry, but I think he died in middle age.

Ruth Slater was my French teacher when I was a freshman at Dexter High School in 1961. Little did I know, at fourteen, of Madame Slater's past friendship with my grandparents, Aunt Teddy, and Mac who did work for her. Nor would I ever have imagined a link to Mrs. Slater in future years when she was a resident at the Dexter Nursing Home. How could I have ever guessed that one day, after her death, I would hold her journals in my hands and read of the events of over fifty years of her life?

Madame Slater was a formidable woman. Formidable and homely, with a lantern jaw, horse's teeth that protruded, and dark framed eye glasses. Madame's hair was wide and flat on top with short gray bangs curled under exposing a high forehead with hair smoothed at the sides to curls. Her stern visage and no-nonsense approach earned her respect and some cruel comments. One boy in adolescent smugness reduced her to tears when he told her she looked as if she had been hit in the face with a shovel. As a man who became a teacher, he has regretted those words for decades, feeling ashamed of the memory of his rudeness.

A widow, she was intelligent and dedicated to her career. When I entered her French classroom that fall of 1961, I was handicapped from the beginning by my unfamiliarity with French and my defeatist attitude which soon developed.

Most of my friends had been chosen in the eighth grade to take an introductory French class. I had not. I felt left out when my friend Carol was chosen. It had never occurred to me to have my mother intercede and request that I be included in the eighth grade introductory French classes. I just accepted my fate.

When I had difficulty with French, it also never occurred to me to reach out for help or study harder. I just decided that I was incompetent and inept. I had felt the same way when trying to learn the incomprehensible "shuffle ball change" in Polly Thomas's dance classes, the times tables and telling time in second grade, the squiggly musical notes in fourth grade flutophone classes, or dribbling with out traveling in six grade basketball. I was a quitter. I just accepted that I couldn't do any of these tasks, shrugged it off, and gave up.

Every day in French class we had a quiz on an unbleached half sheet of arithmetic paper. I sat befuddled or staring at my paper with only a few answers while Madame went around the room, brushing by students with her large hips swathed in a floral print rayon dress.

"Tres bien madamoiselle, tres bien monsieur," she'd say to Carol or Philip Ramsay or other students around me. "Une copie sans faute." She went around the room, leaning over student's desk exclaiming and proclaiming, "Une copie sans faute. Une copie sans faute. Tres bien."

Those of us who didn't get it cringed in our seats, awaiting our turn, expecting the worst. It seemed that every time she came to me, Madame Slater would say, "Tsk, tsk, oh, Mademoiselle Prudie," shaking her head at my lack of skill or preparation as she marked my paper with the correct accent grave or ague over the vowel or wrote the correct conjugation or verb tense or spelling. My ears burned in humiliation, yet it wasn't enough to make me study more. It merely proved to me that French, like so many other learning tasks, was beyond me. That year French and algebra were obscure and overwhelming. My friends excelled while I plodded.

Sometimes, Madame Slater pulled her compact out of her pocket, opened it, and held the little mirror in front of students to show that they were not pronouncing "ou" with properly pursed lips. Her demonstrations caused further discomfort for those of us who were inhibited. I had never guessed that I'd have to go through all this when I had ridden in her car two years earlier.

When I won a trip to the Ice Capades in Bangor for being a top magazine salesperson in the seventh and eighth grades, Mrs. Slater and her esteemed colleague Mr. Vickery, our English teacher, chaperoned us. He was her friend and companion in intellectual pursuits and travels.

Some of the students chuckled and speculated about their relationship. Mr. Vickery and Mrs. Slater were two intellectuals who enjoyed theater, music, art, literature, dining out, and sight seeing. Mr. Vickery was writing a book on the history of Unity, Maine, where he was born. Short, somewhat portly, Charles Laughtonesque, with dark cowlick ridden hair, large flakes of dandruff on his misshapened suit coat, Mr. Vickery also wore wide print ties spotted and stained by food. He was a brilliant man, but his appearance and mannerisms were also a source of students' comments.

When he helped me edit my first draft of *The Little Red Boot*, a story about my adventures at the cemetery with Phillip Ramsay, I had to look away as he spoke, because of the globs of food particles still on his teeth.

After our freshman year, the principal, Mr. Mealey, left for Brewer High School, over an unresolved issue with superintendent Elwin Towne. Other respected teachers—Mr. Vickery, Mrs. Slater, and Mr. Hebert all left soon afterward to teach in Brewer and Yarmouth. I never found out the details of the incident that prompted all the resignations, but the loss of excellent teachers was a blow to Dexter High School.

The replacement French teacher had neither Madame Slater's experience nor her command of the class. I wasn't afraid any longer, but I didn't learn much either. After my graduation, I only occasionally heard Mrs.

Slater's name mentioned. I seldom saw her. My Uncle Mac did some carpentry, wall papering and painting for her at her house located between R.C. Whitney and Sons' garage and LaGasse's I.G.A. Market.

In the early 1980s, Mrs. Slater was confined to the Dexter Nursing Home at the same time Aunt Teddy was. Aunt Teddy was older, but she was still herself. When I went to visit, Aunt Teddy, she'd occasionally say, "Poor Ruth. She can't remember a thing."

I had a shocking realization of how bad it was one day in March when I went to the nursing home to take Aunt Teddy for a ride on the Ripley Road, out past the former entrance to my grandparents' cottage and ours and further down the road past the entrance to the former Wassookeag Summer Camp.

I was hoping to find some pussy willows for Aunt Teddy just as she had found them for me years before. I thought the soft furry buds of spring would give her hope that spring and warm weather were coming. I wanted her to know that I had fond memories of those days at her house on Lower Main Street.

Before we left the nursing home, we walked through the common gathering room where the patients flanked the room like so many moveable objects. I am still chilled and saddened at the memory of the sight of the once formidable Madame Slater looking pale and vulnerable, restrained in a large chair on wheels with a tray snapped in place. She looked like a large, ancient version of me in a 1948 black and white photo, sitting in a square wooden baby tender.

"Take me. Take me with you. I want to go too," Mrs. Slater whined, sounding pathetic as her voice trailed off. "I want to go; I want to go."

Aunt Teddy stopped, bent over Ruth and patted her hand and said in the soothing voice she would use for a little child. "You'll be all right, Ruth. You have to stay here. We'll be back soon. You be good now."

As we walked out of the door, Aunt Teddy in her nineties, shrunken to four feet five inches, shook her head and sighed, "Poor Ruth, she doesn't know a thing. She doesn't even know who she is."

Ruth Slater had been a brilliant woman. She taught English and French for Grampy, and later, Mr. May at the Wassookeag School Camp. She and her deceased husband had been close friends of Winnie's and Grampy's, spending the evenings visiting at Honeymoon Cottage. The children lay awake in their cots listening to my grandparents, Wilford and Ruth talk, joke, laugh, and play cards into the wee hours of the morning.

When Mrs. Slater died, she left everything to her friend, Renee Hebert. As they were cleaning out the house, they found fifty years of journals that Ruth Slater had written. In them, she chronicled the daily events of her life as a teacher and resident of Dexter. There is little reflection and no pouring forth of emotion or inner thoughts, but the spiral bound notebooks are fascinating to read. My sisters and I read them after Mrs. Hebert loaned them to Daddy.

In the notebooks, Mrs. Slater described weekly gatherings for cards, dinner, fancy luncheons at Winnie's and Grampy's. She interspersed her perfect cursive penmanship with newspaper articles from the Eastern Gazette and the Bangor Daily News. In the 1930s and 1940s, the Gazette published descriptions of luncheons and bridge parties or evening soirees that Winnie and Grampy had, as if they were N.Y. society events with the guest list and menu detailed. It is hard to believe, but it must have made an invitation all the more coveted.

After her life of travel, literature, plays, art, and writing, it seemed tragic that Mrs. Slater should meet that fate she did. Although I lacked determination to study for her French classes, I have thought of Madame Slater far more over the years than I have of the other French teacher who took her place.

My connections with this cast of characters from Dexter influenced me in many ways. When I read short stories or novels, I saw many parallels and similarities with the lives of the literary lonely. It made me wonder more about the lives of all the different people: Knight Otto, Reynold Pierce, Harold Weymouth, Tim Hill, Jere Abbott, Gracie, and Ruth Slater. The memories have chafed my mind for four decades.

THE ABBOTT MEMORIAL LIBRARY

In 1953, when I was in the first grade, our whole class walked with Mrs. Gordon down Pleasant Street to Abbott Memorial Library so we could each get our first library card. Our classroom had few books, and visiting the library was a way to open new worlds for us.

Going to the library was an exciting, but scary experience. The elderly Hamilton sisters were the librarians. They wore black lace-up shoes with perforated designs on the instep and sturdy heels just like my teachers. The sisters garbed themselves in long black dresses from a previous decade and their somber attire and personalities made them seem quite formidable. Leaning on canes, they slowly made their way around the library or the yard of their family home across the street from Pleasant Street School. Their yard was always overgrown with a tangle of bushes that hid the front of the weathered Cape Cod style house. It was one more place to hurry nervously by on my way home.

On our first class library visit, we sat in the children's room at the library and the bent black forms of the Hamilton sisters kept shushing us as we looked through the books we wanted to borrow. My choice was from a collection of biographies. There was an entire row of little orange books with black silhouette illustrations of the characters on a few of the pages. The books published, in the 1920s or 1930s, were fairly worn out when my friend Carol and I discovered them.

I went back each week to borrow another orange book about little girls who became famous, successful women. I read about Florence Nightingale, Clara Barton, Jane Adams, Dorothia Dix, Abigail Adams, Louisa May Alcott, Marie Curie, and others. After reading about Louisa

May Alcott I read her book *Little Women* and I started *Little Men*, but for some reason I didn't find it as engaging.

Over the years, Carol and I went to the library after school on a fairly regular basis despite our apprehension of the stern librarians. In those days, a girl had to really want to read to brave a trip to the library. After the Hamilton sisters retired, they were replaced with the Champeon sisters, who often dressed like twins. I was friends with their nephew Skipper, but that didn't make a visit to the library less forbidding. The Champeon sisters demeanor was all business, not folksy and friendly

In addition, the atmosphere was formal and somewhat daunting. The huge old oak door was twice as heavy, tall, and wide as a normal door. It opened with a certain creaking noise and the handle, as it was turned, made a particular click that echoed in the building. When I had an overdue book, the distance from the door to the front desk seemed very long. With each step, the tap of my shoes on the marble floor sounded like an intrusion in the mausoleum-like edifice. Walking across the marble, up to the twelve foot long desk to face Miss Champeon positioned behind the iron bars, gave me a knot in my stomach. The light from the old brass lamps illuminated the area as Miss Champeon silently stamped my card and figured my fine.

The design of the front desk was intimidating all by itself. The desk was built with wrought iron, like the teller windows of the banks in the cowboy shows I so avidly watched as an aspiring cowgirl. I felt like a bank robber sheepishly returning the loot when I stood facing the grill work with an overdue book in one hand and a fistful of my allowance in the other. Peering up over the counter, passing my books through the opening, and awaiting the verdict on my fine seemed to take an interminable length of time. Having the temerity to borrow another one of the librarians' books took even more courage.

Carol grew brave as the years went by, and ventured behind the desk barrier to look through the shelves for interesting books. Eventually I joined her, but I felt uncomfortable. It was easier for me to borrow books from my grandparents' library or from the shelves at home. It was Carol who first read *A Lantern in Her Hand* when we were in the seventh grade. After she told me the story was about a girl who grows up in a prairie sod house, I borrowed the book. Reading it had a profound effect on me. Following the main character from childhood to old age, I saw how quickly the years slip by, how people grow and change, how they endure hardship, yet strive on. I liked Beth Streeter Aldrich's book and ranked it near the top with my sixth grade favorites, *Honest Dollar* by Maine author Dorothy Simpson and *Blue Willow* by Doris Gates.

My previous favorites were Nancy Drew mysteries, Dana Girls, Judy Bolton, and Trixie Beldon stories. Every time I went to Bangor, I bought a new hardcover mystery for a dollar at Freeses Department store or Betts Book Store.

I collected each new book with a vengeance. I kept a tally of the books I had read, the books I owned, and the books I planned to buy.

Carol used the library more than I did. Carol borrowed the book about Dr. Sam Shepard, who was accused and tried for murdering his wife. Carol told me all the details as we walked home from school one day and went to return the book to the library. We were still debating his guilt or innocence as we climbed the granite steps and faced the raised letters, ABBOTT MEMORIAL PVBLIC LIBRARY chiseled above the doorway under the eaves. A band of letters made a border around the building with the names of all the great writers of western civilization—Goethe, Auerbach, Shakespeare, and Milton on the front, Lafontaine and Hugo on the south side, Dante and Cervantes on the north, Virgil, Horace, Homer, and Aristotle on the rear.

Inside the library stood two large old wooden book cases that turned in a circle to display books on four sides. I liked the sound the bookshelf made as it rotated with little beads tumbling at the base. Sometimes I spun it around slowly as I looked for a book that caught my eye.

Miss Hazel Champeon worked at the high school library on week days, but after school joined her sister, Elizabeth, at Abbott Memorial. They both worked there on Saturday morning.

When we were in high school, we heard the story of a scandalous affair discovered by Miss Champeon. After Carol and I heard the news, we tried to imagine how prim and proper Miss Elizabeth Champeon reacted when she returned to the library one Saturday afternoon and accidentally discovered the woman who cleaned the library and a local businessman locked in an amorous embrace.

I always wondered afterward, how long it took for the information to make its way along the grapevine of gossip after Elizabeth or Hazel told the first person. In only a matter of hours the whole town was buzzing with the shocking news. After the incident, I always felt sorry for the man's wife who had to hold her head up and go on attending the Literary Club meetings, as if the affair never happened.

Books and libraries have always been important to me. Certain images and my emotional reactions as I read, have stayed with me over the years. The memories of books and characters seem like a hearty stew that has fed me over the years and given me understanding of life and people.

Although I've outgrown my interest in cowboys and cowgirls and westerns and historical fiction, I still greatly enjoy reading memoirs and literary works. My years of reading books from our home library, my grandparents' library, and the Abbott Memorial Library provided me with a melange of language, the rhythm of words, images of scenes, and insight into the human condition, from which I still draw nourishment.

SUMMERS AT LAKE WASSOOKAG

In the summers of my childhood, there were two constants—moving out to our cottage from our house in town, about two miles away and time with my grandparents. Winnie arrived in Dexter early in June bearing gifts from the doll store in Newport. Grampy stayed in Rhode Island until business at the school was completed. Then he arrived in Maine a few weeks later.

During the summer, Grampy spent most of his days in his office cottage next door, attending to plans for the upcoming academic year or figuring out how to juggle the bills. At noon, he joined Winnie at their cottage for his meal on a tray in the spacious living room where I sat reading or playing cards with my sisters.

Winnie had to keep saying "Lloyd, your luncheon is ready...Lloyd..." while Grampy was at the burgundy leather covered, refrigerated bar pouring amber liquid into a short, wide glass up to the top red stripe. I could feel the annoyance in her voice. When he finally sat down at his place, Grampy covered his fresh peas, green beans, and leftovers with black dots of pepper. Then he began to eat, ruminating slowly, savoring each morsel.

Every summer, I savored the fresh vegetables my father bought at farms in near by Garland or Ripley. Daddy returned with bushel baskets and pecks of produce for our summer meals. He didn't garden like his Papa Hill, but Daddy appreciated fresh vegetables and sometimes gave them away or was reimbursed by friends and neighbors along the lake shore. They could count on peas from Lester Wyman's, strawberries from Doug Britten, potatoes and corn from John Briggs, plus tomatoes, cucumbers, carrots, green as well as yellow wax beans, and lettuce from other gardens in the area.

My sisters and I would help our mother shell peas and snap beans for lunch. Daddy liked to come home to a big meal at noon, which meant my mother was cooking during the heat of the day.

Our green shingled cottage was thirty feet from Winnie's and Grampy's. The two green buildings with white trim were not identical. Their cottage was much nicer. Ours had mismatched furniture, more suited for kids in damp bathing suits. Our cottage had an old and a new section. My father mistakenly let Grampy oversee the construction of the addition. I heard Daddy complain many times of "Llaich's expensive way of having everything built with brass screws and no concern for costs or economizing."

Winnie's and Grampy's cottage had hardwood floors partially covered by Navaho rugs. The rugs' geometric pattern of red, black, green, and oatmeal background coordinated with the furniture which had a Mexican hacienda look. Around the room, blonde wooden chairs with tooled-leather backs and seats provided sitting space. The couch had a round table in front of it and was the focal point of the room. Often a vase of roses from Jere Abbott graced the table.

When I sat on the couch perusing a book of collected *New Yorker* magazine cartoons, I was ever diligent to keep my short legs jutting straight out lest the buckles of my shoes snag the peppercorn-green, tapestry-like upholstery on the cushions. Winnie and Grampy stressed the importance of placing my ginger ale glass on the rubbery, green leaf-shaped coaster to protect the table from water circles.

We followed all rules of decorum at Winnie's and Grampy's cottage and at the school. Grampy was a stickler for proper behavior, etiquette, and grammar. No gum chewing. Say "yes please" or "no thank you." One day he admonished Winnie for uttering a breathy "ayah" to a caller on the telephone. I absorbed that lesson as I sat reading the adult cartoon books.

I loved those cartoon books. I think they were an education in themselves. I learned to understand the subtle nuances of the humor and to recognize specific artists. Charles Adams was a bit weird and gruesome at times, but I read all of his. Many of the cartoons had nude women in them. One of my favorites was by Whitney Darrow, Jr. showing a bespectacled, pointed nosed spinster with her hair in a bun. She stood at an art museum with ten children in front of a large painting by Manet called *Luncheon on the Grass*.

In the painting, a nude woman sits on the grass with trees in the background. Beside her are two men clothed in Edwardian suits. One sits and the other one, wearing a beret, reclines on an elbow. Another woman clad in a slip bathes in the water behind them. The cartoon teacher's comment to her students is, "Well, it was sort of like a cook-out." I loved the understatedness of most of the cartoons and I knew them by heart. Some of them had gallows' humor or were beyond my understanding, but Winnie or Mac would explain the joke's caption, when I said, "I don't get it."

Winnie had a record by Tom Lehrer of Cambridge, Massachusetts. His humor was outrageous, but we loved to hear his distinct gravely voice crooning ditties about murder, mayhem, and the macabre. We knew he exaggerated and the songs were tongue-in-cheek. The music was upbeat and catchy, but Lehrer's lyrics were ghoulish. In contrast, I was uplifted by the soothing classical music Winnie played and by the jaunty music and lyrics from *Oklahoma, Carousel, South Pacific*. For years afterward when I shampooed with golden Breck, the phrase "I'm gonna wash that man right outta my hair…" ran through my mind.

When Danny Kaye sang the songs from Hans Christian Anderson's tales about *The Ugly Duckling* and *The Poor Little Match Girl*, I found beauty in the sadness. I found irony and honesty in the tale of *The Emperor's New Clothes*. Having Winnie read that story deepened my understanding of the folly of people blindly following fashion, not thinking for themselves.

As we sat on the glassed in porch, overlooking the water, snuggled on the couch with Winnie, she read Daddy's gift book from Jere Abbott, *Fairy Tales From France*, as well as, *The Wizard of Oz*, and Marjorie Torey's *Three Little Chipmunks*, a book about Cheeky the chipmunk who disobeys and is sent to bed without supper. One summer when I was about six, Winnie gave me a book about a grasshopper. The book had a plastic insert that made the grasshopper hop as the pages were turned. That book and the flavor of the banana tooth paste I used after hearing the story are forever linked. Winnie read to me about the adventures of Peter Rabbit in Mr. McGregor's garden and all of the other stories in my *Better Homes and Gardens Story Book*. I learned about bad table manners from the story about The Goops who licked their fingers and ate with knives.

One summer, my cousin Nancy Lea read a slim book called *Blue Angel*. It was written by my childhood heroine, Dale Evans. When Nancy emerged from the other room sobbing, she told me the story of Dale Evans' and Roy Rogers' baby who was born with a birth defect and died. Then, as Nancy read us the sad part, I felt a lump in my throat. I thought of Dale Evans as a cowgirl, not as a mother of so many kids.

I admired Dale Evans even more after hearing that she and Roy Rogers adopted children in addition to having their own. Dale Evans did what my friend Carol and I had only pretended to do with our doll children when Carol's bedroom became a deserted town with orphans for us to care for. Dale Evans brought security and happiness to children in the world.

In a way, Winnie was like Dale Evans. Winnie brought happiness into our world, and I think we children also brought it into her life. Grampy was preoccupied with work in the office with his secretary Yolande, so Winnie had lots of time for my sisters and me and our visiting cousins. Sometimes, on a cold or rainy afternoon when we couldn't spend the day swimming, Winnie made butterscotch candy or molasses pull candy for us. We hovered around the stove as the confection neared the crack stage, and each got a chance to taste the hair-like, brittle thread or the tiny ball of candy if it had hardened when it hit the cold water in the custard cup.

When it was done, we sucked the chewy candy so we wouldn't pull out a filling. We listened to records and sidled into the kitchen for another piece when the first became just a sliver.

One summer, Winnie lost all her fingernails and toe nails because of a fungus infection. Once it healed the nails never grew back. The soles of Winnie's feet peeled and flaked and were painful. She soaked them and needed someone to trim off the dead skin that hung loose like pieces of mica or sheets of phyllo dough. Ordinarily, I'm not the type for nursing ministrations, but for some reason I didn't mind trimming the layers of dead skin from the soles of Winnie's feet. Maybe the praise and comments from others who marveled that I would do such a task spurred me on.

While Winnie lay on the cushioned recliner by the waterfront, I carefully trimmed away dead tissue, trying not to hurt her foot. Dark clouds loomed in the distant sky, signaling a brewing storm. I knew we must never be outside in a thunderstorm, especially in the water, just as we had to wait a full hour after eating to avoid getting a cramp and drowning in the lake. We hurried to cover the lounge furniture with canvas tarps at the first crack of thunder. Then we rushed inside as the sprinkles fell and lightning arched and zigzagged across the sky.

The wind whipped the trees and leaves, littering the lawn with debris. Whitecaps rolled in from the center of the lake and crashed, splashing against the rock wall. My sisters and I read or played cards as rain battered on the roof. After the storm passed, we went back outside to play. I noticed the crisp, wet cleanness and peacefulness that followed the storm. I felt relieved that the storm was over. It was a feeling similar to my tightened stomach easing when Grampy and Mac or my parents stopped arguing. I guess I liked both family relationships and the lake to be smooth.

In fact, the lake's roughness or calmness dictated my daily activities and moods. The sight of tranquil Lake Wassookeag propelled me from my bed faster than if a daddy-longlegs were crawling up my leg under the covers. Stirring in my cot upstairs under the cottage eves, where my windows brought the panorama of the lake into view, I sprang from my lazy slumber once I saw the clear reflection of sky and trees on the lake. An early morning glass-like lake was a transitory experience to be savored before the breezes picked up and changed the smooth surface to ripples. All too soon those ripples could grow to waves lapping the shore. On the rarest of hot August days, the lake was like a mirror from sunrise to sunset. But I didn't want to take any chances.

Some mornings I sat on the dock, still in my nightie, caught up in solitary musing, eating toast glistening with Auntie's sweet, homemade strawberry jam. Other days I might dress hurriedly, and go sit by the rocks, enjoying my time alone before my sisters and parents awoke from their downstairs bedrooms where venetian blinds darkened the windows. For a while the beauty of the lake was mine alone to experience.

Sometimes our dinghy beckoned me to row out from the shore to find the spot where I could no longer see the bottom in the blue depths. Occasionally a bass jumped, pursing lips about an unlucky nymph freshly hatched on the lake's surface. A loon gliding by in search of breakfast called out to its missing mate, making the eerie, shrill noise that would wake others in the cottage. I watched as its throat vibrated visibly, like a balloon expanding with each breath. Then the loon ducked under water to pursue another bass and I marveled as it reappeared on the surface yards and yards away.

Those long lazy days of childhood summers from 1951 to 1958 meld together into a composite of memories when my sisters, our friends and I clambered and hopped over boulders along the shore, searched under rocks for crawfish, swam, caught sunfish off the dock, or made trails.

Making trails in the woods beside the cottage occupied us for weeks after Mac gave us the tent and set it up. The tent became our destination in the afternoon when we were chilled from hours of swimming. I lay resting on one of two folding canvas army cots, while the sun streamed in giving a golden orange glow through the tent. Our collection of comic books lay piled on a green wooden table Mac had made. Reading *Richy Rich*, *Little Lotta*, *Katie Keene*, and *Donald Duck* comics was relaxing after work was done on the trails and our vision for the woods was closer to reality. We had gathered old bricks and made a small fireplace for toasting marshmallows. Then as the day progressed, we raked around the tent area. During the process of dumping debris deeper into the woods, we noticed old rusty cans and broken beer bottles that had been thrown into the woods. We gathered them all up for Phil Gudroe to take in his big blue truck when he came to get the trash. With his rippled muscles exposed by his short sleeve navy blue tee shirt, Phil lifted the barrels and dumped all the debris into his truck. He always had a grin on his face and a teasing friendly comment.

Daddy said he couldn't pay to have Phil haul everything away as I wanted to do, just the glass and cans. We chose an area behind the tent to use as a dump for fallen branches and rotting trees. Then Randy, Sally, our cousin David, and I raked a winding path through the woods over to the picnic grounds.

We cleared a trail to the waterfront and found remains of mussel shells, opened by raccoons during a midnight feast by the lake. We tugged and pulled rotted moss-covered logs to one area, pausing to examine the hard shelled beetles and segmented, multi-legged creatures that scurried for cover as their home was disturbed. The worms we saved for catching sunfish. Finally, my sisters and I gathered sticks and limbs to use for a campfire. If the limbs were too rotten and mossy, they went to the newly created dump away from the tent area.

Near the end of our week of trail making, a truck from Fay and Scott Landis Machine Corporation arrived with a load of lumber scraps for the lobster cookout fire. We headed for Grampy's office cottage to "borrow" some wood for signs to mark the trails. Grampy's tool shed—the domain of Mac and Louis Chabot—supplied what we needed—hammers, nails, paint, and small brushes for lettering.

Despite our attempts to be careful, we covered our hands and clothes with paint. Then our efforts took a different turn, because we got new ideas. Mac helped me saw the wood. I nailed together pieces for a little doll's table and a small chair for my Ginny dolls, then painted them.

Once the furniture was finished, and the sign lettering dry, we went back to nail signs on the trees along the trails. My sign warned of the toll bridge, where a small plastic collection bucket hung from a broken branch. Randy's sign marked the pile of debris with a chunk of wood stating "Dump" with a scull and cross bones beneath. Arrows indicated various paths where other points of interest were marked by a sign.

In the evening Randy, Sally, Susie, our cousin David and I toasted marshmallows over a campfire made with dry twigs and newspapers. When I wasn't careful to keep the stick raised above the fire, I had a flaming charred ball at the end of the stick. I discovered that waving it around didn't put out the blaze. It sent the hot charred blob flying. Marshmallows that slipped off the stick, plopped into the fire and oozed into flames. We all preferred a golden, slightly brown marshmallow, but sometimes impatience interfered with perfection.

For us, playing was working at a project. On many afternoons we dug clay from the lake bottom, under the gravel layer, to make ash trays and little mud pots. Our hands were worn rough and finger nails broken from digging the firm clay, rolling it into snake-like strips and winding them around the flattened clay bottom. We shaped and molded our creations, then painted them after they had baked on sun-heated rocks, feeling like potters in early civilization.

One summer when Lynn Milone was visiting in 1954, she and I spent the entire day playing with Trixie Beldon paper dolls. We made camp tee shirts and shorts for the paper dolls, using her grandmother's bond typing paper and some colored pencils. We drew and cut out entire summer wardrobes for the group of paper doll characters and pretended away the afternoon at what we called The Triple Y Camp.

On another day that same summer, I spent an entire rainy, overcast day away from the lake, at my friend Mary Batson's house. Mary and her mother were creative people. Millie Batson was a clever seamstress and she made all of Mary's clothes. Mrs. Batson also made beautiful doll clothes from the left over fabric. In addition, she earned extra money by sewing clothes for the Vogue Doll Corporation. Each week, she received in the mail a sturdy brown mailing box strapped by canvas belts. Hundreds of cut out pieces nestled in the box for Mrs. Batson to sew in her home production line.

That rainy day when I visited, while Mrs. Batson sewed, Mary and I created a doll house. On my own, I never would have attempted something that required such skill and precision, but Mary was smart and good at math. She was able to visualize and conceptualize how to draw, fold, and cut everything we made. We furnished the house entirely with oaktag furniture, fabric scraps, and pictures we cut from the Sears' catalogue. I left the Batson's with a four room cardboard doll house and a feeling of pride.

When I was twelve and my sister Susie was six, she chipped a bone in her foot. It was quite an event, because none of us had ever broken a bone. Susie sat ensconced on the cushioned lounge, a heavy piece of outdoor furniture with two wheels on one end. She had her new Curious George books to look at and we took turns reading to her. The world was at her bidding, and old pictures show her gesturing and pointing for her needs and wants. Winnie ordered an Eloise doll for Susie and when it came, none of us could believe our eyes. Winnie had ordered the large size cloth doll, not realizing what that meant.

A cardboard box the size of a child's coffin arrived with a bill for forty dollars, which was expensive for a doll in 1959, especially in Winnie's and Grampy's diminished circumstances. Winnie couldn't send the Eloise doll back just because it was too expensive. A few years before, when Randy had an attack of appendicitis one spring in Newport, Winnie had gone to the doll store and bought Poor Pitiful Pearl with long straight sandy hair just like Randy's. So four feet tall Eloise, with her large moon face and yellow yarn hair, stayed. She was like a member of the family.

We all loved the Eloise doll with her impish grin. She came dressed in a white Peter Pan collared blouse and navy pleated skirt, looking like the character in the Eloise books Winnie had given us for Christmas.

One August Winnie planned a surprise birthday for my friends, Lynn Milone and Mary Kay Coughlin, who were visiting. Mary Batson's birthday was around the same time as was Carol's, so they were included. Winnie used the cast iron cake pan shaped like a lamb lying down. The white frosting with coconut looked like lamb's fleece. She also made ice cream and we each had a chance to turn the crank on the old green wooden ice cream maker. Mac helped us add the rock salt and the ice, and turned the crank when it became too difficult for us. A few years later, someone gave Winnie a new varnished wooden, electric ice cream maker. It hummed along by itself, and it made the job easier, but it wasn't as much fun to watch. There was little to do except lick the dasher when the ice cream was done.

For thirty years, Winnie had built a reputation for her parties. Mrs. Shurman, a family friend, once said Winnie was responsible for making them feel welcome by introducing her to people in Dexter when the Shurmans arrived after the war to reestablish Dr. Shurman's medical practice. Ruth Shurman told my sister, "Your grandmother was the Perle Mesta of Dexter."

Winnie and Grampy were famous for their summer parties where they invited all of their friends on the lake shore. Once again a truck arrived from Fay Scott Landis Machine Company with a load of wood for cooking the large kettle of lobsters. My sisters and I walked over to the office cottage to watch the deliveries of tables, chairs, food, and blocks of ice for the old red Coca Cola lift-top cooler. Sometimes, we went with Daddy to the nearby town of Newport to get the lobsters that had been delivered from the coast.

For many years, Grampy hosted a lobster party for all the men in the Dexter Club. Every businessman in Dexter was there. I remember hearing about how the Club admitted new members—with each member putting a ball in a box. Afterward, if the balls in the box were all white, the applicant was in. If there was one black ball, he was rejected. I don't remember hearing who was black-balled, but some men had been in the past.

Dexter was a town of four thousand people during the 1950s post war prosperity. Each of the men in the Dexter Club had worked hard and risen above his origins. It was a time when the Protestant men of English, Scottish, or other European heritage were the leaders of the community. At that point, many of the Franco-Americans, whose families had moved from Canada, were laboring in the factories and mills. It would take another generation for their children to become the professionals in Dexter and other Maine communities.

The prominent men—members of the Dexter Club—were in their thirties through sixties. They were all there at the party: Henry Larsen and Norman Plouf of Fay Scott, Paul Barstow of the Dumbarton Woolen Mill, Luke Atwood and Don Champeon of Amos Abbott Mill, the store owners, lawyers, and the town's three physicians—Dr. Taylor, Dr. LaBarge, and Dr. Shurman.

They gathered after five o'clock, parking their cars on the side of the cottage access road and in our driveways. I felt the hum of excitement in the preparations all afternoon. That night I lay awake in my hot upstairs bedroom under the eaves. My metal folding cot with the lumpy mattress and the silvery frame squeaked with every move as I turned, trying to get comfortable. Mosquitoes hummed at the old wooden screens, and, as the evening breezes stirred with cool air from the lake, the laughing voices of the men at the office cottage wafted into the stillness of my room. The men, in jovial spirits, tongues loosened by whiskey and bourbon, sang in harmony, "Mademoiselle from Armentier…parlez vu…" I fell asleep to the strains of "Alouette gentil alouette, alouette je te plumerai…" sung in answering rounds. Later, the repeating refrain of *Good Night Irene* filled the night.

I drifted off to sleep listening to the soothing, happy sounds of the people I knew in Dexter. In the distance, I heard the cries of a pair of loons echoing over the still lake. The combination was an odd serenade.

On other Saturday evenings or Sunday afternoons, Winnie and Grampy and my parents had smaller shore parties, and friends from our side of the lake came for a lobster feed. Between our cottage and Winnie's and Grampy's near the shoreline rock wall, there was (and still is) a large gray picnic table that could seat about twenty people under the shingled roof supported by four posts. That was where we all gathered, with extra tables and benches added to accommodate all the guests and family members.

In the summer, it seemed that everyone converged on Dexter. That was the exciting part, that so many interesting friends and relatives from away came to Dexter. Even so, it never occurred to me that Dexter was unique. Now I know that the town and memories of growing up there have a strong pull for many people. The small town quaintness, generations of long time residents, and the crystal clear lake were so much a part of my life that they seemed ordinary. The far away cities where our friends and relatives lived seemed much more special.

Every summer Aunt Jinny, my mother's sister, Uncle Sig, and their four boys came to visit. The Osterhus' lived in Bogata, Columbia, then Caracas, Venezuela, and later they left South America for Africa and moved to Libya, because Uncle Sig worked for Esso Oil Company. We were excited when Aunt Jinny, Uncle Sig, and the boys flew into Bangor airport once they were back in the United States.

Jinny, Uncle Sig, and the boys flew into Bangor airport once they were back in the United States.

Doug was the eldest. He was my sister Susie's age, exactly six years younger than I, since he was born on my February 16th birthday. I thought it was unique that my mother had four girls and Aunt Jinny had four boys then and the eldest in each family had the same birthday.

The other boys, Philip, Monty (named after Great-Grammy Ellm's deceased husband Lamont), and Peter were blondes like Uncle Sig whose family came from Norway. After they bought the Bucknam cottage across the lake, the Osterhuses stayed all summer. I liked to play games with them, especially Peter, who was a toddler. I entertained him with my new card shuffling skill, fanning the cards back into place. With each maneuver, he gurgled and chortled at the noise the cards made as they flapped into a stack.

The Milones came to Dexter every summer from Chillicothe, Ohio to visit Mrs. Hale, Lynn's grandmother, who was not well. After she died, they continued to come to Maine for two weeks every summer because of their closeness to the Hatch family. When Lynn's mother, Helen, was a young woman, she had attended house parties at Wassookeag School

When our Rust cousins arrived we had fun from morning until night. David was my age and we spent hours playing with the little red boat Uncle Don made. Finally, with blue lips and wrinkled fingers, we emerged from the lake to warm on the rocks in the sun. One day Nancy Lea took pictures of me, Randy and Sally after Nancy curled our hair with beer and bobby pins. When our hair dried after a few hours, and it was free of the criss cross bobby pins, the curls had bounce and body from the beer.

David's and Nancy's brother Donnie went to Camp Winona for several summers. In August when he returned, he brought me a wide metal cuff bracelet covered with red plastic gimp and PRUDY spelled in white gimp. I cherished the gift he had made in arts and crafts and wore the bracelet every day, even to bed.

One night, after a family lobster party, Donnie, John Dyer (Barry's older brother), and Nancy gave my sisters and me airplane rides, holding us by a foot and a hand. It was a glorious starlit night; fireflies punctuated the evening with fluorescent green dots, and I sailed through the air in a dizzying circle shrieking to go faster while Donnie spun round and round and John swung Randy. Eventually we were hurt when we bumped into each other and that ended the rides. We sat on the damp grass nursing our bruises, and watched the fire flies blinking green in the darkness under the starry sky above.

At the end of the summer of 1956, we moved back into town early because the nights were cold and it was time to get ready for school. One day Daddy returned from John Briggs' farm with bushels of corn and other produce and my mother was less than pleased with the abundance he brought home. When he bought things, be it sneakers, peach blossom or horehound candy, rotten bananas, pencils or pens, Daddy bought in bulk if the price was cheaper. His customers emptied the candy dish weekly, Winnie or Nanny Hatch would make banana bread, and plenty of people knew he'd deliver them fresh vegetables from local farms.

My friends and I decided to sell the extra produce. We set up a small table, propped the bushel baskets of corn on edge for better display of our wares, and waited for people to stop on their way home for lunch.

Phillip said, "We've got tons of blackberries on the hill behind our house. Maybe we could sell them too."

Carol, Gene, and Phillip went to pick berries while I stayed at the stand in case we had customers. My friends returned an hour later with berry stained fingers and lips and six baskets filled with luscious glossy blackberries. We arranged the baskets on the table and waited. Business was slow, so we decided dispatch Carol and Gene on bicycles with samples of corn to homes up and down Forest, Maple, and Main Streets. Pretty soon the money started rolling in. Gene came back, breathless, fifteen minutes later, to get another bag of corn. My father ended up driving to the farm for more produce. We ate some of the berries during a lull in the sales and divvied up the money at the end of the day, each of us caressing dollar bills and feeling satisfaction for our efforts.

Summer was over, school was starting, and we kids were rich with pocket money to spend at Ben Franklin. Carol would buy lots of little things and I would choose one big item that would last and be worth my hard earned money.

Dot Whitney (Doug's mother), Aunt Barbara, Hazel Spencer, Donnie Rust, Shirley Hatch,
Sally, Randy and Prudy—1953

Prudy holding baby Susie—1953

Sally, Lynn, Prudy, Randy on towels. Susie standing.

David Rust and Bobby Milone fishing, Miles Jr., Lynn Milone,
Prudy and Susie on the dock. Sally in the boat Uncle Don built

The Burton girls standing near the sign for cottages—1953

Sally and Randy wearing new school clothes—1954

Prudy after Nancy used beer and bobbie pins to curl my hair—1954

Winnie in the cottage—1960

Prudy and Randy at Winnie's and Grampy's cottage—1954

Mac at the refrigerated bar pretending to imbibe with both hands

Prudy in Winnie's and Grampie's cottage.

RED DYE #5

When we baby-sat at Carol's house, we were on our own. To say that we baby-sat stretches the facts a bit. I don't think we ever actually checked on Carol's brother and sister, the seven-year-old twins. They never came downstairs to bother us, and once they were in bed we never went upstairs to check on them. When Carol's parents left for the weekly party at their friend's house, we had our own party. We had the house to ourselves, reveling in the feeling of freedom, the excitement of doing what we wanted to do.

We were the quintessential teenagers then. After years of watching older cousins, neighbors, and baby-sitters, we knew how to act. Years of reading *Calling All Girls*, *Seventeen*, and *Teen* magazines showed us how to be teenagers. Old enough to emulate those we admired enviously for so long, we approached the teen years with a studied, concerted effort to be just like our idols.

As seventh and eighth graders we were placed at the far end of the high school, but we were there nevertheless, observing, practicing to be teenagers. And one thing teenagers love is to be alone in a house with no adults around.

First after Carol's parents left, we made the living room ready for the evening by opening the fiberglass drapes. This way we had the reflection of the darkened window for practicing the newest dance steps. Dee Dee Sharp's latest hit record plopped down on the turn table and playing at full volume. We began the dance step, grinding our toes into the carpet, twisting our heels, waving our arms as we perfected the Mashed Potato.

We knew all of the dances—the Twist, the Pony, the Bristol Stomp, the Stroll, the Locomotion—from hours and hours of viewing *American Bandstand* after school. We watched the show with a critical eye, to see who Carmen and Yvette Jimenez danced with. ("Carmen thinks she's so great," we'd sputter.) We laughed scornfully at the record ratings when Bandstanders said they liked the record, it had a good beat, and they surely would buy it. What sheep they were! It was a crummy record. We would never be duped into buying it; but we kept watching the show, learning the latest steps.

Practice makes perfect, and so we danced in the window's reflection until the record ended and the *Platter's Golden Hits Album* dropped into position. It was Carol's parents' record, but Saturday night baby-sitting always meant *Smoke Gets In Your Eyes* and *The Great Pretender*. Often we held a hair styling session while the records played. We teased our hair, back-combing it to its fullest beauty with the top layer smoothed over the ratted spikes and a smooth little curl at the front of each ear.

One night, with our hairdos finished, Carol said, "Wanna read a good book? I found *The Carpetbaggers* hidden in the cupboard the other day. It's got some juicy parts you won't believe." She climbed on the counter and opened the top kitchen cabinet. As she reached for the book, an open box of red, powdered Rit dye fell to the floor, spilling its contents on the new, beige fake fieldstone linoleum.

"Quick," Carol gasped, "get me the dishcloth."

I reached into the sink, grabbed the wet dish rag, tossed it to her, and she began to wipe up the red powder. Instantly, we realized the mistake.

Our initial mild concern turned to panicked horror as we realized that the wet dishcloth had activated the powdered dye, turning the linoleum bright red. This was the floor Carol's mother had scrimped and saved for.

"Oh, no," I groaned. "What are we going to do now?"

"Get some rags from the closet," Carol shouted, as she rinsed the dish-cloth and began wiping up the dye again. In a frenzy, I hurried to the closet and began searching for large enough pieces. "Quick," Carol yelled.

I scurried back with an arm load of rags and we attempted to mop up the dye. The area in front of the cupboards and sink was distinctly red while the rest of the cobblestone remained a quiet beige. The circle of red spread wider and wider.

"Wet the rags," Carol ordered. "Get some Ajax. We'll keep wiping the area until we lighten it up." This made the large spot on the floor less red, but the pink circle had widened. "My mother will kill me," Carol moaned. "All she talks about is how long she had to wait to have the kitchen redone. She'll have a fit when she sees this. Oh, my gawd, why didn't we just sweep it up in the first place?"

There was nothing else to do but take the red rags and go over the entire floor, giving it a pink tinge. We worked frantically, wiping and wiping, widening the circle of pink, covering every inch of the floor-under the cupboards, around the stove, the refrigerator, and the washing machine, into the corners of the floor, up to the three doors, and under the table— scrubbing, wiping, swishing the reddish-pink water over the beige cobblestones. Working against time, our hearts beat faster and faster as we neared the moment Carol's parents would come home.

By then, the entire floor had a rosy hue. We grabbed more clean wet rags and went back to the original spot, working feverishly to lighten the pinkness, scrubbing, spreading, blending the obvious.

Finally, we stepped back, trying to survey it with the eyes of her parents. It didn't look too bad. We had made it. The wet slickness of the floor was drying. The newly pink-tinged floor looked okay, although the seams were a bit dark. Maybe her parents would never notice the new color.

We cleaned up the sink and scrubbed our blotchy red hands with Ajax. Carefully we gathered all the tell-tale rags, the empty box of Rit dye, and took the entire soggy mess to the trash cans in the garage. Breathing sighs of relief, tense from the ordeal, we broke into uncontrollable giggles. Convulsed with laughter, we imagined the story we'd tell our friends of our adventure the night the dye for the cheer-leading underpants spilled on the floor. Then we went to bed before Carol's parents came home.

The next morning as we came down the stairs remembering the floor, we looked at each other and tried to erase the looks of chagrin. Neither of her parents mentioned anything during breakfast. Maybe we were safe.

I went home with a sense of relief. We had saved our skins, the floor, and unnecessary grief for Carol's mother.

On Monday, I saw Carol at school and asked if her parents had noticed the floor. She said, "I told them I felt sick so I didn't go with them to church. The floor still looked pinkish to me," she continued, "so, I washed it all over one more time while they were gone. I just made it back upstairs when they came home."

Carol went on to explain that she had such a knot in her stomach that she couldn't eat lunch on Sunday. She stayed in bed until 2:00, when she thought she was home free and decided to get something to eat.

While she was in the kitchen making herself a nice, thick turkey sandwich, her father came up behind her and said in his usual, dry sardonic way, "Carol, I just want to know one thing—who got stabbed last night?"

The red-stained rags in the trash cans had given us away. So did the light pink floor with dark pink seams. Mr. and Mrs. Whitney weren't happy about the new floor, but the damage was done.

We were quite relieved that Carol's parents accepted the new floor color with resignation and humor, although Mrs. Whitney did complain for a year afterward that every time she washed the floor the water had a pink tinge and the seams never faded.

Carol and I still see each other. The memories of our growing up together, our discoveries and our coming of age in a small Maine town give us history and strong bonds that separation can't harm. Our friendship has spanned almost five decades. We've grown and changed, matured as women with accomplishments and new experiences, but when we get together we always end up saying, "remember when...."

We remember age eight when we cleaned Carol's room with our ritualistic game of deserted ghost town, pretending the dolls were ill fed, ill clothed orphans who had survived a disaster. We saved the children and brought beauty and order to the world and Carol's room, although it took several hours of play and became a worse mess before we finally achieved our goal.

But, we had a vision and a sense of mission. Just as we had mission on that night we spilled the powdered Rit dye on the new fake fieldstone linoleum, only then, we were driven by panic as well as a need to restore order and beauty.

Today, in our own ways, Carol and I continue to work toward beauty and order in our lives and in the real world with other people's children who are in need, just as the orphaned dolls were. My role as a teacher in the Maine Migrant Education Program and Carol's dedication to Patty and the Big Sister / Little Sister program had their genesis in our childhood when we wanted to make the world a better place for doll children.

The Teen Years at Lake Wassookeag

When my cousin Nancy Lea Rust was sixteen and I was eight, I listened intently as she and her friend Kathy Barstow talked excitedly about the boys at Wassookeag Camp. With effusive, effervescent squeals and giggles of delight, Nancy and Kathy raved about the boys they met on the camp road, in town, and at Lakewood Summer Theater. The Barstow's cottage was right beside the camp, twenty yards from the study cabins where the boys had their morning classes. It was very convenient if the boys' canoes drifted toward the Barstows. Each day Nancy and Kathy lay sunning in their one-piece bathing suits on the gray wooden deck by the shoreline, talking and waiting. Sometimes I was with them.

I listened as they talked about how Diana Taylor had arranged to meet some boys and that Penny Cleaves and her sister Chippy had a secret rendezvous with the boys. (Ironically, Chippy ended up marrying Louis Chabot's son Maurice. Eight summers later he taught math at Wassookeag Camp and I was in his class trying to improve my algebra grade. That was later in 1962 when I had the privilege of walking through the camp for classes. The older teenage girls never had that opportunity.)

It was pretty exciting to listen to the teenagers and imagine the romance of it all. It was almost as exciting as watching a Doris Day and Rock Hudson movie.

In the summer before sixth grade, I met my first Wassookeag boy while watching a Little League game. His name was Preble Ware, and I remember nothing about him, except his name which is sprinkled through my diary in just the way an eleven year old would imagine a teenager would write. I was used to admiring boys from afar because of our visits to Hatch

Prep. My cousin Nancy seemed to have such fun with the boys at Grampy's school while it existed, but just as I was ready to emerge into the social whirl of handsome wealthy boys, Grampy retired from the school.

Still, I had the next best thing for two months, with a hundred fascinating boys sleeping in dorms just six cottages down the lake. The sight of them sailing, canoeing, or water-skiing sent a tingle through my body. Lake Wassookeag came alive in June when the boys arrived and was as sad and still as the cemetery when they left in August.

When I was a teenager, it seemed as if the boys' being at the camp which Grampy established, somehow conferred status on Dexter and on me. I felt a bond that transcended reality. It seemed as if my destiny was to meet a handsome, rich, intelligent Wassookeag boy from away who would discover wonderful things about the person I really was, things I didn't even realize myself. He'd be so entranced that he would sweep me off my feet and carry me away to places filled with glamour and excitement. At the very least, I hoped he'd meet me, like me, continue to write to me, remember me, and come back to reunite with me later in life because I was so special and unforgettable. (I saw a lot of old movies on TV.) But, before I was swept off my feet, I had to first meet the boys.

From the summer of 1959, when I was twelve, until the summer of 1963, I did everything possible to complete my mission. I watched both the clock and the lake. When the boys had their ten o'clock break from classes, Carol, Cathie, or my sister, Randy, and I asked our neighbor Joyce Crosby if we could borrow her brown canvas and wood-dinghy. We casually and coincidentally rowed the boat back and forth in front of Wassookeag camp hoping to be seen or for a chance to see the boys. We usually rowed in deeper water out beyond the green wooden float with the white tower for diving. It was the same tower and float built in the years when Grampy owned the camp, before it was sold to Mr. May.

We were rather brazen as we rowed past the camp. Somehow it didn't seem terribly wrong since Grampy had founded the camp. In old brochures, I saw pictures of Uncle Don, Nancy Lea's father, posing at the waterfront with the other male students in their old-fashioned, one piece, wool bathing suits with tank tops. Other pictures showed a panorama of the lake with the diving tower raft and Chris Craft at the dock.

My father finally bought a new fiberglass dinghy at Dexter Hardware so we wouldn't bother Joyce Crosby with our transparent request to go rowing. Dr. LaBarge also bought a matching dinghy for his children, so we rowed in the other direction to see our friends when the Wassookeag boys were in the study cabins.

Later, when the boys walked to town at two o'clock, Carol or Cathie and I just happened to be at the end of our cottage road timing our emergence for a walk to town. If the boys weren't in sight on the road, we'd start over again, retreating down our cottage road, waiting, then casually sauntering toward the paved road. The excitement and anticipation of hoping to see the Wassookeag Boys made the moment they appeared seem like a hard-won prize. Actually, we usually just walked eight or ten yards in front of them or behind and were too scared and embarrassed to say anything to them.

One year the upcoming eclipse prompted us to talk to the boys as we walked on the sidewalk down Zion's Hill past Senator Brewster's home with pink roses hanging over the shale rock wall. The people at the Junior Chamber of Commerce had figured out that Dexter, which is on the 45th parallel, was the heart of Maine and labeled us "Eclipse Town, U.S.A." Committee members began promoting the event in the spring. By July the event was in full swing.

Anticipating what it would be like to experience a total eclipse was very exciting. Carol and I went in the Rexall for an ice cream, to my father's office for money, and to the Ben Franklin. The Jaycees had booths, and the whole town had a festive air. More than the usual number of boys were in town that day, and we summoned enough courage to talk to them. As the moon slowly covered the sun in a series of smaller and smaller crescents, and the sky darkened, we stared agape, in awe of the event and the workings of the universe. For a few moments, even the presence of the boys didn't matter.

On the afternoons that we didn't walk to town, we kept busy swimming and visiting with our friends. We watched the Wassookeag boys sail across the lake and water ski behind the old mahogany Chris Craft.

Tenney Wheatley, Diana Taylor's new boyfriend, waved to us as he drove the boat speeding by. Diana was petite with long sandy colored hair pulled back to expose a widow's peak. I thought she was lucky that she didn't have a high forehead and need to have bangs like I did. Diana's parents' cottage was beyond ours, right beside the LaBarge's cottage. For one summer, Diana kept her horse Wendy, a mare, in the converted garage on the edge of the woods. Cathie and I revered her status as a girl of such privilege. Some of the adults thought it not quite proper that she had a boyfriend so much older, but everyone liked Tenney, especially Dr. and Mrs. Taylor.

Tenney, tall, broad shouldered, and handsome with a toothy smile, was in his early twenties—very old and sophisticated. A recent graduate of Hamilton College, he often smoked long cigars. Orphaned by his elderly parents' death, and the recipient of a large inheritance (so we heard), he had a new fancy white Oldsmobile convertible with red leather interior. It was thrilling for Cathie and me to ride in Tenney's car with Diana to the horse show at Avis Shaw's on the Corinna Road. Fabian's *Like A Tiger* blared on the radio and we left the world of adults behind as we drove away with the convertible top down and the wind in our hair.

Our favorite afternoons were spent in the cottage living room with Tenney and Diana listening to the Kingston Trio and the rollicking lyrics about Charlie riding the MTA. We also liked the song that actually had the words, "...I don't give a damn..." in the verse. There was something magical about being twelve and being in that room at the lake with the whine of power boats in the distance, the Kingston Trio on the Victrola, and Diana and Tenney getting ready to go out for a date at the Lakewood Theatre.

How I loved the romance of being in another dimension, in the company of teenagers. By the summer of 1959, I was twelve and only six months away from joining the ranks of the teen world. Until then, I could do some of the things that teenagers did, but I still had one foot in childhood, so I wasn't entirely the vapid boy chaser.

The old doll house Aunt Teddy gave us was in my upstairs bedroom at the cottage, and I still got out my Jill and Ginny dolls occasionally, especially for the Ginny Doll Club meetings with Candy Wiley, Carol, and my sisters. I also leaped across the large rocks on the beach when the water was low and helped my sisters find crawfish under the rocks. Carol, Cathie, Candy, and I went to Mr. and Mrs. Lewis' local Girl Scout camp across the lake with other Dexter girls. Carol and I also went to Camp Kirkwold in Readfield, Maine during the summer of 1960 and 1961 because our parents were a bit concerned about the boy craziness. Although it was relatively harmless, we did make a spectacle of ourselves on Lake Wassookeag in that dinghy.

That was the first and only summer we had a gathering for the boys on the Wassookeag baseball team. I convinced my parents and grandparents to have a cookout. Grampy made the arrangements with Lester May, and the boys arrived at our cottage in their dark chinos and white dress shirts with the sleeves rolled just right, below their elbows. We were all a bit awkward and a little shy once we were in an organized social situation. We invited some other girls and included my younger sisters and their friends. I took black and white photos of us all with my Brownie camera—the Dexter girls and the Wassookeag boys.

Their names and the places where they lived were a litany with a magical ring, still etched in my mind more deeply than the list of prepositions.

A few weeks after the cookout, when the docks and diving tower float were moved to the shore during the last days of camp, my sister Randy and I rowed closer to camp than usual. We wanted to say a last good-bye to the boys who played on the Wassookeag baseball team and attended the cookout.

Dickie Boothby and Danny Millett were canoeing and Danny jumped into the water fully clothed. I snapped a picture of him hanging onto the back of our dinghy. He was about eleven years old at the time and his parents weren't too pleased when they found their son was being pursued so persistently by townies. My parents got a letter from Mr. May and the Milletts, after we sent Danny the picture of Randy posing with him on the cottage road near the Barstows' cottage, with her arm half way raised to put around him. Of course I was the one who orchestrated the pose. Randy was chided in the Millett's letter for her boldness, when in fact she was the studious, shy type.

In my box of old letters, I found one dated Thursday August 13, 1959 written by Bill Kirshner, on the evening of the party when he had returned to study hall at camp. He spoke of the dance we all would be attending at Lakewood on the upcoming Saturday (a week before he and the other boys would go home). He very graciously thanked me and my parents for the "wonderful time tonight." He also said, "I doubt that you like me half as much as I love you …In a week and a day I'll be going home. I shall never forget you."

I had forgotten that I ever received that letter just as I am sure that Bill has forgotten that he ever wrote it. I remembered his name over the years, but it was one of a string of names of Wassookeag boys. Ironically, years later I found out that a Skowhegan friend, Warren Shay, grew up in Scarsdale with Bill Kirshner, Al Knork, and Jeff Escher (a Wassookeag boy I met in 1963.) Warren and I discussed it, but I had forgotten that they knew each other. It is amazing that so many paths have crossed and people and events have circled around in the labyrinth of time.

We didn't realize at first, nor did we think it mattered once we knew, that most of the boys at the camp were Jewish. We found out after my grandparents saw the guest list and we found out when we mentioned to the boys that if they went to church on Sunday, we could meet them there.

We knew that for some people there was something forbidden about Protestant girls and Jewish boys, because we overheard my family and other adults talking disapprovingly about Henry Larsen. Mr. Larsen had disowned his daughter after she married a Jewish man she met in New

York City. Liz had a "fantastic job" at Columbia Records, and I often heard comments at the cottage about her wonderful career and marriage. When I saw Mr. Larsen kneeling in church and going to communion, I used to wonder how he could cut his daughter off and forbid his wife to have contact, just because Liz married a Jewish man.

A few years later, when I read *The Cardinal*, I still didn't understand how some people could be so against a couple having different religions. At twelve, I understood even less. I had seen the movies *The Diary of Anne Frank* and *Exodus* at the Park Theater in Dexter, but I was still putting together pieces of information that I didn't quite understand.

At any rate, I wasn't thinking about the horrible history of WW II or that those boys' parents might have been survivors of Nazi prison camps. That was worlds away and not part of my experience.

We were only twelve, and our involvement was merely infatuation. They were cute boys, and we were interested girls. Besides we were friendly with the only Jewish family in town, the Shurmans, and religious difference didn't seem to matter. Valerie Shurman, who was my sister Randy's age, joined us at the party, not because she had followed the games or chased boys, but because she was a friend, and she rounded out the list of girls. We needed to have an even number of boys and girls at our party.

My grandparents enjoyed the opportunity to help plan and orchestrate the party, although on a much smaller scale than in the heyday of Wassookeag School Camp when it was Grampy's.

In the summer of 1962, Daddy had a "good night" at the horse races and bought a new boat and motor so we could water-ski. The owner of Dexter Hardware owed Daddy some money, so they struck a deal. Before that, we had a small aluminum boat with a seven-and-a-half Johnson that would take us to the islands on either end of the lake to fish and explore where the water was shallow with yellow blossomed lily pads, frogs, and lots of sun fish.

That first boat was replaced by a fiberglass boat with a twenty-eight horse power motor. The newest boat, which replaced that one, had a canvas awning and a forty horse power motor. Randy, Sally, and I perfected our water-skiing. Randy mastered the art of dropping a ski after a swing by the LaBarge's camp then a sweep by Wassookeag Camp, she continued for a spin down the lake on the slalom ski, a rooster tail arc of spray behind her.

My mother patiently drove the boat for an hour while we and our friends each had a turn. I liked the route past Wassookeag Camp just beyond the diving tower. Usually we took off from the dock in sitting position so we didn't have to get wet until the drop off. If I took off from the water, I could usually get up, but I couldn't master the feat of dropping one ski. I tried several times, then decided that the thrill of success wasn't worth the reality of ears, nose, mouth, and eyes full of water, and head cold symptoms for a week. I was satisfied with being on two skis and going outside the wake. That was enough of a challenge, especially if the water was rough. Ever a quitter, I added one more thing to my growing list of things I couldn't do.

Times were changing. Once I became a teenager, they changed even more. We still moved out to the cottage each spring, but I made my mother take the long way around, up Highland Avenue past the La Barge's house, so we wouldn't go through Main Street with a station wagon full of possessions. I was mortified that someone I knew might see us, that we would look like gypsies.

My summer days were times of leisure. We still had visitors from away. I found that I hated the good-byes. Someone was always leaving a void as they returned to their out-of-state home. I hated the end of August when all the family visitors had gone back, and no more would be coming. The Wassookeag boys were gone and fall was in the air. The lake was often smooth as glass with a few red tinged leaves reflected in its mirror image. The approaching end of another summer, departing friends and family left me feeling empty. The anticipation of returning to school with a new wardrobe was scant compensation.

I had moved beyond the long days of play in the woods and in the water. I had become a laconic teenager sunbathing, reading, and visiting with my friends, with an occasional evening baby-sitting for the Crosbys. The industrious child, who made clay ash trays and created trails marked with signs in the woods, was of another time.

If I could go back for a day, I wouldn't choose the teenage years. Instead, I'd be in the cottage with Winnie, sitting on the green South Western style sofa, reading *New Yorker* cartoons and sucking on her home-made butterscotch candy, while Danny Kay sings "…The king is in the altogether, the altogether. He's altogether as naked as the day that he was born." Winnie would be in her tooled leather seat at the table as Mac prances into the room whirling about with her three-quarter-length coat thrown over his shoulders, a straw hat on his head, bowed legs exposed beneath his bathing suit. Then he'd pose for a picture with my sisters and me in dresses from Aunt Teddy's trunks.

Carol and Prudy before going to Lakewood Theatre—1963

SNEAKERS AND STEINBECK

One sultry evening as an adult, I retraced the route I had often traveled during my adolescence. I felt as if I were only partially in the present as I came closer to the former Wassookeag Camp and I remembered the days when my heart beat faster as I got closer to the camp full of boys.

The road, a victim of time and neglect, had changed drastically. What was once a bustling exit road from the private summer camp was altered by encroaching alders, bushes, vines, and fallen trees. I looked for the little green wooden cabins each with the name of a prestigious prep school or Ivy League college emblazoned on the front. But, these miniature classrooms no longer nestled among the trees along the camp road.

More than thirty years earlier, I was an unlikely student at the Wassookeag School Camp. It was the opportunity of a lifetime to enter those hallowed grounds in the summer of 1962. At fifteen, I didn't need to resort to the transparent subterfuges of previous years. Instead, I walked with feigned nonchalance, always with a feeling of trepidation that some adult would stop me and ask what I, the only female, was doing invading that male bastion of learning. I was ready with an answer and an explanation. But no one asked for the first few days.

After an academic year of frustrating incomprehension, lack of diligence, and quavering fear in the formidable Madame Slater's French class, I was receiving semi-private tutoring at Wassookeag School Camp. It was hardly a punishment for me to repeat French that summer, nor was it a penalty to take Algebra again. This was the highlight of my year, to be able to walk down the access road, through the camp, and past study cabins with boys and teachers readying for class.

As I walked through the camp I tried to keep my eyes straight ahead in a fixed stare, but I still noticed the bustling activity. I arrived on the grounds minutes before the dismissal bell for changing classes brought one hundred young men into my path. Some boys relaxed by the waterfront, others prepared to take out canoes. I kept walking along the road past the large green building which contained the kitchen and dining hall where my great-aunt once cooked when my father was young.

Continuing on my way to my assigned study cabin for class, I had a better view of the waterfront. Large green wooden docks on metal barrels creaked and rocked in the wake from a passing boat. Farther out, the high towered diving float swayed at its anchor, and the shiny mahogany 1930s Chris Craft rocked at its mooring, waiting for the afternoon to pull waterskiers across the lake.

One day after class as I walked home, Dave Ferguson and his friend sauntered confidently over to ask who I was and why I came through camp every day. After I replied, "Prudy Hatch," with an explanation of my reasons for being there, Dave asked if that was my real name. Reluctantly, I answered that actually my name was Prudence Frame Hatch. I was embarrassed by the name I have since come to like for its uniqueness, if not its connotation. They chuckled at the formality of my name, and said it was "quaint." They also were interested to hear I lived in a nearby cottage.

Not only was I embarrassed by my name, but I was ill at ease standing on the camp grounds talking to two suave, debonair seventeen year olds. As I stood talking to the boys, I was also acutely aware of the holes in my sneakers. They were the latest style Keds of black hopsacking with a squared toe. I had pleaded with my mother to buy them for me at Standard Shoe store in Bangor, not realizing that the stiff burlapy material would have the consistency of gauze after only four weeks of wear. So there I stood, primly, nervously, in my collarless, red print blouse, black, stitched-down pleat skirt, and my sneakers with holes in the toes, praying that these boys from the city would not notice.

In the seconds after I told them my name, Dave Ferguson had introduced himself and said, "This is my friend, John Steinbeck, IV." When I showed no sign of awe or recognition, he said, "His father writes books."

"Oh," I said, registering my ignorance. I can't remember if I added "I don't think I have ever heard of him," or if I just said "Oh" and feigned knowledge. I was uneasy because of the idiotic concern and embarrassment over the holes in my nearly-new hopsacking sneakers. That was compounded by the realization that I probably should know about John's father who wrote books. There was a trace of patronizing smugness on Dave's face, and I didn't enjoy feeling like an ignorant hick.

During the next few minutes, I did manage to regain some of my composure as I answered their questions about Dexter—what there was to do for fun in such a small Maine town, and how I knew so much about Wassookeag.

Hoping to elevate my stature a bit, from that of hick to that of a girl who had been privileged to some cultural exposure and a few encounters with people of some import, I explained that my grandfather had established the camp in the 1920s and that he had sold it in the 1940s to the present owners. I briefly mentioned the Hatch Prep School in Newport, Rhode Island and my grandfather's retirement as headmaster. I told Dave and John about Lakewood Summer Theatre where the Wassookeag boys were allowed to go on Saturday nights and that my friends and I rode with family members to the theatre which was located near Skowhegan.

That afternoon, I asked my mother offhandedly, "Have you ever heard of John Steinbeck?"

"Of course," she said explaining that she had copies of most of his books in our living room book case.

I didn't read the books that summer, partly because of my homework in French and the unfathomable Algebra I, but mainly because I was busy with my friends—the old and the new. My cousin Miles and friend Lynn, who were visiting, became acquainted with Dave, Chris, and John.

Dave, his friend Chris, and sometimes John soon began to sneak out of camp. Instead of going to town, they walked to our cottage or they paddled a canoe off limits down the lake. I don't remember how they were able to elude the counselors, but I think their age of seventeen gave them some privilege. However they managed to escape, I began to look forward to seeing Dave more often as July wore on.

At first, Dave had tried to get me together with his friend Chris Washburn. Three years before I had watched Chris from afar at baseball games and developed a crush on him. Tall, muscular, blond haired, and as handsome as a Greek god, Chris returned to Wassookeag in the summer of '62 with a vintage red Austin Healy as his chariot. He was also conceited and fancied himself as a ladies' man. During one of the boys' visits, the conversation came around to whether Chris had kissed me that summer of '59.

They were incredulous when they heard that I had never kissed a boy and did not plan to until I was sixteen. Chris coined the phrase that I had "virgin lips," something unheard of in their fast paced crowd. For a while I was interested in Chris. Then Dave and I became interested in each other. As the summer progressed, Dave seemed to take it as a personal challenge to initiate me to the world of kissing

Dave had a girlfriend back in Ohio where his mother owned a women's clothing store. As the summer wore on, I began to see Dave even more. I thought he was suave, and I would take whatever crumb of affection came my way. I was infatuated with him. His sleek stature, neatly trimmed, thick dark hair, and goatee made him seem very sophisticated.

We saw each other almost daily during August. We walked and talked. Sometimes John accompanied Dave. They talked about writing and the fact that John, like his father had a talent for it. They discussed John's father and his communications with his son.

I learned that John's father was traveling the country that summer of '62 with his Standard Poodle Charlie and writing the drafts for a new book. As the summer passed, I learned more about Steinbeck's writing. As

I learned about John's and Dave's philosophical, intellectual, and moral ideas, I gained a new awareness of a world outside of Dexter.

During one conversation when we walked along the cottage road, Dave and John talked about the parties they had and how everyone in their crowd smoked and drank. John spent a lot of time in New York City where his mother lived and in California with his father. Dave and John alluded to the intimate relationships they had with their girlfriends. They both were more sophisticated and experienced than I was and that was part of the allure.

As Dave and I talked and became better acquainted, I developed a romanticized image of him as the older, sophisticated, experienced man, since he had told me he and Sandi had gone all the way, regularly. He seemed like a modern day Rhett Butler. Dave's girlfriend Sandi was in Ohio. Their relationship wasn't all rosy. He told me how they argued sometimes. I began to imagine that he might grow to like me. We became more romantically linked in my mind, but I was interested in a platonic, intellectual romance. I'm not really sure what his motives were, but it was the beginning of my new stage and a persona I created for myself. The fact that I had "virgin lips" became a badge of honor.

With that in mind, I patterned myself partially after the character that Doris Day played in *Pillow Talk* and other movies with Rock Hudson and Tony Randall. I acted coy, interested, aiming for cute and perky, but more often being distant and quiet, shy and introverted. I wanted to appear just friendly enough so it would be a challenge to win me over. I hoped my personality and attitude would make me irresistible. Dave seemed to fall for it and me. I documented every nuance, conversation, and movement of our blossoming romance in lengthy letters to my friend Lynn Milone who had met Dave earlier in the summer and was from his home state of Ohio.

One afternoon Dave attempted the ultimate—a kiss—and I could see it coming. I was so flustered and embarrassed as I saw him moving closer, that I turned my head and said, "Oh, no." I had seen so many movies and built the possibility into such gigantic proportions, that it was not just a simple gesture of affection. It was a momentous occasion I was afraid to experience, yet in a way, I was dying for the kiss to happen. Just as I was possibly ready to allow him to try again, and to be calm, affectionate, and responsive, my father arrived to take me to my Algebra lesson with Maurice Chabot at the Cleaves cottage.

I said an embarrassed good-bye to Dave and rode out of the yard with my father, still swooning and dramatically tipping my head to rest on the car window, so overcome was I with emotions, theatrics, and romance. Once we were on our way, I had to act normal with my father, not like a girl who had almost been kissed. When I arrived at my class with my fellow student Gene Kortecamp, the theorems, integers, and equations were even more enigmatic that afternoon. All I could think of and picture was Dave's handsome face and lips coming closer.

Years later, I discovered in my collection of letters and momentos, two Lakewood Theatre Playbills from July 28th, 1962. The play was *The Gazzebo*, starring William Bendix. One of the playbills must have been the one Dave held in his hands all night. Both booklets have the imprint of my Tangee Natural coated lips in the left hand corner.

That same summer I arrived at the Lakewood Summer Theatre for an August performance. The Wassookeag boys had arrived by bus and were all milling about outside The Shanty, in front of the steps to the entrance of the theatre. I stood on the slate patio in front of the Inn, watching the scene as if it were a play. John and Dave, resplendent in Weejuns, khaki summer suits, blue button-down collar shirts, ties, and neatly trimmed goatees, leaned against the window boxes of red geraniums and ivy. I didn't feel bold enough to just walk over to join them and strike up a conversation, so I stood on the patio and listened.

They were harmonizing some popular tunes. As I listened, their deep adolescent voices grew stronger with the lyrics. Everything seemed to freeze for a few moments as they sang the verses to *See You In September*.

As I thought about the words, somehow it seemed as if Dave's girlfriend could lose him to me in the romance of a starry, moonlit night at

Lakewood. I over-looked most of the song's message and from that moment on connected it only with Dave and John.

On another Saturday night in August, my sister Randy and I rode to Lakewood with the Heberts, ostensibly to see the play, but mainly so I could see Dave. The Wassookeag boys all sat with their counselors in the balcony. I sat with Randy and the Heberts in the orchestra.

I didn't see the last act of the play. That night, after the second intermission, I didn't return to my seat, instead I walked with Dave by the waterfront. I worried what the Heberts might think, but I couldn't miss a moonlight stroll.

My dress was a sleeveless rayon print paisley with swirls of sapphire blue, green, and a touch of brown. Designed with a fitted bodice, the gathered skirt, with pleats at the waist, created fullness at the hem. It was one of the most flattering dresses I had ever owned as a teenager, and I felt quite sophisticated for a change, not awkward and unattractive.

We bought that dress at Cortell Seigal in Bangor so I could wear it to my cousin Nancy Lea's wedding, which took place in early August on the day Marilyn Monroe's suicide was announced on the radio. For the summer, my hair was cut short and layered, but long enough for me to tease and style almost as well as Vicki did at Mr. Barnard's in Bangor. I definitely wanted to look stylish on the last Saturday that Dave and I would be together.

As intermission began, Dave joined me, and we strolled toward Lake Wesserunset under a starlit sky. I shivered though the evening air was warm. I felt nervous and giddy with the thrill of anticipation, but gradually I talked more easily because my inhibitions and introversion were loosened by the beauty and magic of the evening. We lost track of time, missed the buzzer for the last act, and decided to continue our walk and conversation.

"This is my last Saturday night in Maine, he said. " Next week at this time I'll be back in Ohio."

I didn't want to think about that or about him and Sandi.

Perhaps I didn't talk much. I just basked in Dave's presence and the glow from the full moon. I clutched the flat, black satin evening bag that I had appropriated from my mother, and still use today for dressy occasions. We walked and talked, and my whole being pulsed with the warmth of closeness.

We didn't hold hands or touch or kiss. We were just together. We might have discussed my idiosyncrasies and phobias, the shyness, and desire for a platonic relationship. Or maybe the memories of that night have melded with other conversations and relationships with the three boyfriends that followed in subsequent years. When we finally heard the hum of voices outside the theater, we walked back toward the bus so Dave could join John and the others for the ride back to Dexter. I found the Heberts and my sister and rode home in dreamy silence, knowing I should explain my absence, but not wanting to break the spell by speaking.

Dave and all of the Wassookeag boys left for their homes the next day. That afternoon I went into town to see a friend. I couldn't bear the unnaturally quiet lake without the sound of the Chris Craft and male voices on the camp waterfront.

That fall of my high school sophomore year, I went on a Steinbeck binge, eager to rid myself of the ignorance that had become such a burden and happy to immerse myself in a literary tie with the Wassookeag boys. I read *The Grapes of Wrath* first and felt such compassion for the Joad family in their life as migrant farm laborers. I thought it was Steinbeck's best book, but each of the others left an impression too.

As soon as *Travels With Charlie* was published, I read it, savoring every detail in the chronicle, feeling somehow familiar with the author through my brief acquaintance with his son. The next summer John's brother Tom went to Wassookeag. I read a few of his stories in the camp newspaper, but didn't get to know him, because I was interested in a boy named Jeff from Scarsdale, who was my last Wassookeag boy.

Years later, in 1988 or 1989, while reading the *Morning Sentinel*, I noticed the name John Steinbeck IV in the obituary section:

'John Steinbeck IV, a writer and son of the Nobel-writing author of *The Grapes of Wrath*, died of complications from back surgery Thursday, according to an Encinitas, California, news report. He was forty-four. Steinbeck died at Scripps Memorial Hospital. No other details about the surgery were disclosed. Steinbeck had been working on his autobiography, *Legacy*, in which he intended to examine the genetics of chemical addiction and trace what he believed to be his father's alcoholism to his own. The younger Steinbeck had been a recovering alcoholic for three years. A free-lance writer, he was published in many magazines, including *The New Yorker*. He wrote a non-fiction book, *In Touch*, about his experiences in Vietnam, where he embraced Buddhism. Steinbeck was born in New York, where his father moved from to California. At eighteen, Steinbeck was drafted into the army and completed a tour in Vietnam, part of which he spent as a combat reporter for Armed Forces Radio. He later returned to Southeast Asia to work as a free-lance journalist, primarily for CBS, in Vietnam, Laos, and Cambodia. Steinbeck was in Vietnam in 1968 when his father, who won the Nobel Prize for literature in 1962, died of heart failure.'

I reread the obituary twice that day, letting the details wash over me. As I drove to my work of teaching migrant children, my mind tingled with dozens of memories and images, but the strongest one was of that night at Lakewood Theatre. I could still see Dave and John in all their suaveness and sartorial splendor, standing confidently outside The Shanty, singing the words to *See You in September*.

I thought about how, for more than thirty years, I had been transported back in time when the radio station played that special song from the summer of '62. Life had changed so much. Wassookeag Camp and all the buildings were gone. The glorious days of Lakewood Theatre were gone. The hockey rink of childhood and adolescent neighborhood play was gone. All of my old schools were gone or changed. My grandparents who founded Wassookeag Camp were gone, as were my great-aunts and uncle who once worked there. Now one of my peers was gone.

Today, when I drive through Dexter, and see one of the Dartmouth-green cabins from Wassookeag Camp, which were sold off as tool and storage sheds in the 1970s, I am overcome by a sense of loss. The cabins that once held Wassookeag instructors and summer students, now hold rakes and shovels caked with dry mud. I find myself wondering which of these sheds was the Cornell cabin, where I day dreamed of nights at Lakewood Theatre while being tutored in French.

I never developed much of an aptitude for algebra, geometry, or French, but I became a keeper of memories, not fixated on the past, but holding thoughts of the past for safe keeping until I could put them on paper and examine the effect on my life.

LAKEWOOD SUMMER THEATRE

Lakewood Theatre peaked in the '50s. Then in the '60s began a slow slide toward its eventual denouement. The Lakewood summer community on the shores of Lake Wesserunset thrived for more than sixty years. In the early days tourists arrived by trolley car and cruised the lake on a steam boat.

In the '50s and '60s people drove to the theater for plays, to the Inn for lunch, dinner, and the famous Sunday night buffet where food was elegantly displayed. Guests came for the week-end or extended visits in the quaint guest cabins or bigger cottages.

Actors from Hollywood and Broadway traveled to Maine for week long engagements at the theatre. Artists from the renowned Skowhegan Art School, strolled through the Lakewood grounds. The flamboyant artists and actors gave a delightful, Bohemian ambiance to Lakewood. The waitresses, set-up girls, and busboys were college students. Hundreds applied, but only fourteen waitress, three set up girls and three bus boys were hired for the summer of thirteen weeks.

My early memories of Lakewood blend together in a series of images and scenes starting in the summer of '51 when I was five. Because I was the eldest, I was chosen to go with my grandparents for a week-end at Lakewood. We stayed in one of the cedar-shingled bungalows situated along roads that meandered about the spacious grounds. A canopy of pines and birches provided privacy and enhanced the rustic charm. When I stepped out of the car onto a carpet of pine needles, the soft scrunching sound and woodsy scent were inviting. It seemed like an enchanted woods with small cabins scattered under the trees. I felt as if I were in a new little world.

The theater stood majestically with white colonial columns and six paned windows flanked by green shutters gleaming against the white siding. I loved being in the throng of people gathered before the curtain call in front of the theater on the patio, or the wide long flagstone steps, or the paved area in front of the theater. That stage set is frozen in my mind in a collage of summers. Men and boys dressed in summer suits, navy or Madras blazers. The women wore sheaths and swirling summer dresses in a dazzling display of floral prints and bold solid colors as they stood in clusters chatting before act one. No one dressed casually in the evening or for the matinee. That first night, I stood quietly with my grandparents, listening and watching while they talked to their friends.

A noise, like the humming of hornets pierced the sound of chatter. The theater buzzer signaled that the play was about to begin. Conversational stragglers followed early arrivers to the inner sanctum. In exchange for a chance to see the play, local women from the Skowhegan and Madison, area armed with flashlights, ushered people to their seats, handed out programs, and chatted with familiar season-ticket-holders until the lights began to dim for the performance.

I had learned to dress appropriately when I traveled with my grandparents or visited them at the school in Newport. When I went to Lakewood with Winnie and Grampy in 1951, my mother packed my nicest clothes—my white dressy shoes with a strap and perforated petal design, my white anklets, and a cotton party dress with hand smocked stitching creating a maze of tiny diamond shaped gathers on my chest. I would be dressing for dinner at the Inn and the theatre. In the daytime, I had colorful matching shorts and tops to wear for walks around the colony to the Shanty or the Inn gift shop. Going to the theater to see the actors in a play was a special treat.

That summer when I was five, one of the waitresses baby-sat for me at the cabin. I attended the play until the waitress finished her shift at the

Shanty snack bar or at the Inn. Then, she took me back to the cabin during intermission because the eleven o'clock final curtain was too late for me. I was tired, but wanted to stay with Winnie and Grampy and not go off with the unknown waitress, even though she seemed nice.

One night I sat beside Winnie and Grampy with my feet propped on the edge of the varnished wooden theater seat in front of me. When the people in that row arrived and a man sat down, my toes, encased in the white leather shoes, became wedged in the small space as the seat was opened. I didn't say anything to Winnie. I suffered in silence until intermission, after trying in vain to free my shoes from the crack that painfully held me prisoner. I tried to concentrate on the play or the actors on the stage and hoped for a way to seruptiously ease my feet from the trap. To block out the pain as I sat waiting to be free, I became more keenly aware of my surroundings—the colorful sights, the humming sound of voices, and the unique scent in the theatre.

The smell of Lakewood Theater was distinctive. It was a combination of an old wooden building closed and unheated all winter, then refreshed by spring and summer breezes from Lake Wesserunset wafting through the doors and windows. Added to that, were mingled scents of hundreds of people discreetly perfumed and coiffured, and the smells of musty theater props and costumes. This combined with the scent of fresh paint, wooden seats, hardwood floors, old carpet runners down the isles, and the faint lingering odor of cleaning products.

The scent of Lakewood Theater was none of these individually, but if it had been bottled and placed on a counter with ten other odiferous potions of distinctive bottled air, I, and most other Lakewood regulars, could find L'Air du Lakewood Theatre with little difficulty.

Inside the theatre the walls were painted a warm, dark moss-green, accented by white molding and woodwork. The atmosphere was unique to Lakewood. The theater's small size and the location of our seats near the front contributed to my feeling of excitement and involvement when the curtain went up and the actors appeared. The grand finale curtain call caused a warmth of appreciation to envelope me as the cast held hands, bowed in unison, beamed their thanks to the audience and each other, then stepped aside for the featured celebrity to come running out and bow for another exuberant round of applause.

I knew the joyful feeling derived from applause. When our perform-ances in Aunt Teddy's shed ended, we smiled and bowed to a round of Aunt Teddy's, Auntie's, and Aunt May's clapping hands. The shed on Lower Main Street was our small version of Lakewood.

When the orchestra played for musicals, the musicians' presence added to the excitement of the show. Our seats were only a few feet away from the orchestra, and I watched them closely during the performance. The nuances of their expressions as they waited for cues, and their involvement with the music captivated my attention. As they played, I watched the pianist's fingers flutter over the keys and the percussionist wipe perspiration from his brow. I felt the music in my soul just as the people on stage did.

Inside the theater entrance foyer, a vivid red carpet covered the floor. Lighted glass displays featuring distinctive clothing from Dunham's of Maine and Hathaway shirt company added to the elegance. The walls were covered by hundreds of eight-by ten inch black frames containing autographed, black and white photos of famous actors and actresses who had appeared at Lakewood since 1900. As the years went by, I recognized more and more of them, because I watched countless old movies on chan-nel eight's Sunday Suburban Showcase.

Some of the older famous actors who appeared at Lakewood include: Ethel Barrymore, Charles Coburn, Keenan Winn, Vincent Price, Groucho Marx, Fay Ray, Cyril Richard, and Cornelia Otis Skinner. My mother told me that the 1930s were the best time for theater at Lakewood, because of the quality of actors and plays. When I was a teenager seeing plays in the 1960s the quality might have been reduced to game show hosts and pan-elists, but theatre goers still bought season tickets.

As the theater changed from featuring Broadway actors and a resident company in the 1930s to become a showcase for television actors in the early '50s and '60s, Lakewood featured packaged shows from New York City. In those days, we saw Henry Morgan, Tom Post, Peggy Cass, and Kitty Carlisle from the TV show *To Tell The Truth*. We saw Allen Ludden (of *Password* fame) and Betty White, who fell in love with Ludden at Lakewood and later married him. In 1962, my friends and I saw William Bendix, who was in the TV show *The Life Of Riley*, and in 1964 Nancy Walker was a featured performer. A few years later she was Rosie the waitress in Bounty paper towel commercials.

Another actor, Tom Tempest, appeared on stage at Lakewood from 1927 to 1952. Winnie and Grampy and I passed him on our way to the Shanty to get a newspaper for them and a vanilla ice cream cone for me. We stopped to chat because my grandparents knew him in the old days when they owned the Wassookeag School Camp. He sat in an Adirondack chair in the small island of grass and white birch trees between the Inn and the Shanty. He wore tennis whites, and a sweater with the traditional navy and burgundy border at the V-neck. White haired, with craggy features, a wrinkled face, and a wispy voice, Tom Tempest made me feel a little scared, but he seemed revered by Winnie and Grampy who spoke of what a fine tennis player he was when he and they were younger. The vision of him has lingered all these years after only one chance meeting, not so much because he was the essence of Lakewood, but because he was old and near the end.

Tom Tempest was gone in 1954 when Randy, Sally, and I accompanied our grandparents to Lakewood for the week-end. Grampy had arrived back in Dexter for the summer in the long, shiny black Cadillac that he used at the Hatch Preparatory School in Newport. The day of our excursion to Lakewood, my sisters and I slipped into the plush automobile with its soft gray flannel interior. We unfolded seats from the back of the front seat into the spacious passenger area, but didn't touch the button for the automated window between driver and passengers.

We knew we must not play with the silvery window buttons lest we repeat the accident of putting the window up as one of us looked out to say good-bye to our parents. So the three of us sat quietly and obediently in the back seat with our short feet sticking out straight during the ride through Ripley, Harmony, and Athens to our final destination of Lakewood in Madison. As the older sister, I was eager to show my sisters around the familiar resort and theatre.

When we arrived, the bell hop helped situate us in the white trimmed cabin with cedar shakes that gleamed a glossy brown the color of the molasses pull candy Winnie made. A black and white photograph shows the three of us girls, Prudy, Randy, and Sally, wearing identical outfits, posing spaced apart against the side of the limousine. As we stood for the photograph, I smiled a missing tooth grin and my fingers rubbed the puckery fabric of those green and yellow seersucker shorts and shirt with a Floridian palm tree print on the front.

We accompanied our play clothes with patent leather shoes and anklets, probably because our canvas play sneakers were too dirty and worn for a week-end at Lakewood. In another photo, Grampy posed with us by the rear of the car. I wore my favorite dress with a vibrant band of red around the middle of the skirt and bright colors at the top for a Mexican look. We were on our way to the Inn for dinner, before the play.

Twinnie Richards and Libby Mills, daughters of the original owners, greeted the Hatches from Dexter, exclaiming about the "lovely little girls." I felt so poised and privileged and proud of my such-a-big-girl status as we were seated in the dining room, dressed properly for dinner—three well behaved little girls glowing from the attention.

That was the one and only year we all went together to Lakewood with Winnie and Grampy. After that, we were each going to have a special time by ourselves with them at Lakewood. Since I was the eldest I went with them in 1955. The atmosphere in our bungalow was cozy, with warm knotty pine tongue-and-groove boards on the interior. A uniformed bell-hop settled us in, putting our luggage on the folding wooden rack at the end of the bed. Winnie, Grampy and I relaxed before dinner. Ice cubes clinked into their glasses as they fixed gin and quinine water for Winnie, whiskey for Grampy, and a gingerale for me. I opened *Life* magazine and looked at the photographs.

Winnie and Grampy were discussing an article in it about donating one's body for medical science. Winnie avowed that she fully intended to will her body to science, and when I showed concern about the possibility of her death, she assured me it would be a long time before that happened. I was proud that she planned to do something so good and helpful. Fifteen years later, when I sat in the second row of Dexter's Universalist Church at Winnie's funeral, I wondered if anyone remembered the noble thing she once told me she would do. Everything was different then, but the memories of the happy days of the '50s sustained me.

Winnie always let me buy something at the Inn gift shop. The shop was filled with beautiful scarves, Margaret Smith handbags of distinctive flowered fabrics, and decorative items for home entertaining. When I was five, I bought a miniature gray suitcase for my Ginny doll, with a tiny pink plastic comb and mirror which I took to Rhode Island later that summer. For a dollar, I also bought crepe paper balls with faces painted on the outside and surprise trinkets hidden in the folds and strips of paper. As I unwound the strips slowly, anticipation built as I discovered wonderful treasures.

Mrs. Swett, a friendly lady, ran the gift shop. She was about Winnie's age and had an unusual first name—Fanchia. Her deceased husband Herbert, a Bowdoin man like Grampy, was the founder of Lakewood. Her daughters, Twinnie and Libby, and their husbands were gracious and happy to see the Hatches and the rest of the regular crowd from Dexter. Decades later I met Mrs. Swett at a cocktail party in Skowhegan and told her of my memories. Her face lit up and she spoke nostalgically of her summers at Lakewood. Meeting her was one more coincidental connection with the past.

That night in 1951, we sat on peach colored wing back chairs and coordinating couches in the spacious lobby lounge with mellow wood walls the color of spiced pumpkin. When Bea Boardman, our cocktail waitress, appeared from The Trolley Room Bar, she brought me a gingerale with a cherry and a tiny floral print paper parasol that fit in my Ginny doll suitcase. I noticed how pretty Mrs. Boardman looked in her flamboyant, colorful, gypsy style skirt and off-the-shoulder blouse. She flashed a pleasant smile, bantered with the guests, and her dark hair glistened in the lamplight as she set drinks on the table before us. She and cocktail waitress Madeline Lloyd chatted with the guests until the dinner table was ready for us.

At the Inn's dining room, we liked to sit on the glassed in porch where sunlight streamed in. This part of the Inn had a view of the water and was more popular than the darker inner room. Lakewood's dining room was a vision of color with its well-dressed patrons and its furnishings. Each table had ladder-back, rush-seated chairs painted in vibrant yellow, red, or blue with multi-colored floral designs. At Winnie's and Grampy's lake side cottage in Dexter, I had a special little red chair with similar Tyrolian look floral designs. The sight of that chair in my home, even today, makes me think of the Lakewood Inn. I feel the gentle memories of those simpler days—of the beauty, of my innocence—before I knew what was to come—the deterioration and loss—in my grandparents' lives and in the vitality of Lakewood.

Outside the open dining room windows, the leaves rustled gently in the lakeside evening breeze, swooshing like a silk petticoat. Couples strolled by the shorefront and a few children played in the water. Inside the Inn, set-up girls and waitresses in yellow cotton print dresses scurried about and bus boys carried away trays of dishes. The chatter of guests sometime rose above a gentle murmur. Around the dining room, sat many couples from Dexter who came weekly for dinner and the play. Our Dexter neighbors—the Atwoods, Barstows, and Taylors—were Lakewood regulars, as were many other people from our town.

I have a page from the June 21, 1965 edition of the *Bangor Daily News* featuring the gala celebration of Lakewood's 65th opening. Grampy and Luke Atwood posed discussing the event. Under the picture, the text says it was Grampy's 39th consecutive opening night attendance. The summer of 1965 was a time when everything was coming apart financially for Grampy, a year or two before the sale of the stucco house on High Street and the humiliating move to a trailer. Nevertheless, he was there at Lakewood for the opening night in his old Louis of Boston summer sport coat, looking dapper despite the specter of financial doom and my grandmother's poor health. Grampy knew how to keep up appearances.

In the summer of 1957, when I was ten and my cousin Nancy Lea was eighteen, she had a coveted job at Lakewood Inn as a set-up girl. A summer at Lakewood as a waitress was like an extension of a college sorority. Waiters and waitresses had only breakfast and lunch off one day a week in a rotating schedule, to lie in the sun at the beach, to swim, or go boating. Then they were needed to serve dinner. Friendships developed and romances blossomed. If the student workers performed well, they could return each summer and earn tips while having free room and board and a small salary of seven dollars a week. The glamour of having new stars arrive each week for the featured play also made the job desirable. Getting an autograph or a chance to talk with the actors added to the allure of being hired to work at the Lakewood Inn.

Enid Tozier, a petite no nonsense woman, was in charge of all the waitresses, and she trained them well. The college girls were her charge and she chaperoned and oversaw their every move, making certain they didn't attend any cast parties and be exposed to the licentiousness of some of the guest actors. We saw her issuing instructions to pretty girls in floral print dresses when we were there for dinner.

A font of knowledge about Lakewood, Enid Tozier told me, "I worked at Lakewood for twenty-five years from 1939 to 1964 and knew the owners, the visiting actors, and the staff."

Sometimes we rode over to Lakewood for the matinee and to see Nancy when she was off-duty to find out how she was doing. Nancy and her waitress roommates led a carefree life until the family inspectors arrived. Winnie and Aunt Barbara were very concerned that Nancy Lea kept hundreds of dollars from tips and wages in a shoe box under the bed. The adults were appalled by Nancy's lack of concern and scolded her about the fact that her money might be stolen. Winnie thought the girl's cabin was a disgrace with shorts, shirts, underwear, uniforms, shoes, bathing suits and towels tossed carelessly about. She clucked and scolded, but she wasn't really mad.

Nancy Lea went back to Lakewood the next summer to work as a waitress, which meant she could earn more money than as a first year set-up girl. By then, she had finished a year at Elmira College. I went to visit her at Lakewood and to a play once or twice with my grandparents. On a few Sunday evenings, our whole family went to the famed buffet at the Inn. None of my sisters ever had a chance to stay alone with Winnie and Grampy at Lakewood, and I didn't again either, because the financial picture was beginning to change. I felt a sadness that everything was so different for Winnie and Grampy, but as a self-centered teenager, I also had other things on my mind—being with my girlfriends and finding romance, replacing one kind of romance for the past with another more tangible variety.

Once I was in high school, Lakewood became a place to meet boys. Going to see the plays was the vehicle. Several Saturday nights each season, Carol and I rode to Lakewood with family friends or my grandparents.

My most memorable evenings at Lakewood were in the summers of '62 and '63 when I was with the boys from the Wassookeag Camp who were bused to the plays. Those teen years were days of anticipation, of longing for romance and I played my role, costumed in clothes from Cortell Siegal instead of from Aunt Teddy's trunks.

My photo album shows Carol and me posing in the summer of '63, before we left for Lakewood. We had spent the afternoon at the lake in

Dexter, adding a deeper glow to our tans, making lengthy preparations. With our hair teased to perfection, wearing a little make-up, our fanciest dresses, and high heels, we felt like models for *Seventeen*. That summer I wore my white silk-look oriental sleeveless sheath with a sparse floral design of colors that I knew looked great with my tan. I hoped I would look alluring enough to wow a Wassookeag boy.

That was the summer of my last Wassookeag boy—Jeff from Scarsdale, New York. I was attending French classes at Wassookeag School Camp for Girls which was in its first season across the lake from the boys' camp. One Saturday evening Mr. May, the camp owner, reserved the club house at Lakewood golf course for a dinner dance and social for the Wassookeag Camp boys and girls. We danced to a record of Trinny Lopez singing, "If I Had A Hammer" rather than Big Bands as my father once had. On several other Saturdays that summer my sister, Randy and I went to Lakewood for plays and to see Jeff and Steve, her heart throb of the summer.

One evening while my sister and Steve talked, Jeff and I strolled by Lake Wesserunset and didn't hear the second act buzzer signal. We missed the last two acts of *The Unsinkable Molly Brown* as we walked on the water's shore, speaking with teenage fervor about philosophical, intellectual and personal ideas, and the constellations above us. Jeff was smart, and he wanted to be a doctor like both his mother and father. I was a wannabe intellectual, eager to soak in his genius. That night was not my last as a theater going teenager at Lakewood, but it was the beginning of the end of an era, for me and for Lakewood.

In the summer of 1970, my husband and I attended a play. That was the summer when Eddie Bracken, comedienne, would-be entrepreneur, bought Lakewood from the Swett family and had financial difficulties. A year later the Swett family regained ownership after foreclosure on Bracken Associates. One Saturday night I entered the familiar Shanty and was dismayed to find that the large, old-fashioned green marble soda fountain had been removed and replaced by a room full of vending machines.

I stood in the Shanty, in theater clothes, lamenting the modernization and loss of something that was unique. I felt such an emptiness and a chill of foreboding as I looked about the room. Someone had made the drastic change in the erroneous belief that mechanization would save salaries and expenses. Instead, it hastened Lakewood's demise, by taking away the ambiance, coziness, and charm of the Shanty.

Fifteen years later I saw the photographs that our friend Bill has of the early days at Lakewood. His collection once adorned the walls of The Trolley Room at the Inn, where guests gathered for cocktails served by Bea Boardman and Madeline Lloyd. Bill's old photographs are a testament to the other changes wrought by the decades at Lakewood. Some of the photographs were taken in the early 1900s when the trolley delivered guests from near-by Skowhegan. Other pictures are of the steamboat on which people cruised the lake before arriving at the resort. When I saw those pictures of early Lakewood, I realized more fully that each generation had to accept change in the name of progress.

In the early 1970s, Katie and Joe Denis tried to revive the theater and Inn. Skowhegan was in a state of excitement the week John Travolta arrived to appear in one of the productions. He was a hot commodity that year because of his fame as an adolescent idol on the TV show *Welcome Back Cotter* and the movie *Grease*. Having Travolta appear on stage was quite a coup for Lakewood. It attracted the younger set who might never have gone to the theater otherwise.

Under the Denis's management, Lakewood survived a couple of seasons. Times were a changing. Television, people's different interests, and the pace of life contributed to Lakewood's demise. Looking back now, I see that it was inevitable, but sometimes I still long for simpler and more elegant times when Lakewood was in its prime, before we all became so jaded by reality.

In 1973 my cousin Nancy came to visit, and we drove out to Lakewood to recapture the memories. It was as sad and depressing as could be expected when one tries to revisit a place of childhood memories. Many of the birch trees were dead or dying or gone. The Inn and theater were in need of a fresh coat of white paint. No people strolled by in tennis attire. The Shanty was shabby and contained the bank of vending machines flanking three sides of the room like silent inert robots. We drove through the winding dirt road past the cabin where Nancy and her waitress friends had stayed.

As Nancy and I walked into the Inn, we talked of the old days and the changes we had seen. We knew it was the end of an era, just as we knew it was the end of an era of log drives on the Kennebec River below our house. That summer of 1973 the river was jammed for the last time with logs on their way to the mill. From that date on, the river would be free of rotting logs and bark and open for recreational use, but from that day on hundreds of eighteen wheeler trucks would roll through town daily instead of delivering logs the old way—by the river.

In 1978, Lance Crocker and some partners bought the theater. They had grandiose plans to restore Lakewood to its days of glory. My husband and his partners were doing the accounting work so we had season tickets. We took our sons to see *Jesus Christ Superstar, Oliver*, and other shows. I still went to the Shanty during intermission to get my usual spearmint Lifesavers, but the place wasn't the same. Souvenirs were no longer for sale. The screen door to the Shanty still had the familiar squeak when I opened it, but the echo of the flagstone seemed louder because the place had lost its ambiance and was less busy.

Crocker and his partners survived for a while, but finally failed miserably causing the end of Lakewood as people had known it. That fall the Lakewood corporation went beyond Chapter 11 and declared bankruptcy. One bleak November Saturday in 1980 an auction was held to sell the buildings and their contents. I couldn't bear to go. I felt a futile sense of sadness all day, when I thought of everything being divided and sold.

The following morning I read the details in the newspaper. Someone bought all the framed autographed photos of the actors for one thousand dollars. Everything was parceled out to different people—the Inn, the

Shanty, the theater, the Colony House, the bungalows. It was a sad day for many people.

Our friends, Bill Laney and his sister Marge, went to the auction at Lakewood that I avoided. They remember the day as somber, chilly, overcast, and depressing. They walked through the Inn, where items were spread out for viewing before the bidding began. Bill hoped to buy the trolley photographs. As people walked by numbed by the cold and the finality, strains of piano music echoed in the cold dreary building.

Richard Webber, who had summered at a near-by cottage for years, sat at the keyboard as the essence of Lakewood was sold off in pieces. Dressed in his sheepskin coat, sitting erect at his favorite station, Richard Webber played *As Time Goes By*, *Autumn Leaves*, and other nostalgic songs. A retired English teacher who loved the theater, he was an old friend of the Swett family. In the end, Richard Webber was an actor in one of the final scenes of Lakewood, and the music he played couldn't have been sadder if it had been a funeral dirge.

Even though some people tried to revive the Inn and the theater in the 1980s, the attempts were ill fated. During the 1990s a loyal group of local theater buffs formed a community of amateurs to present plays. They continue to work valiantly to make improvements at the theater each year. Their organization, Curtains Up Enterprises, has renovated the historic theatre and purchased the Inn. In the summer of 2000, the completely renovated Lakewood Inn Restaurant will once more be open after nearly facing the fate of being torn down.

Dreams of returning Lakewood to its days of glory, and visions of what is possible with hard work, have motivated that group of people to save the buildings. Lakewood Theatre may never be what it once was, but the essence of it will be there in a new form. The amateur performances fill the void for many people, but not for me. The memories of the old Lakewood and of past evenings spent there, are too rich for me to replace with new realities.

I haven't attended a play there in decades, just as I didn't attend the auction. I prefer to remember Lakewood Theatre in its prime with a full house of patrons caught up in a dramatic or comedic production.

I envision the theater lobby, its walls resplendent with photos of Tallulah Bankhead, Ethel Barrymore Joan Bennet, Loyd and Jeff Bridges, Imogene Coco, Joan Bennett, Richard Dysart, Edward Horton, Darren McGaven, Kathleen Nolan, Betsy Palmer, Zasu Pitts, Arthur Rubenstein, Arthur Treacher, Tom Tempest, Vivian Vance, Dick Van Patten, James Whitmore, Humphrey Bogart, and hundreds of other performers, famous and obscure. The ghosts of seasons past linger on. Many of the actors are dead now. Others have gone on to fame, fortune or folly and failure, but they all no doubt remembered their summer engagements at Lakewood— The State Theater of Maine.

Prudy, Randy, Sally with Grampy at Lakewood—1954

Prudy, Randy and Sally in front of Lakewood guest cottage—1954

A DIFFERENT DEXTER

Dexter is definitely different now. I feel the difference with resigned acceptance as I drive into town and see what time has wrought. As I approach Dexter on the Corinna road, one of the first changes is that Avis Shaw's barn is gone. The fields, once fenced off for horses, stand empty. I think of my friends Cathie with her horse Pollyanna, and Diana with her mare Wendy, and of the shows where they once won ribbons, the young horsewomen, beaming with pride at the newly won awards pinned on their horses' halters.

Further up the road on the left, the street just doesn't look right. Don Brown's Market has been renamed Dexter Variety. The new owners purchased the store from the Warks who had torn down the adjoining rental house where my classmate Gary Gilbert once lived and where we had a sixth grade boy / girl party on his birthday. I wore a colorful blouse and a favorite, print polished cotton skirt flounced to its fullest with nylon net petticoats. We stiffly and shyly practiced our ballroom dancing skills that night, in 1958, in Gary's house which was attached to Brown's Market. The color of the large building matched the owner's name.

When I was a girl, we bought most of our groceries at Brown's Market and Lagasse's IGA on the other end of town. Until the early 1960s, Main Street also had a small A&P store and a small First National grocery store, but Don Brown's was the place where Winnie and my mother shopped. He delivered boxes of groceries if Winnie telephoned an order of items for a party.

My sisters and I often tagged along to help shop and get a treat. Randy usually chose a small jar of Gerber baby food custard for a snack. Sally liked animal crackers. I selected a small bottle of Baker's red cinnamon bits to eat on the way back to the cottage. The store smelled of the freshly washed, old wooden floor that creaked with age. The odor from the dark oily floor and cleaning solution combined with smells of fresh produce in various stages of ripeness and the aroma of meat in the white refrigerator display case. Sometimes, I peered through the glass at the disgusting, white, jiggly tripe. It looked like the inside of a foam rubber pillow that had come apart. Winnie said it was the cow's stomach. Thankfully she bought a rib roast instead.

Reggy Reeks worked at the market and he liked to tease us. Don Brown's name was like one word—Donbrown. He was a kind man, white haired, and quick to smile. Winnie loved to cook and entertain and she shopped there regularly for food. His father, old Mr. Brown, Sr. was in his eighties. He was stooped and failing, yet kept busy in his long white apron, stocking shelves and sweeping, helping his son manage the store that had once been his.

One day they were concerned because they had trusted the bread or potato chip delivery man and cashed a check for him only to have it bounce. Later, they learned that he had left his job as a route man and disappeared. It was an expensive lesson.

Now Dexter Variety is in the remaining section of what was once Brown's Market. It's a small white building that looks like an island in a parking lot. I prefer the memory of the sprawling brown buildings where Gary Gilbert once lived and Don Brown sold food and household goods to families in the leisurely way of a friendly local store. In the 1960s, a large competitor, The Red and White Supermarket (a forerunner to Shop and Save) was built further up the road.

Spring Street gets more and more seedy looking. Continuing on up the street, two houses beyond the left hand Lincoln Street turn-off, is a structure of red, white, and blue vertical strips of metal siding. It has a car wash and an office squeezed onto a small lot where someone hauled tons of gravel to fill in the sloping area and create a site for the building, which is an affront to the few genteel houses remaining on the street. Dr. Stewart's white colonial, where I went to be fitted for my eye glasses, is across the street from the car wash, and just beyond the car wash and office complex stands the other attractive older home where a chiropractor now lives.

Neither of those owners of lovely old homes was pleased to have their property devalued by the garish metal sided car wash, but Dexter has no zoning because people voted it down, fearing that their right to do what they wanted with their property would be infringed upon. As a result, Spring Street, the route that anyone going north must travel, is a pathetic hodgepodge of rundown houses that are victims of neglect, poor taste, and shoddy materials.

Oddly enough, that red, white, and blue building with the office in the front and the car wash in the back, now contains the customer files that were once in my father's Main Street office. The insurance company is under new ownership now, and the ground floor entrance makes it easier for the elderly and handicapped to enter, but I venture to say that the atmosphere is much different. Most people probably just mail in their bills and the money, and they surely don't pay five dollars on account each Friday.

I doubt that the atmosphere of the office is like that of a town gathering place. The accounts receivable are no doubt lower, and it's probably a more professionally run office, but I suspect those old timers who are still alive don't stop in, the way they did when the Hatch Agency was upstairs on Main Street and my father stood behind the oak counter. I doubt that many children stop by on their way home from school for pens, pencils, or rulers, and a look at the Dexter disaster and accident photos.

The kids ride by in busses now since the old neighborhood schools are gone. Elementary students are in the former high school on Abbott Hill, just as in my school days when we attended schools that had once been high schools before they were replaced with bigger, more efficient buildings. It's all part of the relentless cycle of change.

Across the street from the car wash / insurance agency and the chiropractor's house, is a church that was built on the site of the Spring Street School from which my grandparents graduated, and where I attended third and fourth grade. The school was torn down in the 1970s, and the layout of the land is different. Fill was hauled in to make the construction site higher. The old trees that I remember playing under during recess are gone. They once provided shade and a circle of splayed roots that we swept between with a handful of plantain stems as we played house all recess long. We'd gather sticks and little rocks to divide the rooms. We'd use acorn caps for dishes or make little pipes out of the hollowed out acorn bottoms.

Recess seemed so long, and perhaps it was because we could also go home for lunch. Sometimes I stayed at school for hot lunch. I liked the food, especially when they served what we kids called "Welsh Rabbit" on crackers or a scoop of mashed potato covered with brown gravy and meat, accompanied by apple crisp for desert. The canned grayish-green spinach wasn't very good, but having a nickel for a chocolate fudgecicle or an H Bar—chocolate coated vanilla ice cream on a stick—took away the bitter taste. The hot lunch ladies were friendly and knew me and my family. One of them was my Aunt Etha Ellms who was married to my Grandfather's brother. She would have a big smile and say, "Well, howah you today Pru-day?" and give me a good serving or just a little of the food I didn't like. After lunch, we had forty-five minutes for play around the tree root houses.

Beyond the church where the school used to be, there is a succession of dreary houses in need of paint and restoration. Someone has established a used car lot on the lawn of a big old house that has lost all traces of the character it once possessed. Another house offers a continual yard full of junk for sale.

Further up the road, one house has improved. Mrs. Fields' flower gardens of dahlias, peonies, petunias, and impatiens bloom profusely all summer, filling the entire front yard with color and providing something beautiful to look at amid the squalor of SprFing Street. Mrs. Fields' house looks better than ever.

Just before Mrs. Fields' flower filled yard is another symbol of modernity—the ubiquitous mini-mall—created in an area where once old houses and a small family owned grocery store stood. Beyond Mrs. Fields' house on the left, is the Sterling Hotel, a place where my father, on more than a few occasions, stopped to imbibe.

I have an article from a 1954 *Eastern Gazette* with the headline "Harvey's Car Takes To Bushes" printed above a photograph of my father's 1954 Olds parked at an angle in tall grass and bushes with trees in front of it. The headline under the photo says "Quick, Watson, The Needle!" The seven paragraph article beneath goes on to detail the editor's tongue-in-cheek humor and reporting of events in a sleepy town where anything is noteworthy.

"This week produced a red-letter page in the police records for the solution of two startling cases, which had the ear-marks of an audacious crime wave in Dexter."

"Case 1: A valuable memorial candlestick was missing from the Methodist Church when parishioners assembled for Sunday morning services. Case 2: Harvey Hatch's automobile suddenly vanished when he stepped into the Sterling Hotel (to make a telephone call). Police swing into action to recover the property and bring the culprits to justice. Five roadblocks were established surrounding Dexter to halt the automobile thief, with state police aiding in the action."

"Chief Knox and Officer Curtis questioned several suspects in the candlestick mystery. Pastor Hartwell Daley of the Methodist Church incorporated thoughts upon juvenile delinquency in his sermon. Eventually someone noticed the tire tracks heading down the hill by the Sterling Hotel. It didn't take a bloodhound to trace them to the foot, where Harvey's car was resting in the bushes with the front stove in against a tree—damage $500 (covered by insurance, naturally). Spontaneous locomotion was the verdict."

"Also, after a day out of town, a Methodist parishioner on hearing of the hue and cry, reported she had taken the candlestick to be engraved and thought Pastor Daley would have realized where it was."

I remember the excitement of Daddy's runaway car, and years later, I still find myself stealing a quick glance down over the hill by the Sterling where the overgrown field, bushes, and grass have been tamed and a house erected. Daddy always left his keys in the car. On another occasion, a few years later, his car was stolen one night from our driveway by some fugitives who took it to Houlton. Once the car was found, we had a family trip in my mother's car to Aroostook County. I was in awe and chilled fear to be riding home in Daddy's car that had been touched by real robbers, who left their Milky Way wrappers on the floor. After that, Daddy didn't change his ways. He still left his keys in the car and still went to the tavern in the Sterling, down on Spring Street.

Beside the Sterling was Bailey Motors, the last section of which was razed in the early '90s to create space for a Rite Aid drugstore. That building was abandoned in the late '90s and another Rite Aide was built near Fay Scott. Thus Bailey's garage and then the former Bailey house were both torn down for Rite Aid stores. The first Rite Aid, an ugly gray big box now stands empty.

Dexter, like so many other towns today, doesn't have many owners in the stores. That element of Main Street local businessmen and women is fast becoming a rarity. Now the money goes out of town rather than being circulated around to local businesses to make the town more self-sufficient. It's another sign of the times.

Bailey Motors was no longer selling cars when I was a child. They sold gasoline and provided storage space for cars in the winter. The old showroom was a place where our church, Messiah Mission, held rummage sales. Since the Episcopal church in Dexter had fewer than twenty-five members, counting the children, we all helped with the fund-raiser. I loved organizing and tagging the clothes, sweeping and picking up the area, and helping count the money. Working at the sale gave me an awareness of how some poor people lived in Dexter, and I felt proud of the generosity of the church ladies when they offered some needy family extra or free clothes.

Across the street from Bailey Motors was Dr. Taylor's office, where Daddy carried me wrapped in a blanket on the morning I slipped in the tub and grabbed the hot water faucet, turning it on, and scalding myself. I have a blurred image of that morning and the trip to see Dr. Taylor when I was three, and he took big silver tweezers to peel back the shriveled skin. It must not have been too bad because I have no scars from it, only the lingering memory.

Most of the time, Dr. Taylor made house calls when my sisters and I had mumps, measles, chicken pox, or scarlet fever. Mr. Marsh came by later and tacked a sign saying "Quarantine" to the clapboards on our house. I also saw Dr. Taylor in the hospital when I had pneumonia and was confined at Plummer Memorial for a few days. I was staying with my grandparents and after I became sick, Winnie called Dr. Taylor, who lived next door. When my parents returned from Boston, they brought beautiful red cowgirl boots. I outgrew them too fast. My mother put them on the top shelf in the cellar way and only took them down after I begged and pleaded to try them on and see if they would possibly fit again.

Dr. Taylor's former office, once an attractive white house on a hill, is one of the most butchered houses on the street now. The current owners enlarged it to ungainly proportions and re-sided the resulting structure with what appears to be Texture 111, that short lived grooved plywood-like material that looks okay for about a week. To further disguise and enhance it they applied swirls of stucco-like material and strips of brown wood on the seams for a pseudo Tudor effect. In addition, the lot and hillside behind have been bulldozed and gouged beyond repair with nothing planted to beautify the site or prevent erosion on the steep banking behind it.

Further up the road is Dr. Shurman's former office. Now the school superintendent's office is located there. Across the street from it, is the Big

Apple store. It dominates one corner and a tan-sided dentist's office stands where Kelton's restaurant once called to the locals. In the early and mid-1950s, Dexter's businessmen gathered for coffee in the morning or for lunch, families or people traveling through had supper, and the teenagers gathered after school to play the juke box, have a Coca Cola, and smoke cigarettes with their friends.

In 1957 when my mother, sisters, and I were in Newport, R. I. Daddy called from Dexter. While we were away, he came home Sunday morning after breakfast at Kelton's to discover that our cat had delivered six kittens. Sickened by the sight of the slimy newborn creatures, Daddy told us he lost his entire breakfast of juice, fried eggs, bacon, toast, and coffee.

Another event with Kelton's restaurant is when I had been at Carol's playing. We had covered ourselves in perfume and by the time Daddy came to get us and take us to Kelton's for a special treat of lunch, I was physically ill, nauseated by the sickening odor of the strong perfume. I went in the restaurant bathroom to scrub my neck with wet paper towels in an attempt to wipe off the offensive scent. Daddy let us choose a song from the small display case at our booth. Whenever I hear *The Yellow Rose Of Texas* my stomach feels queasy and I can almost smell the Tabu perfume.

At some point, the restaurant's name changed to The Scenic, because of the large wallpaper murals of woods and water. In the eyes of some adults, the Scenic and Kelton's before it, were a den of teenage iniquity in the afternoon. As a child, I certainly thought that only teens who were "fast" hung out there after school smoking and carousing.

That whole block where Kelton's or The Scenic and several other stores once stood, was destroyed in several spectacular fires that devastated the area and hurt Daddy's insurance loss ratio. Several small stores were sandwiched between the restaurant and Titcomb-Davis Clothing store for women. The most recent fire in 1978 wiped out the L-shaped section that rounded the corner and started down Main Street engulfing the building where the first Reny's and Fossa's store were located.

The Fossa family operated the store for sixty-five years. Jimmy Fossa and his wife, Ernestine, ran the store his father, Mario, established in 1918. That's where my father bought the candy bars he sold to Amos Abbott Mill workers.

As a kid I loved Fossa's store, where I could buy caramel Sugar Daddies, Smith Brother's cough drops, and full, luscious red lips, buck teeth, and black mustaches made of sweetened wax. Those treats also provided my ticket to Dr. Badgers' dental chair further up Main Street, a few houses below my friend Gene Kortecamp's house. I'd sit in the dental chair, gripping the arms, nobly thinking I was saving Daddy money, and sparing myself the needle by not having Novocain. As Dr. Badger's drill whirred its high pitched whine, I thought of the all the candy I bought at Fossa's and vowed not to go there to buy any for a long time. But eventually I did, just as Daddy still secretly stopped in at the Sterling for a shot or two.

When the fire destroyed the block where Titcomb-Davis, Reny's, and Fossa's were located, Fossa's was rebuilt with white siding instead of the conforming and more expensive brick. In addition, an incongruous sloped shed roof completed the replacement building, leaving an empty lot for parking where the clothing stores once stood. After Jimmy Fossa died, the building was sold. Now its siding looks weathered and shabby. A new printing business is located there now and the owners are making changes and fixing up the structure.

Around the corner on Main Street, untouched by the fire, stands the block that my father bought when he had to leave his office further down Main Street so the bank with a drive-up window could be built. After that, in the years after my parents were separated, Daddy's office was up over Reed's shoe store. His apartment was down the hall from the office, up over the Big L variety store.

The evolutions of the upstairs rooms in that building create a weird kaleidoscope of memories, syncronicities, and connections. Aunt Teddy used to attend the Gossip Club there. A 1915 photo shows her and friends holding sewing and sitting around the fire place, that decades later, was in

Daddy's office. Winnie went to those rooms for treatments with Dr. Wendall. Years later I had a permanent given by hair dresser Jerry Page whose salon was there. A few more years later, the Messiah Mission held church services in those rooms, after it moved from Mrs. Card's parlor.

Following that, the Draeskes, family friends, took possession of the block and renovated the rooms to use when they weren't in Palm Beach or at the lake. After they moved out, Grampy Hatch lived there for a while before going to the boarding home. Last of all, my father lived there for ten years until the day he died. The area that became my father's dining room and kitchen was once the room where Father Gardner put on his vestments.

Further down the street on the left was the Ben Franklin Five and Ten Cent store. Ben Franklin sold Evening in Paris perfume in the cobalt blue bottles, as well as handkerchiefs, Whitman Publisher's June Allison paper dolls, Trixie Belden books, and miniature china animal figurines.

The distinctive, tantalizing odor of Spanish peanuts roasting lured me into the store, up to the glass case. Daddy was often tempted, and so were Carol and I when we visited his office above Ben Franklin. We gobbled warm peanuts from the paper bag so fast that the brown skins fell to the floor around us like confetti.

Carol and I stopped by Ben Franklin for peanuts one summer day when Mrs. Bentley was sick and couldn't give Carol her usual piano lesson. The dollar for her lesson was too tempting to save, and as we went up and down the isles that summer of 1958, we spotted just what Carol needed—a bra. On the display counter, sectioned by size with narrow glass partitions, we found an alphabet of sizes printed above the jutting cone-shaped cotton mounds.

We walked left past the mounds of cup sizes E, D, C, B, and A to the double or triple A and found the perfect one. There were no dressing rooms, but 30 triple A seemed fine. The conical shape of spiraled concentric stitching on the thick cotton held its shape in tiny points like the metal brassiere of a Norse Goddess. When we bought the bra we felt like conspicuous thieves sneaking up to the counter to pay the ladies who knew us and our families.

In her green striped Girl Scout jersey, it was obvious that Carol still had some growing to do, but at least we both had bras now. I had a Loli beginner's bra that my mother bought for me earlier in the summer when we were in Bangor shopping. It was made of cotton jersey-like undershirt material and didn't project as much as Carol's.

When we were a few years older, Ben Franklin was also where we spent a quarter for a little red plastic container the size of a box of matches. The Mabeline mascara had a tiny slide out drawer with a tiny brush that we wet with water or saliva before applying to our lashes. That and Tangee Natural lipstick completed our cosmetic needs, except for a cobalt blue jar of Noxema, a little white jar of Arid or Mum cream, and an eyelash curler.

One night thieves broke into Daddy's office above Ben Franlkin. A 1965 article from the *Dexter Gazette* shows my father sitting in his large, doorless safe, on the sidewalk. The side of his head rests in his hand and he wears a chagrined look on his face. The caption says, "That's all there is; there isn't any more! Lloyd Harvey Hatch considers himself a lamentable replacement for the $1,900 which was stolen from the safe of his insurance agency Friday night." In the text of the article that follows, a Ben Franklin employee says she heard someone moving upstairs in the office at about 7:30.

The thieves, who were never caught, had rolled the 600 pound safe away from the wall, tipped it over onto a mat, and pried open the door with a heavy instrument. No one down stairs in Ben Franklin suspected a thing. They thought someone was cleaning. Besides, the stores and Main Street were busy, bustling with the activity that was typical for a small Maine town three or four decades ago when everyone went downtown to shop on the evening of pay day.

The former Ramsey and Gates furniture store, later became home for Ben Franklin. Now the building's tin ceiling and hardwood floors have been restored and the building turned into a pharmacy with a soda fountain, reminiscent of the one at the former Rexall. Locals gather at the counter savoring icecream shakes and soda's and the nostalgia. The people from away, who also own the print shop and Jere Abbott's house, have brought new life to the community. Their monthly newsletter even offers more human interest stories than the current Gazette, which mainly features advertisements.

Just down the street from the former Ramsey and Gates Store, stood the most popular gathering place in the town—the Park Theater. The movie theater was our window on the world away from Dexter. I have a huge jumble of memories of the movie theater spanning the years when I was about four until I was about sixteen—twelve short years of childhood that seemed like they would roll on forever. My first movie memories are of *Fantasia* and *Twenty Thousand Leagues Under The Sea*. Others include *The Seven Little Foyes, A Bell For St. Mary's,* and *Lily*. I loved the music from *Lily* and Winnie bought the record so we could hear it over and over. I laughed with my friends at scenes from the movie with Lucille Ball and Desie Arnez towing a camper trailer when everything spilled from the camper. In the following years I watched prison movies about "the big house," big sky westerns, Elvis, Troy Donahue and Sandra Dee.

One Saturday in my cowgirl days, I saw a newsreel with Will Rogers talking and telling stories with a drawl. I was fascinated by the way he twirled his lariat and did tricks with the rope as he talked. I walked up Main Street afterward with my own weighted crepe paper lariat, twirling it in a circle to step into and out of. I bought the lariat at Fossa's, or perhaps they sold them at the theater. Wherever I got it, the toy made fancy twirls and made me feel like a real cowgirl as I walked up Main Street hill practicing. My thick bobby socks kept my new beaded moccasins from slipping off as I jumped.

Main Street veers to the left and changes to Zion's Hill straight ahead. At the base of Zion's Hill people make a U-turn so they can go back up Main Street to find a parking space on the other side. In the fifties and sixties, both sides of Main Street had diagonal parking and the spaces were usually filled. Daddy kept his car in front of the office and received many tickets, but he needed his car handy. In a way it was thought of as Harvey Hatch's parking space—at least by Daddy, if not by Chief Harold Knox. With all of his errands, Daddy needed his car handy in front of the office. He'd make a trip to Whitney's to see the boys at the garage to talk over the latest results at the horse races or to get their $2.00 bets to take with him to Lewiston or Scarborough or Bangor. In the fall or winter they'd hash over the state of Dexter High's football or basketball teams.

Then Daddy would go back to the office until he had to get one of my sisters or me at school or had to go show a house he had for sale. Daddy couldn't stay at his desk or the oak counter for long. He had to be out and about Dexter, or, depending upon the season, to drive to Garland for peas at Lester Wyman's or to Ripley for corn or potatoes at John Brigg's or strawberries at Doug Britten's or to Exeter for maple syrup. Daddy always came home bearing gifts—food, fruit, baked goods, gum, or free samples from the mail—pens, pencils, or other advertising gimmicks. Once Daddy came home with a bushel basket full of inexpensive sneakers for us and was offended when my mother lacked his enthusiasm for the purchase.

One of the most thrilling ways I ever traveled the route through the center of town was on foot in a human chain weaving down Zion's Hill and through Main Street chanting jubilantly after the Dexter Tigers were victorious over the rival Dover-Foxcroft Ponies. After the playoff football game at Crosby Park, my friends and I, who were just barely teenagers, grabbed the hand of someone at the end of the chain of students. Fifty or more students (mostly female) joined in the celebration and snaked our way down the hill after the winning touchdown.

Excitement was in the air on the afternoons when Dexter won a football game. Cars honked, students cheered, and townspeople paused on the sidewalks. Shopkeepers watched from their doorways and waved from their windows. The whole town pulsed with energy and pride in the sports heroes. The D.H.S. cheer-leaders, dressed in matching red corduroy slacks, white blouses, and white sweat shirts, with little red silky scarves knotted at their necks, jumped and cheered in their white canvas sneakers.

The cloudless sky was cerulean with the September sun warming us. An afternoon football game drew most of the community out of their homes and yards. Along the street near Crosby Park, maple leaves glowed orange, red, and yellow on the stately trees above us as the chain of students wound under them. Time slowed down that afternoon, and the serpentine chain of teenage cheer-leaders and the football fans snaked down Zion's Hill, cavorting through the center of Main Street. Traffic backed up in a long line of cars with drivers tooting horns behind us, and the losing team had to endure waiting in line as Chief Knox directed the traffic and stopped everything for us.

There was nothing more heady, exhilarating, and carefree than the experience of being part of the human chain weaving down steep Zion's Hill. Breathless from the running to keep up, trying not lose our grip, we yelled the victorious chant, "We won! We won! We had a good team and we won. We won! We won! We had a…" Over and over, we all chanted with wild abandon giving more importance to the high school football game than anything else. The local gladiators, bruised, sweaty, and dirty, were back at the school locker room showering. Main Street pulled the town together in celebration of a sport that generations of young men had played, giving Dexter its reputation as "a football town."

Across from Ramsey and Gates Furniture, was Koritzky's Department store, where Daddy's friend Max Glazier worked, and we shopped there for shoes and clothes when we were little. In the shoe department, a plastic Wonder Horse on a wooden platform with springs to make it rock or bounce occupied all the little buckaroos while their siblings were fitted for saddle shoes or brown Oxfords. Our little sister Susie got a Wonder Horse for Christmas one year, but I was too big to ride it then and my cowgirl days were over. In 1959 or so, Koritzky's went out of business in Dexter. Then Dexter Hardware occupied the store when I was in seventh grade.

One of my most distinct memories is of the day I was on top of the three story, flat roofed building with Mrs. Wilson's sons and another boy. The thing I can't remember is, why I ever went with them on such a fool-hardy adventure or how I ever got away from them once we were on the roof. Perhaps I felt safe with them because their mother, Mrs. Wilson, had a private nursery school in her home on Pleasant Street which my sisters Randy and Sally attended.

That Saturday after the matinee, I went with the Wilson boys to Daddy's office to get them free pencils and pens and then tagged along with them afterward. For whatever reason, I found myself with them, behind Koritzky's climbing up the steep bank below Highland Avenue and leaping onto the flat roof.

I soon was filled with feelings of regret and foreboding. The boys were being boys, showing off for each other. I remember realizing that they were urinating over the side of the building because of their joking laughter and their positions back to me. I didn't want to see what was usually zipped inside their pants and I wanted to go home. It was that same sinking feeling I had when Philip and I were stranded in the cemetery in the deep snow, only this seemed worse. I was scared, nervous, worried, and regretting my foolish decision to go with older boys to explore.

I remember using false bravado and my wits to get me out of there. I kept my distance on the other side of the building and somehow, eventually, was safely on the street, on my way to Daddy's office or our house on upper Main Street. I know I was about eight years old. I also have a faint memory that someone saw a bunch of kids on the store roof and came to get us down or perhaps we were heard walking about the roof. Whatever happened, I came through the episode physically and visually unscathed, but more savvy about the wisdom of being the lone female with a bunch of older boys.

Reny's is now located in the former Dexter Hardware. It is the Main Street shopping Mecca for many, with its various departments and bargains. Another spectacular fire caused significant damage to two blocks of stores in the 1980s. As a result, Reny's became larger once the damage was repaired. The old Rexall Drug store and the Dexter Club above it were so damaged that the top floor of the building was torn down. Gone is the section where we had ballroom dancing lessons, the thirteenth birthday party for my friend, Cathie LaBarge, with boys in suits and girls in party dresses, and where wedding receptions and class reunions were held. Our parents gathered there for New Year's Eve parties and our fathers met for Monday night dinner, drinks, and card games while others played pool.

In the 1950s, the Dexter Club was selective about its membership. I learned what it meant to be black-balled. These days, anyone and everyone can belong to the club, and the mystique and eliteness of belonging have gone.

The Dexter Club was also a place Carol and I secretly visited after school and on Saturday afternoons and evenings in our sophomore year of high school. Our friend Steve Bassett's father was president of the Dexter Club, so Steve had access to the key. In the winter of 1963, we sat watching television in the Dexter Club lounge as Skip Chapelle shot baskets at the University of Maine. I didn't care much about the basketball game, but Carol, Doug, and Steve did.

We enjoyed the freedom and the furtiveness of our clandestine use of the club. The boys also liked using Bartolo Sciliano's personal pool cue that unscrewed and came apart to fit into its own leather case. Steve and Doug used the cue carefully, then put it back on the shelf near the piano. Years before, Mrs. Gudroe worked the keys on that piano while my friends and I had waltzed around the room during our ballroom dancing classes. However, we didn't dance during our high school visits at the Dexter Club.

For months we had the place to ourselves, until someone became suspicious that teenagers were sneaking into the club. Perhaps they found out because one Saturday night, when Carol and I were supposedly at the movies, we were actually spending an evening at the club. We left the upstairs rooms to go buy soda and chips at Fossa's. As we were about to open the door and step on to the Main Street sidewalk, Carol and I paused briefly to discuss the best method of exit. Carol thought we should slowly inch the door open and then, after carefully scrutinizing the sidewalk and street, we would step out. I favored a bold, exit to get it over with quickly, wrongly figuring that it would attract the least attention.

Unfortunately, as I hastily thrust the door open and we leaped onto the sidewalk, Mareka Carter and her husband, friends of Carol's parents, drove by and turned to notice us bounding out of the Dexter Club doorway. We knew she had seen us, and we also knew she was on her way to the same party that Carol's parents were attending. Later that evening when the movie was over, Mrs. Carter rode along with Carol's father to give us a ride home.

"How was the movie girls?" she asked pointedly.

"Oh, it was good," Carol said with forced enthusiasm.

"Really? What was it about?" Our antagonist pursued.

Carol managed a suitable answer by the time they dropped me off at my house. I didn't envy Carol for her ride home. She managed, but shortly afterward our secret was revealed. Steve Bassett nearly choked at the dinner table the night his father commented that someone had apparently been breaking into the Dexter Club and using the facilities, as well as using Bartolo Sciliano's prized pool cue. The revelation curtailed our use of the club.

The town office building, with Dexter's version of Big Ben on top is a three story structure that housed the Central Maine Power office, as well as the municipal office for the town manager, secretaries, and the police. Sandwiched between those ground floor offices is a doorway that leads to offices above. Dr. LaBarge's office was upstairs, as was the water company where The Wiggly Woman worked.

We children watched her, fascinated by her long, wispy black hair that hung down her back like a fringed shawl, swaying as she walked. Her shoulders and entire torso twitched back and forth as she walked to the house where she lived with her elderly father. She was short and

Kewpie-doll-like, with rosy cheeks, a enigmatic, Mona Lisa smile, and a terrified, furtive look in her eyes, like that of a captured creature. She seemed shy and seldom spoke. Her walk was nervous rather than sensual, with one shoulder and then the other quickly turning in, causing some to call her Miss Twitchit. She seemed scared of people, even children.

As a child, when I was on the second floor of the town office building, I looked from the dark center hall of the second floor into the office where The Wiggly Woman worked. I saw her walk about the office in her straight black skirt and sheer pink nylon blouse, shoulders moving back and forth as she went from her desk to the files.

At the time, I was with Winnie while she had her hair done at Madeline Pratt's beauty parlor. I smelled the strong aroma of chemicals from permanent wave solution, dyes, and shampoos in large brown glass jugs. Pictures of Breck Girls and their sleek beautiful hairdos covered the walls and the back pages of all the magazines.

Further up Main Street, across from the traffic light on Church Street, is the Abbott Memorial Library and on the little street near the library is the Universalist Church. The interior still looks much as it has for over a hundred years. A large, newly refurbished Estey pipe organ graces the chancellery, in front of a sea of pews or so it seemed when I was little, rehearsing in my colorful crepe paper flower costume for a Spring pageant under Carrie Palmer's direction.

At the Universalist Church I attended Sunday school classes, nursery school, and years later, participated as a guest in youth group activities with the Methodist teen group joining the Universalist. Before we switched to the Episcopal Church, when I was in the fourth grade, and still attending Sunday School at the Universalist Church, certain events there created images that are forever imprinted in my memory.

I remember reciting and hearing other people say nursery rhymes especially, "Peter Piper picked a peck of pickled peppers…" I'm not sure what year that was, perhaps it was the nursery school year, but I think it was Sunday School. I remember complaining at some point a few years later to another child about what we were learning at Sunday school. Even then, I had strong opinions of what was good, enjoyable, fun, interesting, and appropriate, but was too meek to voice them other than to a friend.

When I was in the third grade, I went with my friend Brenda Willard and her mother to the Cambridge Baptist Church, just up the road from Carol Whitney's grandfather's general store. At the Sunday school the children gathered for a class and placed felt shapes on a flannel board to tell Bible stories. I was drawn in and could see by comparison that such interesting Bible study was missing from the classes at the Universalist Church.

I was quite chagrined and embarrassed later when the Universalist Sunday School teacher asked me what I liked better about the other Sunday School. Apparently, my outspoken critique had been overheard or reported to her. Then, as now, I was better at expressing myself on the sidelines, rather than openly in a confrontation.

In Dexter in the 1950s and 1960s parades and celebrations were a big thing. The survivors of World War I and World War II paid tribute to those who had fought on foreign soil to defend freedom, and in Dexter they did it well. When I was a Brownie, attending meetings at the old fire hall, and later a Girl Scout going to meetings at the new fire hall, we marched in the parades.

For Memorial Day and the Fourth of July, children decorated doll carriages and bicycles using colorful crepe paper strips and clothespins for playing cards to flap against the spokes. The high school and N.H. Fay School bands, along with Waterville's R.B. Hall band for adults, played patriotic marches. Old soldiers and young did their distinctive boot shuffling march through Main Street, bearing flags in their ceremonial pilgrimage to the war monument. They placed a wreath at its base, and the chaplain or minister evoked a prayer for those lost in the war.

As young teenagers, we thought them stuffy and overly patriotic with their uniforms, solemn faces, stiff marching, and covering their hearts with hats in hand. The remaining Doughboys were elderly by then, and each year fewer and fewer of them marched in the parade. The W.W.II men, those who fought in Korea, and those in the reserves marched in full military dress. The VFW ladies, mostly old and over-weight, seemed proud and connected to the memory of something we could not fully understand, despite our seventh grade study of both wars and the music that inspired those on the home front and on the battlefields of Europe. I never grasped the full import of it all until the spring of 1995 and the following months as the 50th anniversary of the War's end made it real, with the personal televised stories of old soldiers, who were once fresh faced boys and young men, and later, the fathers of my contemporaries.

One Memorial Day as we gathered by the monument and the chaplain read a prayer to those who died, my friends and I were whispering and someone laughed at a crucial moment in the solemn remembrance. I can still remember the embarrassment when an adult had to turn with a stern look and an audible shushing reprimand to the rude students. Because of what I learned in Mrs. Mealey's seventh grade class, I was trying to listen and feel the sadness that young men had died, but still I was a part of the group.

After the invocation and placing of the wreath at the base of the monument, the crowd slowly dispersed to follow the bands, the soldiers, and other marchers for the final tribute. We marched by Alice Dugas' beauty shop, Dr. Taylor's new office, and across the street to the pond by Amos Abbott Mill where the minister said a prayer for those who died at sea. There another wreath wrapped in red, white, and blue ribbons was thrown into the water. As the scent of lilacs wafted in the air, people stood in respectful silence while one of the band members, who had quietly moved to the far edge behind a tree, played taps on his trumpet. I felt a tingle of patriotism and awareness of the import when I saw a few people with handkerchiefs dab at their eyes before the crowd dispersed for the day, and those who had cottages on the lake went to open them for the season.

As I retrace a route through the Dexter of past and present, I am struck by the significance of the area where the Universalist Church, the library, the town hall, and the Civil War memorial are all located. In the 1970s, the old town hall received a much needed new coat of paint, compliments of Vaseline Intensive Care hand lotion. As part of their advertising campaign, a film crew traveled to towns around the country filming ordinary people gathered as a community to paint a local building. In the segment, townspeople gathered on the street near the church, behind the library, and in front of the war monument. They clapped their work-worn hands (smoothed by Vaseline Intensive Care Lotion) and sang the same song that others in communities around the U.S. sang, "Working hands, working hands…"

When I saw the ad, I remembered all the Memorial day parades—a time of pride swelling in chests wearing tight old military uniforms. In the 1970s, those veterans were in their late forties or early fifties. Now, I realize that most of those men, like my father, are gone forever and the sense of belonging to the vital working and growing community of Dexter's prime is also gone. Those who remember the past work to bring forth a new Dexter.

Fall 1992

Throughout August the acceptance letter for the writers' retreat lay on my desk, on top of the untouched stack of stories to rewrite. Every time I passed the desk, my spirits were buoyed just to know that I'd be at the retreat in September.

In anticipation, I looked through the folders bulging with drafts, lists of ideas, images, and partially finished stories, wondering which story I would start. Two years had slipped by since I had last worked on my collection at a writers' workshop. In moments of solitude, while I ironed, cleaned, gardened, or drove, I let myself think of the writing. I created phrases in my head, shaped ideas into words for stories, but they were lost because I didn't have a pen or tape recorder handy.

When I thought about the writing, I kept going back to the idea of rewriting the story of my egocentric adolescence and the summer of '62 when I met John Steinbeck IV. I searched the folders for his newspaper obituary and became obsessed with finding it. Although it seemed lost, I wouldn't give up. I spent three hours at the newspaper office looking at microfilm, searching unsuccessfully for the words, "Elsewhere" and "John Steinbeck IV" underneath it.

As I scanned the microfiches, it was eerie to be reminded of all the people who had passed on, to see the same "In Memorium" pictures and poems that I have noticed in the paper for twenty years.

In a way, the futile search for the elusive article was just another way to postpone writing. I found the obituary weeks later in my 1990 U.N.H. poetry folder, but by then summer was over, school was in session, and I was too busy with my job.

That summer of 1992 I hadn't let myself work on the drafts, partially because I knew if I started writing again, it would be all-consuming. Before I could write, I had to finish building a rock wall for my perennial garden.

I carried rocks from the woods, and when that proved exhausting, I backed my Blazer under the power line and loaded it five times. When that wasn't enough, I bought some rocks at a demolition site, and my husband helped me get a load at an old gravel pit. The garden site kept growing.

I was inspired by the vision of how beautiful the area would look. In addition, I had ordered two truck loads of loam for the project and the dirt had to be used up before the snow came. In fact, my deadline was sooner. I gave myself until August 26, because once the gardening was completed, I had to prepare for going back to school. By early September, teaching preparations were behind me, and I needed to focus on our son's Labor Day week end wedding and to finish the garden.

Although I didn't write a word during that time, I rationalized that I needed to garden more than I needed to write. Gardening had become therapy for me. In June, after a school year of working with disadvantaged children and their families, I needed the peace and tranquillity of digging in the soil, arranging plants, creating a colorful garden, and having some control while making beauty and order in the world.

I lost track of time as I worked. With so much restorative solitude and contemplation while I toiled, I began to think of the past. I built up the soil with peat moss, manure, and new weed riddled loam and I thought of Winnie's garden's of zinnias, marigolds, and geraniums at the lakeside cottage.

As I dug in the soil, transplanting phlox, potentilla bushes, coreopsis, impatiens, and daisies, thoughts of my father crept into my mind. I could see him in his diminished condition and wanted to banish the vision of his vastly changed looks and personality. Whenever I telephoned to talk with him, he seemed disinterested, eager to be off the phone. I knew it was because of the effects of the stroke, his depression, and other illnesses that made him weak, but that knowledge didn't take away the sadness and hurt feelings after the conversation. His voice was no longer slurred by the effects of alcohol, but now with the ravages of stroke. I forced myself to think of better days in the 1980s when he was sober, attending AA, and feeling well—Harvey Hatch in his prime. That was the man I wanted to remember, the man who was a font of historical facts about Dexter and its people.

Lately, he seldom spoke of the old days in Dexter or the people. With the stroke, he lost not only his mobility, he lost his zest for life, and his connection with the past. Sometimes I thought I could carry the torch of remembering, chronicling the stories, the memories, and the events of our family and Dexter.

Then I would be overwhelmed by the idea. There were so many details I didn't have. On the other hand, I was overwhelmed with pages and pages of details in folder after folder of unfinished writing, nagging me, like dusty furniture, unread books on the shelf, or unwatered houseplants. I had, somewhere, a videotaped interview with my father and audio tapes of when he spoke of the '20s and '30s and his father's summer school on Lake Wassookeag. I lost more hours of writing time searching for the safe place I had packed them before the move to our new house.

I efficiently set up more road blocks for writing, but the gardening goals were the most effective. I finished the gardens just in time to prepare for our wedding rehearsal dinner responsibilities.

We had a beautiful whirlwind weekend of wedding activities, with old friends and family. The Hatch side seemed pitifully diminished, and my father's absence was noticeable, but I put it out of my mind and celebrated the day and the reunion with family and old friends.

I wanted to slow down time so I could savor the day and the time with those friends who I seldom see, now that we live in different parts of the country. I realized how fortunate we were that events merged and that we met by chance or fate, to forge friendships that could pick up after months of busy lives and no communication.

I felt sadness and acceptance that Andy's and Adrian's marriage was over. Our children grew up together, hiked the trails of Baxter Park, skied the slopes of Sugarloaf, and swam in Lake Wesserunset. Now they were grown and the relationships had changed.

We visited with Penny and Adrian who were now both single and chatted with Andy who was there with his new girlfriend, Melissa. The excitement of the day took the edge off the awkwardness of seeing our old friend with someone new. Andy and Melissa stayed for a few days after the wedding. We climbed Mt. Katahdin with our son Andy and his wife Angela before their return to Chicago.

Two days after the wedding, I returned to school, still reeling from the activity, hurrying home to cook for a dinner party for Andy Lilburn, Melissa, and mutual friends. I was on the treadmill to disaster, but as usual didn't recognize the signs.

After the second evening of entertaining friends for dinner following a day at school, I seemed to be coping competently with the work load. I was getting back into the routine of teaching children whose families move often.

My job required me to make visits to the homes of all of my students who have been in the program for up to five years and to recruit the new students who had recently moved to the community and qualified for Migrant Education services.

On Thursday of the first week, as I left for a home visit, I backed my new Blazer into the side of another teacher's van, doing $1700. damage to my vehicle and $1100. to hers. That was just the beginning. At 5:00 P. M. I was called back to the school by the sheriff, because coincidentally, the same day, another teacher's new car was victim of hit and run and they thought I had done it. (What did they think that I'd done a demolition derby?)

After I was cleared from suspicion, I returned home, shaken, fatigued and itchy for I soon discovered that I was covered with poison ivy from ankles to thighs and on my arms from weeding. I would wake up in the middle of the night and rub my legs raw with a cold, wet wash cloth, then slather on calamine lotion.

So, itchy and tired I went about my job as best I could, proceeding to lock myself out of the car at one home visit. I had to crawl through the plastic wrapped rear window of the Blazer to unlock the door. The next day I ran out of gas after a day of traveling on back roads and being too consumed with work to notice the gauge. I bought lawn mower gas from a man and was soon on my way.

The week was more hectic than the usual beginning of school, because our program had received grant money from Scott Paper Company to take nine area students to the Maine Conservation camp at Bryant Pond. We rode in a van with another teacher and her students, arrived safely, and had a wonderful weekend learning about habitats and nature. I shared a room with the Migrant teacher from Dexter, and by Sunday, knew I was coming down with the cold from which she suffered. The sleepless itchy nights had lowered my resistance and the Prednisone tablets had little effect.

Exhausted, I stayed home Monday and Tuesday to sleep and ward off further illness. By Wednesday, the cold was worse, but I went to school anyway. On Thursday, since my Blazer was in the auto body shop, I asked a friend for a ride to school. Another friend and her daughter gave me a ride home. We chatted and laughed about the trials, tribulations, and mishaps of the past three weeks.

When we arrived at my house, I invited them in for a glass of juice and a chance to visit more. Our lives had been so hectic that we'd hardly had a chance to visit since the wedding. As we stood on the doorstep, I flipped through the keys for the right one, hurrying because I could hear the phone ringing in the background.

"Come on in," I said as I bounded to the phone to answer before the caller hung up. It was my mother.

"Harvey died this afternoon," she said.

"Harvey died this afternoon." I replayed the words in my head. Harvey? Daddy? I listened trying to comprehend the unexpected news, absorbing the details. As my mother talked I pictured myself at three o'clock sorting papers on my desk at school, getting ready for a staff meeting while my father was carried on a stretcher out of his Main Street apartment, which was just down the hall from his former office. My friend and her daughter stood in the living room waiting and wondering. I felt like a clod listening to my mother while they stood and waited, but I couldn't find a way to tell my mother I had company.

As my mother explained the possible arrangements and arrival of relatives, I turned to my waiting friend who had decided to leave. "It's my mother. My father died this afternoon," I whispered apologetically, holding the phone away from my mouth, my ear, and the detailed explanation I was still trying to fathom.

"It's okay," I mouthed the words, not wanting her to feel more uncomfortable. Not quite knowing what to do under the circumstances, and my detached announcement, she and her daughter left.

I stood by the large window, phone in hand, looking out at the lavender phlox, tall and bright, with a background of green. As the details made the message more clear, I realized I wouldn't be able to go to the writing retreat. I tried to figure out a way to handle it all, make funeral arrangements, mourn, fulfill responsibilities at school, and still attend the writers' retreat.

Calmly I listened to the information about my father's last moments, feeling twinges of guilt for my selfish, yet undeniable desire to still attend the writers' retreat. A fleeting thought crossed my mind, memories of activities and performances that my father missed because of a trip to the horse races. I erased the thought lest I feel like a whiny adult Ann-Landers-letter-writer.

As my mother and I talked and later after we said good-bye, I tried to figure a way to plan the funeral for Monday, which would allow time for arrangements and travel by relatives, and for me to go to the retreat. Finally, I began to let go of the idea, to face the loss of my father, as well as the loss of the opportunity to finally begin working on the collection of stories about family members and growing up in Dexter. I chided myself for the inappropriate thoughts.

I thought I had gotten used to the idea that my father, with his failing health, might not live out the year. He was just a shadow of the man he had been, and I wouldn't have wished him more days of such a life. Yet, preparing myself for this moment didn't make it any easier. That evening was a blur of long distance phone calls, hours on the phone with my sisters, dealing with plans and overwrought emotions.

I woke up the next day, like a child with a new injury, knowing something was special or different. Then in the first seconds of waking, I remembered and my spirits became heavy with the finality of the news. A night of fitful and odd dreams had left me feeling tired. The poison ivy still itched and my nose was stuffy from the head cold.

I got up at 5:30, as usual, thinking that I was not going to Norridgewock to work with students, but to Dexter to make funeral arrangements for my father. As I drove North that morning, I thought about the ordeal ahead, mentally listing each of the things we must do: choose Daddy's clothes and casket, meet with the funeral director and the minister, choose songs that would be uplifting, and arrange for the service, one that was not too religious.

My thoughts were a jumble. I finally had come to the decision that I would leave for the writers' retreat after my mother and I made the funeral arrangements. At moments I felt twinges of shame that I had decided to go, imagining other people's reaction. Yet, it seemed more vital now than ever that I go to Tanglewood. I needed to write, to sort through my grief and memories. This would be the beginning of a memorium to my father, my tribute to honor him as I wrote the stories he had told me.

I hardly noticed the exit signs or towns as I sped up I-95 toward Dexter. My mind sorted and sifted the memories, the realities of my father's death, the stories I had written. My stories about Dexter and family members have usually been precipitated by a death or funeral, or thoughts about changes or losses. In 1980, I wrote my first story, about Mac. That paper became a learning tool as I rewrote it in 1982 and 1984 for four different instructors. During the process, I came to a better understanding of Mac, my father, and grandfather as I questioned Daddy for details.

When I reached Dexter, I drove first to my father's former office which was connected to the apartment where he lived after he left the nursing home. With round the clock CNA caregivers, he was able to live his last months in familiar surroundings of his apartment, just fifteen feet down the hall from where he had done business for fifteen years. Instead of going straight to see my mother at the house where she lived alone, I felt a need to talk first to Norma, Daddy's secretary, to get some balance and receive condolences before facing the ordeal of making funeral arrangements.

My parents had been separated for years. It hadn't been easy for my mother to live with my father over the decades, but she had done a great deal for him in the year since his stroke. She overlooked his cantankerous, irascible personality change and arranged for women to take care of his medical needs.

Talking to Norma, hearing her words of comfort, her honest memories of the good days and the bad, Daddy's good points and foibles, helped me remember my father as he had been before the stroke. As Norma talked about Daddy for the first time I felt tears well up in my eyes.

"Your father had such a memory and such a love for Dexter. People would call up and ask him about a football game—was it 1950 or 1951 when Dick Barstow ran how many yards to score a touchdown and your father knew the answer. People brought in fifty or sixty old pictures for him to identify and he would know the places and the people.," Norma said.

As I started to go back down the stairs of the office, I glanced at the closed apartment door, and thought of the hundreds of times I had climbed the stairs to visit him. I thought of Daddy's old office that had been torn down and remembered how being Harvey Hatch's daughter had such significance when I was little. I remembered how that inspired me to write *THE ERRAND* during my freshman year at UMF as a 36 year old student studying egocentrism in a Developmental Psychology class.

I got in the car, my head still full of images and memories, and drove up Main Street to see my mother who still lives in the house where we all once lived. She and I talked over the arrangements, made lists, then made phone calls. After the calls, we drove down to the apartment where Daddy lived and died. It is the same one where my grandfather lived in the mid '70s in his declining years. The apartment had been remodeled for the Draeskes, a wealthy couple who summered in Dexter, and wanted an interim residence for the fall when it was too cold to be at the lake. They rented it in the '70s to Grampy and later sold it to my father after the old office was torn down and my parents had separated.

When I stood in the 1960s paneled dining room, I tried to picture the room as it looked when it was the chapel for Messiah Mission, the Episcopal church my sisters and I attended as children and teenagers. The apartment kitchen had been the room where the priest changed into his vestments and gave us confirmation instruction.

The room that housed my father's dining room had many other lives. In the 1950s, it was a waiting room where I sat while Dr. Wendell, an odd man in a white lab coat looking like a silent mad scientist, gave Winnie her "treatments." I think he was a chiropractor. Later a hair dressing salon was located there, and Jerry Page gave me a permanent that made me regret the decision.

It was strange to see the dining room with boxes of old photographs on the floor, my old maple bed, with cannon ball posts, standing in the corner by the picture window, and Mac's prints of dogs playing poker hanging on the wall. The faded, drooping linen drapes, ordered by the Draeskes in the 1960s, still hung in the huge windows.

As I was looking around, two of the women who took care of Daddy in round the clock shifts, arrived to meet us and talk of his last day. I steeled my self for the job we must do—selecting clothes for Daddy to wear—but it was obvious that I needed to comfort DeeDee who was visibly upset over my father's death. (I was a typical ACOA co-dependent woman, focusing on another's grief instead of my own.)

During the past two years, DeeDee and Daddy had forged a bond and a friendship as she helped and encouraged him and listened to him talk in the evening when he couldn't sleep. A mixture of feelings flooded me. Part of it was sadness that I had not been as close to my father in the year after the stroke. Part of it was a twinge of resentment that DeeDee was closer, but mainly it was gratitude that she came into Daddy's life to help him through the most difficult time he had to face. She did what my sisters and I couldn't do living an hour or two away and working full time. It was natural that she was close to him and good that he had a non-family friend to talk about his fears and angers after the stroke debilitated him. My time for being my father's keeper was in the 1970s and 1980s when he was drinking and later when he was sober and well, having dinner with us and attending our sons' sporting events.

As we talked with DeeDee, I opened the closet to find clothes for my father. I saw two sport coats—a tweed and a seersucker—and the Glen plaid suit.

"Daddy always wore this suit to weddings and funerals. I guess he should wear it to his own funeral," I said aloud. I looked for the maroon and navy striped tie and reached for a blue button-down-collar shirt with pills on the neckline. Might as well be sensible and leave the nicer all cotton oxford cloth shirt for someone to wear later, I thought.

It's odd the thoughts that run through a person's mind during times like that. I kept thinking of what I had said. "I guess Daddy should wear the Glen plaid suit this last time for his own funeral." It sounded so callous, yet it had an ironic, literary tone. When I reached for the suit, I winced thinking how big it would be since Daddy had shrunken to a skeletal form. I thought of a comment my brother-in-law once made when referring to a man who had a puffed up opinion of himself, "We all go out with a suit slit up the back," Bob had said. I pictured the fine worsted wool of Daddy's suit being cut up the back to make it fit his slender, emaciated body and shuddered. I knew I wouldn't see him in the suit. I had no desire to see Daddy in the casket as my sisters did.

As we put the clothes in a bag, I listened to DeeDee and Mrs. Cote speak of my father. I would have liked to talk and listen more, but my mother was uncomfortable and we had an appointment at the funeral home. Mrs. Cote, who was with Daddy when he died, talked so openly and graphically about his last hours and his death, that I felt a bit stunned. Mrs. Cote used to clean for my mother, so she had known Daddy for forty years.

Since my mother and I were on a schedule, we let Mrs. Cote know that we must leave for the funeral home. We loaded Daddy's clothes into the car as we had done in the past when we were getting him ready for the hospital or the alcohol treatment facility.

When my mother and I entered the funeral home it was through the back, because another family was having visiting hours. We handed my father's clothes to Peter Neal, the mortician, and introduced ourselves. Peter used to be the little kid who was my younger sister's age. Now he runs his grandfather's undertaking business. As we talked, we moved closer to the room of caskets and I steeled myself once again. We chose a moderately priced casket and then followed Peter through the rooms of the old house past the mourners in an area near his office.

Standing near a desk was a portly older man whom I recognized as Jimmy, a boy from my high school class. A vision of myself working at Daddy's first office, flashed into my head, and I remembered the day Jimmy called the office out of the blue.

"This is Jimmy," he said.

"Jimmy who?" I responded abruptly, suspecting a prank by Larry Richards, not knowing who Jimmy was, and nonplussed to be called at the office for a date to the movies.

I went to the movies with him after all, because I didn't know how to get out of it, I felt sorry for being rude, and I was self-conscious about Larry's label that I was a snob. Maybe Larry was right. It was pretty clear on the date, that Jimmy and I were from opposite ends of the spectrum, socially and intellectually. I think we were both relieved to have the night end. It was odd that all those memories could come rushing back to me on such a day, as he and his family mourned the premature death of his younger brother, and my mother and I made final arrangements for my father.

We continued on to visit with the minister, made phone calls to a vocalist, and chose the flowers. Then it was time for me to leave. My mother and I hugged good bye and then I was on my way.

As I drove home to Waterville, I thought of what DeeDee had said about my father being scared to be alone at night. I thought of how he said so much more to her about his feelings than he ever said to me. I was glad that Daddy had DeeDee as a caregiver during his last months. My father wasn't a religious man, although as a child he had attended the Universalist Church. Yet, choosing the right songs and readings for the funeral was somehow important. I wanted some uplifting songs that were a celebration of life and gave people hope.

I thought of songs we sing at the Catholic Church, and was surprised that the Universalist hymnal didn't have as many beautiful songs. As I drove, I tried to sing the songs that are my favorites, the ones my friend Cathie LaBarge Frost sings so beautifully. I kept singing the verses in *Be Not Afraid, I Go Before You*, and *On Eagles Wings*. I felt the trickle of tears and let them come, my throat constricted and singing became impossible. Then, gradually I refocused my thoughts to happier memories. As I got closer to Waterville, I began to think of what I should pack for the writers' retreat. I thought of my sisters and family members gathering on Saturday and Sunday, planning for the funeral on Monday, and once again had doubts that I was doing the right thing by choosing to go be with strangers and write.

When I arrived home, my husband and his golf buddies were on the screened-in porch relaxing, so I quietly went upstairs and gathered my sleeping bag, toiletries, clothes, writing folders, paper, and pens, forgetting my flashlight and rain gear. I chatted cheerfully with my husband and his friends, not wanting to appear maudlin since they knew where I had been.

I didn't want to make them feel uncomfortable, but it occurred to me later that my reactions probably seemed callous.

Half an hour later I was on my way to Lincolnville, knowing that the two day retreat might not live up to my expectations, but optimistic that it would finally get me back to writing. I would not be there, while my family gathered at the lakeside cottage to reminisce and grieve for Daddy, but in my own way I would pay tribute to him. I rationalized that I'd be there Monday for the funeral.

As I drove through South China, I passed the house in which Brian, Chris, Andy and I lived from 1971 to 1973. I remembered how my father used to stop by with his buddies on their way to the Windsor fair and the horse races in September. I had traveled to Lincolnville before, because in the early 1970s Brian, the boys and I drove it with Cathie and Dennis Frost and their children. We bought cooked lobsters at a restaurant take out and took the ferry to Isleboro for a picnic at Dark Harbor, just as my family had done in the 1950s. My sister Randy had gone to YMCA camp at Tanglewood, where the writers' retreat was being held, so I knew the route.

When I arrived at the camp. I saw a friend, Jane Ann McNish, in the parking lot. We chatted briefly about the days at UMF in Leonard Gilly's freelance writing class and of our chance telephone contact the previous year. I had called the agency at which Jane Ann works to ask for information for my students on the effects of smoking, and recognized her voice. By coincidence, she and I had chosen the auto-biography writer's session and made plans to see each other after I registered and found my cabin.

The women in my cabin all knew each other from the previous year. I found one woman particularly obnoxious, loud, and crude. Her brashness and smoking grated on my nerves. She bragged about the ghoulish, gruesome story she was writing, with a bloody plot, cemeteries, and murder. Having spent the last twenty-four hours dealing with my father's death and funeral arrangements, I decided to leave the cabin and go meet Jane Ann at the main lodge.

The dinner was delicious, the introduction to the writing instructors was interesting, and the participants were definitely in the Berkinstock crowd. After dinner we broke into groups, with autobiography writers meeting on the porch. Our instructor, Bill Roorbach, posed interview questions that became more probing and took different turns, leaving some of us blurting out things we hadn't planned on revealing.

One of our assignments was to draw a map of a special place of our childhood. I took an old map from my folder and drew a new one with more details. As I sketched a map of Dexter's Main Street, it became clear that all paths from my friends' houses and mine led to the hockey rink, a place I would later write about with more detail than the little time I had to write at the retreat.

On Sunday afternoon, when the retreat was over, I headed home. My mind sifted through the images of the two day retreat and the conversations, then gradually I focused on thoughts of my father and the next day—Monday, Daddy's funeral. I wondered what I had missed with my family gathered, but knew I had made my choice. They had reminisced and written a eulogy. I had helped my mother make funeral arrangements. We had each done our part.

On Monday morning we gathered at the Universalist Church. My mother, my cousins, my aunts, my husband, our son Chris and his new bride Karen and I filed into the reserved pews with our cousins. Friends of the family had begun to gather outside the church and in the pews. Twenty-one years before I had attended my first funeral—Winnie's. Now I walked into the same church, as a woman, no longer with the fresh face of youth, but with a lifetime of experiences behind me. Tears welled up in my eyes as I saw all the people of the community who had come to pay their last respects to Harvey Hatch.

I listened as the minister gave a eulogy for a man he didn't know, but whom he had an understanding of from talking to family members. Randy and Sally walked together to the lectern and read from a prepared eulogy they had written. It was fitting that they do this for him. I could not have, for I needed to process more of my thoughts before I could gather them on paper. I realized that with Daddy gone, I couldn't ask him about family history or events that were part of his childhood. Now I would have to be the one to tell the stories. It was a way to celebrate Daddy's life and the special people of Dexter.

HARVEY HATCH

Whitney's garage was a vital part of Dexter for many decades. It was one of Daddy's destination points for years. The garage changed in the 1980s when the Whitneys sold the business to a man who expanded the gas station to offer fast food and coolers of beer, milk, and soda. Although the business changed hands, Carol's father, Bob Whitney, and his brother Ray stayed on for a few years.

People bought gasoline and fuel oil from the Whitneys, and they were probably the only Dexter businessmen with a higher accounts receivable than my father. The Whitneys were quietly generous and waited, or overlooked, or forgave bills for fuel oil deliveries, because they knew people were in need and would pay when or if they could. They sponsored little league teams and let school groups and others have fund raising car washes in one of the bays.

When Carol and I were in elementary school, we often went to the garage. After Carol had obtained permission, we opened the large, glass, oak-trimmed candy case for a Milky Way bar to eat after drinking a Coca Cola from the machine. Then we waited for the right moment when the men were busy in the office and the adjoining bays. When it seemed that they were too busy to notice, we sidled surreptitiously over to the Calendar Room in the back corner.

The anticipation, the false starts, the caution, the planning, and the forbidden allure made the door-opening even more exciting. I don't know if the men ever noticed and figured out what we were doing. We gazed in awe at the room full of pictures of nearly naked ladies. The young women posed in all their air-brushed perfection with flawless, peachy flesh tones and voluptuous breasts, clad in see-through pink or black negligees, fancy underwear, or skimpy bathing suits, holding tire irons or wrenches. We were wide-eyed at the sight of breasts thrust forward, backs arched, and buttocks jutting out seductively.

After the garage was sold, Daddy still went there to talk about sports and horse racing results with Bob Whitney, Earl Richards, and the other men who gathered. That was where my father was the day he had the stroke in February of 1990. His speech became slurred and his body was clearly affected. The ambulance came and took Daddy to Dover-Foxcroft to the hospital since Dexter's Plummer Memorial hospital was just a ghost of a building then, owned by writer Stephen King of Bangor. (Dexter lost its hospital in the 1970 era of government mandated SADs and HADs—school administrative districts and hospital administrative districts).

I drove to Dover to see my father in the hospital and saw a changed man. The stroke had left his right side partially paralyzed. He looked weak and frail. His face and lip were slack. The Harvey Hatch that people in Dexter knew would never be the same. The next two years were a sad denouement to his life.

After my father died, the Dexter Town Report featured a dedication to him in the front, just as it had in 1963 for Mr. Marsh, the health officer, and for attorney Bartolo Siciliano in 1972, and for Chief Harold Knox in 1976, and Clarence Pierce in 1979. Those copies of old town reports that were my father's are now in my Dexter archives.

The town report for 1992 says: "This year's Dexter Town Report is hear by dedicated to Lloyd Harvey Hatch, Jr. Harvey was one of Dexter's friendliest and most unforgettable citizens—a true legend in his own time. A Dexter native and a man of exceptional integrity, Harvey spent 47 years of his life on Dexter's Main Street, providing outstanding service to those in need."

"Harvey was characterized by a strong sense of community spirit, generosity, and honesty. He was always there for everyone—his family, his friends, or a stranger in search of information. His knowledge of Dexter's origins and forefathers was a wonderful resource for the citizens of Dexter. Harvey's sense of humor and intense interest in life will always be remembered by those who knew him. May God Bless you and keep you Harvey."

The eulogizing sentiments about always being there for his family were perhaps a bit overstated. I thought back to my teenage years when Daddy was drinking fairly heavily and away at the races often, but good memories tend to dominate after a while. It was comforting to read those words the spring after my father died; to think about how my childhood, my father, and Dexter were intertwined.

As the summer went by several Dexter people told me how much they missed my father. Weeks later when I met with the Heberts to go over the details in the story about Wassookeag, Mrs. Hebert said, "We miss your father so much. He was so good to us. Such a kind man. I loved Mackie too. He always did the work for us. He didn't finish work on time for some people, but he did for us. I know sometimes when he was drinking he wasn't very nice to Aunt Teddy, but I'd tell him, "Mackie, you shouldn't treat Aunt Teddy that way."

After church one Sunday, Jim Peakes, a local attorney, came up to me and said, "You know I used to see your father quite often for business. I went to see him at the nursing home after his stroke and he still had that sense of humor. He told me, "When I was at Bowdoin I thought I might try out for the crew team, because I thought I might have a good stroke, but I never thought I'd have this.""

"I miss your father," Jim said.

Jim's comment made me think about a visit I made to see Daddy in the nursing home. I accompanied him to the dining room with all of the other residents, forcing myself to endure the sight and smells. Daddy was not cheerful, joking, or happy that day. He had found the nursing home was not as he had imagined.

Before his stroke, in the weeks preceding each Christmas Daddy used to go to the Dexter Pharmacy or Welby and purchase all the half-priced, foil-wrapped candy turkeys left over from Thanksgiving to give to the nursing home patients with a pencil, pen, and small calendar, because he said, "They like to have something to open for Christmas." I think he found out later that most of them felt like he did later, so weak, sick, depressed, waiting to die that they probably didn't give a damn about a present, but Daddy cared enough to give it before he had to endure the indignity of the stroke and the nursing home.

That day when I visited the dining room with Daddy, I felt a sense of panic. How could either of us be there in that situation? The CNA handed out plates of food that didn't look appetizing. A man nearby was given his plate as Cindy the CNA said, "Your mashed potatoes are at three o'clock, your hamburg is at six o'clock, and your peas are at nine o'clock.

I realized with a jolt that the man next to us was blind.

It was depressing to see bibbed adults who had once been active and vital members of the community, now waiting resignedly for their food. Some people moaned, others refused to eat and had to be coaxed. Others rocked in place or waited silently staring off at nothing.

"Get me out of here," a voice in my head screamed as I asked Daddy, "How are the baked beans?"

"Awful," was all he said.

I looked at the dry, over-cooked beans and realized he was probably right.

"Maybe you could drink some of your milk," I suggested, "or try some of your coleslaw or your yeast roll."

As my father tried to eat his dinner with his stroke affected right hand, dribbling food in the process, I looked by chance to the wall and ever so slightly caught my breath. A Lloyd Harvey Hatch Insurance and Real Estate calendar was in my line of vision. It was eerie. For four decades Daddy's calendars had presented the months for Dexter citizens. Every year of school a large Harvey Hatch U.S.F.&G. or Fireman's Fund calendar had graced every classroom in Dexter's schools. This calendar on the nursing home wall would probably be the last one advertising his business.

EPILOGUE

Dreams of the past no longer haunt me, although they did give me the impetus to put the memories on paper. Now that I've written about life in Dexter and the people there, I am no longer visited by the dreams.

The events of my past, the threads of my life, are woven into a tapestry depicting simple, yet rich experiences, like those in the medieval tapestries that once graced the halls of the Hatch Preparatory School in Newport.

During the years of my writing and remembering, I immersed myself in the past as I delved through photos and newspaper clippings. I came to a new understanding, an acceptance, and an appreciation of the people in my childhood. I learned to put the past in its place, to remember it with fondness, and to embrace change, if not cherish it.

I also have been learning how to let go of loss, to live life to its fullest, to look for the lessons in life and learn from them. My faith, the grace of God, family and friends, new and old, offer comfort and inspiration.

Being diagnosed with liver cancer in October 1997, has provided me more impetus. Knowing that my time on this earth will be shorter than I once anticipated, I feel an urgency to have my stories see the light of day. I could spend another five years revising and editing and getting more opinions of what to cut, but I won't. The stories must be told and the book shared.

I don't dwell on the past or the future now, although I'd like more time to read and write and be with my family and friends. I'd like to picture myself finishing writing a second and possibly a third book. I'd also like to spend more time at our log cabin on an island at Moxie Lake and at the Lake Wassookeag cottage savoring the summer days. I'd like to make molasses pull candy with my granddaughters, when they are older and watch them dress up in clothes from a dome-top trunk, but mostly, I now live in the present savoring each day given to me.

ACKNOWLEDGMENTS

Many people have helped me along the way as my lists of memories began to evolve into stories. Teachers at Dexter High School nurtured my interest in writing through their instruction which laid the ground work. English classes with Francis Mealey, James Vickery, and Thomas Rowe helped me realize I loved to see my words and ideas on paper. Mr. Rowe's assignment to write our autobiography was an early catalyst, although it was fifteen years before I realized what I needed and wanted to do.

I owe a great deal of thanks to my instructors at the University of Maine at Farmington in whose classes I wrote early versions of some of these stories. Valerie Heubner, Leonard Gilly, Carl Franson, Alice Bloom, Patricia O'Donnell each helped me with early drafts. Professor Daniel Gunn offered tremendous help with my writing with countless conferences, specific questions, and suggestions for pulling together ideas and memories or reordering text. He helped me discover what I really wanted to say.

In Gail Schade's summer writing workshop at Thomas College, I created the first Aunt Teddy story, portions of which are included in this book. My three summers at University of New Hampshire in classes with Ellen Blackburn, Bruce Ballanger, and Makeel McBride helped me produce more stories about family members.

Debbie Larsen Holt typed drafts for me for years, until I finally learned to use a word processor. I'm grateful for Debbie's help and for technical assistance from Nancy Jeannotte, Jennifer Mckenny, Mary Jane Stafford, and my sons, Chris and Andy. I especially want to thank Doug Eugley for all of his technological assistance with manuscript submission.

Two summer sessions at Stonecoast Writers' Conference gave me a chance to work with writers Madison Smartt Bell and Bill Roorbach who suggested changes I wasn't then ready to make.

Until 1993, I had just a small collection of stories and dozens of folders of ideas to develop and lists of memories I wanted to capture. I hired writer Steve Miller to be my writing consultant and we met regularly for over two years. With Steves's guidance and editing I pulled together old stories, wrote new ones, and the book began to take shape.

In the fall of 1995, I met a new writer friend, whose name, ironically, is Carole Whitney. I am grateful for her editing skills and her suggestions for revision. She read the entire manuscript and offered invaluable advice for improving the work further. Carol, Terry Hibbard, Jackie Manning, and I met weekly to critique and edit each others work. Their support and encouragement helped me improve the chapters and develop new material.

When that group disbanded, Sue Laplante, Pete Young, Muriel Fish and Janet Shea each helped me glean further insight through their questions and revision suggestions. My manuscript grew as I wrote new details to clarify the stories and my intent.

Thank you to Jean Berger and Sandy Mahaffey, members of the Newcomers' Book Group, who graciously offered to read the entire manuscript and make helpful comments as the publishing deadline approached. I'll be forever grateful to my writer friend, Peg Shore, who has been my most recent editor, helping me revise and cut material to "let the gems show." She, Sandy and Jean offered encouragement and insight that helped me do the final editing.

I am grateful for the help and encouragement offered by my sisters, Randy, Sally, and Susan, my Mother, my cousin Nancy, Aunt Barbara (who died in December 1999) and Aunt Bunny who is the last of the six cousins.

My friends Carol Whitney, Cathie LaBarge Frost, Mary Ellen LaBarge Fletcher, Kathie Lombard, Gene Kortecamp, Larry Richards, and Gary Gilbert helped by confirming my memories, by adding details, and expressing appreciation.

I am grateful to Marge Reid for her close reading, insightful comments and suggestions on stories. Thanks also to Kate Higley for her supportive humor and input over the decades as we both worked to develop our creativity.

I give thanks to God for putting all of these people in my path at just the right time in my life. I am grateful for His gift to me of creative spirit, writing talent, and the health and energy to pursue my dream.

I especially owe a big thank you to my husband, Brian, who has been with me for 35 years, through the ages and stages of girlhood and womanhood, as I discovered that I was a writer. He paid for it all—my education at UMF, UNH, Stone Coast Writers' Conferences, Maine Writers and Publishers Alliance workshops, the hired private writing consultant, the first word processor, the computer, and all the necessary books, supplies, and materials to help me produce a six feet high stack of writing.

About the Author

On Main Street is Prudence Hatch McMann's first book. Currently, she is working on another memoir about one woman's journey on the road to self-discovery. For eleven years, she taught students in the Maine Migrant Education Program. She is a member of the Maine Writers and Publishers Alliance and a local writers group. The mother of two married sons and the grandmother of three little girls, Prudy lives in Waterville, Maine, with her husband Brian and their Irish Setter.